PRAISE FOR *YENTL'S REVENGE*

"*Yentl's Revenge* is a brilliant, zesty, gutsy collection that will enlighten, expand and occasionally aggravate. The surprise is that the aggravating essays are the ones that prompt an inner discussion, the ones that end up shedding the most light. A provocative book in the very best sense, *Yentl's Revenge* moves our thinking to the next level."

—Rabbi Bradley Shavit Artson
dean of the Zeigler School of Rabbinic Studies

"With stubborn integrity, the writers in *Yentl's Revenge* negotiate their diverse and sometimes transgressive identities across traditional boundary lines: A feminist blends Judaism and goddess worship, an Iraqi Jew upholds her non-Ashkenazic community while challenging its sexism, an Orthodox mother dresses her daughter in the fringed garment reserved for males, a Valley Girl deconstructs the JAP joke, an incest survivor refuses to shield the Holocaust-survivor relative who molested her. Spirited and iconoclastic, these young women critique their Jewish experiences and propose alternatives."

—Rachel Adler
author of *Engendering Judaism*

"Feminism continues to fire up the minds of a new generation of Jewish women activists, ideologues and dreamers. As proof, read *Yentl's Revenge* to sample tantalizing ideas that are personal, political and polemical. Here, revenge is not only sweet, but spicy."

—Susan Weidman Schneider
editor in chief of *Lilith* magazine

YENTL'S
REVENGE

THE NEXT WAVE OF JEWISH FEMINISM

EDITED BY DANYA RUTTENBERG

FOREWORD BY SUSANNAH HESCHEL

SEAL PRESS

Published by
Seal Press
An Imprint of Avalon Publishing Group Incorporated
161 William Street, 16th Floor
New York, NY 10038

Cover design by Christina Henry de Tessan
Text design by Anne Mathews
Cover photograph by Ingrid Emerick

Excerpt from "Sabbath of Mutual Respect" from *The Moon Is Always Female* by Marge Piercy, copyright © 1980 by Marge Piercy. Used by permission of Alfred A. Knopf, a division of Random House, Inc.

Excerpt from "The Chuppah" from *The Art of Blessing the Day* by Marge Piercy, copyright © 1999 by Middlemarsh, Inc. Used by permission of Alfred A. Knopf, a division of Random House, Inc.

"Parenting as a Religious Jewish Feminist" is excerpted from *Life on the Fringes: A Feminist Journey Towards Traditional Rabbinic Ordination* by Haviva Ner-David (JFL Books, 2000). Reprinted by permission of the author.

A version of "Bubbe Got Back: Tales of a Jewess with a Caboose" appeared in *Utne Reader,* issue 102 (November/December 2000). Reprinted by permission of the author.

Library of Congress Cataloging-in-Publication Data

Yentl's revenge: the next wave of Jewish feminism / edited by Danya Ruttenberg; foreword by Susannah Heschel.
p. cm.
ISBN 1-58005-057-3 (alk. paper)
1. Feminism—Religious aspects—Judaism. 2. Women in Judaism. 3. Jewish women—Religious life. I. Ruttenberg, Danya.

BM729.W6 Y46 2001
296'.082—dc21   2001049003

Printed in the United States of America
First printing, October 2001

10 9 8 7 6 5 4 3 2

Distributed to the trade by Publishers Group West
In Canada: Publishers Group West Canada, Toronto, Ontario
In Australia: Banyan Tree Book Distributors, Kent Town, South Australia
In the United Kingdom, Europe and South Africa: Hi Marketing, London
In Asia and the Middle East: Michelle Morrow Curreri, Beverly, MA

To my mother Janie, z"l, for everything

and

To David and Sarajean, with love.

ACKNOWLEDGMENTS

There are too many people to whom I am indebted; the list fully rendered is at least another book.

Thank you to everyone who's been working all these years to make Judaism a safer street to walk down at night. We couldn't be here without you, and we know it.

Much gratitude to Jennie Goode for enabling this project to be, and to Leslie Miller for her spirited, indefatigable editorial magic, and for managing my endless questions. Thanks to Rosemary, Lucie and all of Seal for their help, work and patience. A big thank you to all the talented contributors for putting up with so much of my editorial B.S., and *todah rabah* to Ariella Reback and Susan Sapiro for research help and halakhic input.

Endless gratitude to Dawn Stevenson for much beyond her actual job description.

There are a lot of folks whose encouragement and insights have helped fuel me on this project and keep me on my toes. To name just a few, thank you Bari Mandelbaum, Laura Waters, Emily Wages, Christina Wodtke, Karissa Sellman, R. Pickett, Jes Cornette, Dina Pinsky and Sharon Bernstein—heroes of a very high order.

Thanks to Ben for being wonderful, and for his occasional bouts of big-brotherly advice. And, most importantly, many, many thanks to my father, Biff—for his support, friendship and excellent secretarial work. The letter of reference is there if you need it, Dad.

CONTENTS

FOREWORD

It's Not about Equality—It's about Who's in Charge!

SUSANNAH HESCHEL

I GREW UP IN THE SYNAGOGUE of the Jewish Theological Seminary, the Vatican of the Conservative movement—then the largest denomination of American Judaism, and, like American Judaism as a whole, a denomination in conflict with itself. Wanting to accommodate modernity without relinquishing the authority of Jewish law, many of the movement's practices seemed to be hypocritical compromises with modern exigencies—like ruling that it is legally permissible to drive a car on Shabbat—while many others seemed intransigent and guided by sheer prejudice. The seminary trains rabbis to serve congregations with mixed-gender seating, yet the seminary's own synagogue followed Orthodox Jewish practice in keeping men and women separated.

I started protesting as soon as I could talk, but I was born into a medieval world. Some of Judaism's most prominent leaders at the time told me, "Sure, study chemistry. It'll help you be a good cook." The vice-chancellor of the seminary explained that women could not possibly be called up to the Torah for the honor of making a blessing because he and his male colleagues would admire their legs, not their piety.

The bottom line was women's submission to male authority. Even when changes were made by the Conservative movement in which women were slowly permitted to take a more active role in Jewish ritual and prayer, the decisions were made by men, on the basis of texts authored by men. How was it possible not to be indoctrinated, co-opted, sucked into the mentality that men, as authors of texts and interpreters of law, have exclusive authority? After all, the wives of the seminary's faculty and students never expressed discontent. What gene did I have that made me rebel?

Once, while in college, I took a friend who had never heard of the joyous, raucous holiday of Simchat Torah to services at the seminary. As soon as we arrived, he was handed a Torah scroll and welcomed enthusiastically into a crowd of euphoric, dancing, singing men. As usual, I had to stand in the back, watching with the women. After an hour, I could no longer control my rage and I simply threw myself into the crowd of men and started dancing, too. A rabbinical student angrily grabbed me and demanded, "Who gave you permission to dance?" Calmly, I replied, "God." He threw me out.

Jewish feminism is not about equality with men. Why should we women want to define ourselves by imitating male Jewishness? Nor is it about degrees of oppression, whereby the more traditional realms of Judaism are the "worst" and the less traditional are the "best." As *Lilith* magazine founder Susan Weidman Schneider pointed out years ago, even liberal congregations that have women rabbis often still have an invisible curtain separating women from men. That is, institutional sexism—a 1950s suburban bourgeois mentality that expects women to be stay-at-home moms, available to chauffeur their kids to Hebrew school and volunteer in the community—still prevails in many politically liberal Jewish communities. How many congregations provide daycare? How many have overcome the "Noah Syndrome," which expects all congregants to be members of heterosexual couples?

Feminism is about women's refusal to submit to male authority. The real issue is not equality, but power. Who's in charge? Who defines Judaism, and who determines whether or not we get to dance with the Torah? The point of feminism is to create institutional structures and mental frame-works in which women act as their own authority, determining for them-selves the nature of the Jewishness that best expresses their identity.

What makes the wonderful essays that Danya Ruttenberg has collected in this volume so original and inspiring is their tone: Third-wave Jewish feminists have a choice. Thanks to the hard work of earlier generations of feminists, the spirit of fighting—and the anger—has given way to free choice among Judaism's many different traditions, with the joy that such freedom engenders.

Third-wave Jewish feminists are their own authorities. They choose whether to study Talmud in an Orthodox yeshiva or create new feminist rituals; whether to marry a man or a woman; whether to bear children or not; whether to volunteer on a kibbutz or work for Habitat for Human-ity. The Jewish alternatives have existed since these women were born, and the decision is theirs how to shape the Judaism they wish to express. The victory of feminism is that women are the authorities—not male rabbis, male-authored halakha (laws) or male-imaged divinities.

What a relief to live in a world knowing that there will never again be a time when women cannot be counted for prayer, can find no synagogue in which to publicly mourn, have nowhere to dance with the Torah. As a member of that first generation of women who raged and struggled and fought and wept, I thrill with the second generation and all those to come.

As Marge Piercy wrote in "Sabbath of Mutual Respect,"

> Praise our choices, sisters, for each doorway
> open to us was taken by squads of fighting
> women who paid years of trouble and struggle,
> who paid their wombs, their sleep, their lives.

Susannah Heschel
March 2001

INTRODUCTION

DANYA RUTTENBERG

I'VE ALWAYS HAD A STRANGE RELATIONSHIP with *Yentl,* Barbra Streisand's co-lossal 1983 musical. It's about a woman who dresses in boy-drag in order to study Jewish texts—it's about the love of learning, about being tough and brainy and soulful all at once. Yet despite my embarrassingly dorky identification with our heroine's book lust, despite the fact that I adored the film's bittersweet campiness, despite it all . . . something about the movie was always a little bit unsatisfying.

The plot includes a Shakespearean love triangle between Babs/Yentl, Mandy Patinkin (hunky Avigdor) and Amy Irving (sexy Hadass)—but in the end, Yentl gets neither the boy *nor* the girl. Nor, as in the Isaac Bashevis Singer story on which the movie is based, does she continue living as a man, thereby ensuring her scholastic freedom. Nope. She goes off to America without love, resolution or even a clear direction for further study. But we, the audience, are to understand that she managed to enter the male-only world of learning and that, most important, she found herself . . . and that was enough. And you know what? For a long time, that was plenty.

Yeah, well. Not anymore.

✡

Judaism has changed pretty radically since the advent of second-wave feminism, as much as—if not more than—the business world or the domestic sphere. Forty years ago, "Jew" was understood as "man" when it came to almost every aspect of communal Jewish life, including counting for prayer, leading services and running major organizations. Many things once unthinkable have since become reality: Over three hundred women, for example, have been ordained as rabbis by Jewish seminaries since 1972. In some ways Judaism has become an entirely different religion, one that in many sectors counts women in ritual, rites of passage, prayer and study.

Women who are now in their twenties and thirties were the first to grow up with feminism as a given. As such, many of us have begun to see the possibilities beyond inclusion or egalitarianism—and to ask for more.

Now it's Yentl's turn to run the damn yeshiva. She knows enough. She's got the necessary tools. She has learned the rules well enough to know if and when it's appropriate to flip them on their head. Yentl's back—and this time it's personal.

Today's Yentl can, as many Orthodox feminists have begun to do, learn Talmud to extract the sexism from legitimate Jewish law. Or, she can lead workshops on S/M and Judaism. Or she can do both. She can see infinite ways to address women who want to talk honestly about the place of Judaism in real life—who grapple with body image, queer identity and the media's pervasive role in our culture. Who want to give religion a breath of fresh air—whether through meditation, eco-kosher living or punk rock. Who crave innovation—but innovation that's genuinely Jewish.

Yentl's Revenge seeks to open a long-needed dialogue—to bring out the diverse range of young Jewish feminists' thoughts, strategies, gripes and master plans, to provide a starting point for us to sort through today's pressing questions.

The feminists who came before us have made some heavy-duty changes, but it's now all too apparent how many aspects of Judaism still have a long way to go. Sure, women are more active in synagogue, but female rabbis still face sexual harassment and double standards. We're talking more about women's role in the family, but still must debunk the myth that only goyim have problems with alcoholism, domestic violence and incest. Jews from Sephardi or Mizrahi traditions have too long been alienated in a world dominated by (as contributor Dalia Sofer puts it) a "bagel-and-lox culture." We've begun to question a one-dimensional Zionism, we're less satisfied than ever with the traditional Jewish approach to marriage, we're skeptical about whether the various denominations can address both political and spiritual needs in one neat little package. At the time of this writing, the Conservative movement still refuses to ordain gay and lesbian rabbis, despite a wealth of arguments—well-grounded in Jewish law—that would permit the movement to do so. As author Blu Greenberg has said in another context, "When there's a rabbinic will, there's a halakhic [legal] way." Come *on* already!

It's also time to draw sharper connections between feminism and issues of race, economic justice, the environment and global politics. Obviously, any human concern is a feminist concern, and if Jews are going to live up to that "light unto the nations" moniker we sometimes tote around, we have to at least start dealing with our own baggage. This means addressing the rampant classism in the Jewish community: We're not all rich, so let's not assume that everyone can afford High Holiday tickets and Ivy League educations. It also means looking more closely at the relationship between European Jews and (other) people of color, building stronger alliances and questioning the white privilege we seem to have been handed some post-assimilation era ago. And, of course, there's that "chosen people" thing, complete with our anxieties about The Perpetuation of the Jewish People. How can we read it in such a way that we don't become xenophobic and closed?

As personal as many of these issues are, there's another thread weaving through contemporary dialogue that's more personal still. It's a huge triumph that, by now, women have managed to address almost every aspect of the Jewish ideological, ritual and legal universe; many young Jewish feminists are on altogether new terrain, able to choose from a dizzying range of spiritual possibilities. But the fact that we can now sometimes get beyond the political and address our relationship to the sacred generates a number of tough personal questions: If I can be any kind of Jew, what kind do I want to be? What satisfies me, as an individual? Do I want to observe rituals surrounding menstruation, do I want to wear tefillin, or both? Neither? Am I looking for a Jewish community, and, if so, what kind—and how might that fit in with my life? Now that there are many more tenable options for Jewish practice, young women have the luxury—and the challenge—of figuring out where on the spectrum they want to be.

But it's not just about religion. The range of available choices only complicates an issue with which Jews constantly struggle: How do we forge a comfortable line between culture and religion? What is it to be "too Jewish" to this generation? What is it to be "Jewish enough?" Where are the boundaries between culture and religion, anyway?

For young Jewish women who weren't raised with a strong religious and/or cultural identity, the questions are even more difficult; many of the identity markers we associate with Jewishness are hopelessly outmoded or in the process of rapid change. The Catskills have grown quiet and nobody thinks the JAP thing is funny anymore (thank G-d). Even the old New York–intellectual shtick seems to be fading from the limelight; Woody Allen just isn't sexy as a creepy stepdad. In our attempts to anchor ourselves in this history/culture/religion/whatever, what models do we have to hold on to?

Maybe we just have to make up our own models.

In this collection of essays, questions, dispatches and manifestoes, young Jewish feminists from all walks of life show us what a little brains and chutzpah can do.

Emily Wages muses on the assumption that a woman wearing a *kippah* couldn't possibly be open-minded and left-wing—and that, by extension, neither could Judaism. Ophira Edut helps us to see that old body-image dybbuk in a new, booty-shakin' light. Ryiah Lilith considers why being a Jewish Pagan Witch is not, in fact, a contradiction in terms, and Haviva Ner-David, who is studying for Orthodox rabbinic ordination, writes of her struggle to raise a daughter with feminist principles in a religiously traditional culture. Jennifer Bleyer applies the lessons she learned as a riot grrl to religious practice, and Hanne Blank explains how we can all learn to become "sexual Talmudists." Yiskah Rosenfeld offers a gorgeous reading of Eve—no longer "docile and obedient"—that elevates Eve to the same feminist status as Adam's other wife, Lilith.

It's worth noting that this book's title was not chosen without a question or two. As I mentioned above, and as Loolwa Khazzoom observes in "United Jewish Feminist Front," equating Judaism with the Eastern Europe, shtetl life and chicken soup of Babs' movie is, at best, a big mistake. Of course Jews—and Jewish traditions—come from all points on the map; the range of our customs, prayer melodies, legal rulings and foods is absolutely staggering. Judaism hardly begins and ends with the Yiddish-speaking world.

But here, in the Great Gold-Paved Galut, the Star-Spangled Exile, Babs is the A-1 genuine product: an American feminist Member of the Tribe, a pop-culture mascot whose own Jewishness seems to oscillate from religious investigation to a faint ethnic/cultural pulse bobbing just beneath the surface. As with many of this volume's writers—and, I imagine, many of its fine readers—her Judaism can't be classified as just a religion, or a bloodline, or even a definable culture. It is all of these things, but greater than the sum of its parts, and somehow every attempt to classify it yields, in the great and sometimes annoying tradition of our people, more and more questions. And really, *Yentl* does reveal something quintessential about being a Jew in this strange new world: We watch a film in which one of our pop-culture icons pretends to study Talmud, and feel, somehow, as though we've just participated in a religious act.

That continues to be as close as some people want to get, while others of us are trying to incorporate Judaism's spiritual and religious bits without compromising an inch of feminist principle. As this anthology will show you, there are about as many ways to see this stuff as there are blintzes at a bat mitzvah buffet. *Nu,* please . . . sit down, dig in. Taste the Jewish flavors of tomorrow.

Danya Ruttenberg
May 2001

YENTL'S
REVENGE

The Nice Jewish Boy

A. C. Hall

Naturally, I rebelled.

Naturally, I blame my parents for the need to. Even though they sent me to Hebrew school for bat mitzvah training and to a fairly observant summer camp, at home being Jewish meant you occasionally lit Hanukah candles. Oh, yes—and dated (and by extension, married) nice Jewish boys.

And which Jewish boys would those be? The small town I grew up in had six Jews in the public school system. I was related to three of them.

Besides, I wasn't going to be a Wife. Wives were ladies who applied orange lipstick in the rearview mirror while driving. When I grew up, I promised myself, I wouldn't own a car. I wouldn't wear lipstick. I certainly wouldn't marry. Wives were fools who let their husbands dick around, who had no power because their husbands made all the money.

My first boyfriend was black. We lasted about a week. The first guy I seduced, a different guy, was also black. That lasted forty-two minutes. Then came the nebulous string of working-class ex-Catholics who smoked a lot. Most of them were anti-Semitic. Then came seven years of celibacy, during which I worked on the family-of-origin issues that led me to seek out that kind of man in the first place. All very mid-'80s, but productive nonetheless. By the end of it, I understood it was my family's attitude toward Judaism, not Judaism itself, that repelled me. Lo and behold, I became interested in leading a more Jewish life.

I moved to Seattle and found myself involved with, in no particular order, a congregation with a female rabbi, a Rosh Chodesh (new moon) group, and a *havurah* (community) where the tresses were longer on the guys than the gals but amounts of body hair were equal. I pierced my nose and decided I wanted to be with a woman. Terribly early '90s. Imagine my surprise, then, come 1996, when I fell in love with Cliff.

Everything about us was so "normal" it was galling. We met through a friend. On the Fourth of July, for God's sake. He was a nice-looking, intelligent fellow who favored button-down shirts. With stripes. He said he liked the Mets. I was relatively sure that meant baseball. He appeared pleased when I suggested we split the bill for our first dinner together. None of the "But I asked you out" (which he hadn't; we'd kind of asked each other out) that categorized the painful ends to dates I had been going on since I realized I wanted to be with a man. With Cliff, there was no drama, no trauma.

Damn.

"He's the kind of guy your grandma would want you to go out with," I mused to a friend a few months into it.

As our relationship deepened, I began to admit—to no one but myself—that in addition to some very real political objections to marriage, I held an equally firm belief that it wasn't going to happen for me. Relationships, marriage, normal stuff—other girls got those things.

Not that I thought he would—oh, no, not me—but *if* he were to propose, I had Cliff pegged as the small-velvet-box-slipped-across-the-table-of-a-fancy-restaurant kind of guy. A vacation to Bali came and went. My birthday came and went.

WAITER AT FANCY RESTAURANT: Will there be anything else?

ME: Cliff?

CLIFF: Just the check, thanks.

I complained to my friend Gary.

GARY: Is Cliff a romantic guy?

ME: Sure.

GARY: He's got this all planned out. Just let him do it. Besides, it's the last decision he gets to make.

My therapist agreed. "Just let him do it," she told me.

I let him do it. Over Memorial Day weekend, Cliff took the stage during the Big Jewish Show at Seattle's annual Folklife Festival. In front of an audience of six hundred, he asked if I was in the house, went down on one knee and did it.

I have never told anyone this: I almost said no.

Fear.

Never mind my three months of angst-ridden control fits leading up to "Will you marry me?" If we hadn't been on stage in front of six hundred people, I might have said, "Let me think about it." Instead, I said yes.

We embarked on a torturous year of wedding planning, which kicked off with six months of procrastination. Eventually, I got sucked into tense debates over china patterns and wedding colors. I discovered the fun of playing with makeup. I started wearing lipstick. I read the wedding issue of *Martha Stewart Living*.

I found it helpful.

I was doing some numbing. Like having a glass of wine before a difficult family gathering. I wasn't getting plastered; I was getting through it. Maybe that's why people make such a fuss over the bride—they understand that if they rivet a bride's attention to the ring, the dress, the goal of the perfect day, she will overlook the fact that she is signing up for life. And if, like me, the bride comes from a long line of screwups in the "for life" department, if she harbors fears that she might lack the strength to be anything other than that which begat her, it becomes a fuck of a lot more pleasant for her to focus on flower arrangements.

My impulse was to call it off until I matured. But, wishing to wed before my Social Security kicked in, I breathed deeply and redirected my attention from the wedding stuff to the marriage ceremony.

Step one: Find a rabbi. As a general rule, Cliff and I disagreed about most things Jewish. But I wanted a rabbi, and so did he. Cliff had a typical Manhattan Jew's ability to align culturally and participate in services without demonstrating one teaspoon of religious inclination. I, on the other hand, thrived on spiritual connection, but derived it primarily from Jewish community. Formal services left me brain-dead. I adored ritual, however—as long as it wasn't too much ritual and those elements chosen were meaningful. Having come late to Jewish practice, I didn't bring to it a great deal of "you're supposed to."

We checked out several rabbis who completely wigged us out. Was it their mainstream level of observance or simply the fact that we were looking for a rabbi to marry us? Regardless, we finally happened upon Fern Feldman, a Jewish educator in the process of receiving rabbinic ordination through Aleph, the Alliance for Jewish Renewal. Cliff really liked Fern's gentle demeanor. I saw in her face that she understood when I said, "I don't mind having a wedding, but I don't want to be the cherry on top."

Step two: Come up with a ceremony. Fern outlined the traditional Jewish ritual. Naturally, I rebelled.

"What's this walking-around-him-seven-times business?"

Fern conceded that, yes, the bride circling the groom seven times did have something to do with marking territory. But, she pointed out, you could also look at it as weaving him in circles of protection. "Or," she said, "you could focus on one of the seven *spherot* during each circle, with the intention of bringing that energy into your marriage."

"Fern, no matter how you slice it, in the end, I'm gonna feel like lifting my leg and peeing."

We agreed I would circle Cliff three times, he would circle me three times, and we would join hands for a final, subdued do-si-do.

The remainder of the ritual presented no ideological controversies: blessing the first cup of wine, exchanging rings, reading the *ketubah* (wedding contract), reading the *sheva brachot* (seven blessings), the second cup of wine, breaking the glass, the *yichud.* Back when we Jews wandered, upon concluding the ceremony, the groom immediately took his bride to his tent for a little nudge-nudge-wink-wink. For the sake of my dress, we would forgo that element of our culture. But we would indulge in a yichud, secluding ourselves for the first fifteen minutes of our married life.

I was relieved to discover the number of wedding dictums that were not a part of the Jewish rite. Bridesmaids? Not Jewish. Traditionally, Jews have *chuppah* holders. Thank goodness. The only thing worse than forcing four of my friends into buying expensive, horribly unflattering pink gowns with poofy sleeves would be choosing among them for the honor. Saying "I do"? Not Jewish. Traditionally, Jews read their wedding contract. "I do" snuck in as a result of living in a predominantly Christian culture.

Cliff and I were a little sad. We wanted to say "love, honor and snuggle." But, ya know: not Jewish.

We still had to come up with a ketubah. We were blessed that our friend, Yael Yanich, was a gifted artist with a great deal of Jewish knowledge. We commissioned her to create the marriage contract. Fern knew of a text that was both egalitarian and in accordance with Jewish law. The text was Aramaic (a language that is similar to but predates Hebrew). Yael laid out the words as a square, then surrounded them with imagery from the Song of Songs: stars, lilies, pomegranates, grapes and deer.

I asked, "What's with the Bambis at the bottom?"

"'Your breasts are like two fawns,'" Yael quoted, gesturing evocatively.

Above the Bambis was an empty space for the English translation of the Aramaic. The literal translation talked about Cliff giving me the shirt off his back and other oddities, so he and I agreed to write a personally meaningful interpretation of the literal translation. My first attempt was fairly boilerplate. "In accordance with the ritual of Moses and Israel . . . we pledge to dedicate ourselves to each other as lovers, friends and partners . . . to establish a Jewish home . . . " and more along those lines.

Cliff read it. He looked disappointed. "It's a little . . . impersonal."

"What about this part: 'To support each other in becoming who we are yet to be and to retain a sense of humor as we change and life changes.' That's personal!"

A slight tiff. I left him at my computer for a while. When I came back, the den was dark except for the small, yellow lamp lit on my desk. The computer screen glowed from between the cavernous stacks of wedding-related paperwork. Here's what he had written:

> We promise to dedicate ourselves to each other as lovers, friends and partners; to share hopes, dreams, insights and fears; and to maintain an unyielding commitment to trust and intimacy. We pledge to support each other in becoming who we are yet to be and to retain a sense of humor as we change and life changes; to love each other deeply without losing sight of our individual selves; and to remain continually aware that our time together is precious. In so doing, we shall establish a Jewish home that reflects the best elements of our heritage, including a love of learning, the bonds of community and the spirits of generosity, compassion and activism. We also shall endeavor to spice our union with acts of spontaneity, wit and love that may not always be comprehensible to those unfamiliar with our ways. Let no day pass without time for us to reflect upon these promises to ourselves and to our community.

Even today, I cannot read our ketubah without melting into very girlish tears. The tears, perhaps, of a scared child who saw hurt called love and therefore refused to risk loving, who, as a still-scared woman, was realizing she was now very, very loved.

One huge project remained: making our chuppah. I had drawn great strength from the line in Marge Piercy's poem "The Chuppah" that reads,

"It is not a coffin / It is not a dead end / Therefore the chuppah has no walls."

ME: I have an idea for our chuppah.

CLIFF (NOT TAKING EYES OFF TV): Can't we just borrow some white thing?

ME: Never mind. I'll take care of it. Did you finalize the invitation list yet?

CLIFF (BURROWING INTO COUCH): After the game.

I had two colors in mind: blue for Israel and purple, a color often associated with the Goddess, not necessarily in that order. I, however, have close to zero artistic ability, so I co-opted the formidable talents of my Rosh Chodesh group. I invited them, their partners and their children to a painting party hosted by resident artist Yael. Cliff got caught up in all the excitement. "Aren't any of my friends invited? It's my chuppah, too."

We ended up with thirty-one folks, including the young'uns. We wanted uniformity in size and color, but within that, room for personal expression. Yael passed out squares of white cotton and paints and stepped nobly into the role of art teacher. When the paint dried, friends batiked every design with wax, dyed each square a rich sky blue, arranged them among strips of purple fabric and quilted the whole shebang. The end result was a huge, soft canopy, strangely similar to a Chagall window. I was increasingly eager to stand under it. I had no idea at the time, but my remaining hesitancy would be washed away by a mikveh.

I had taken the ritual bath once before, with my Rosh Chodesh group. In a hot tub. Our concession to halakha was a tiny vial of rainwater poured into the jet-made bubbles. Not one of our twelve-woman crew believed our periods made us impure and therefore in need of cleansing to ready us for sex again. We did it partly to explore and partly to have fun. I hadn't given much thought as to why I wanted a wedding mikveh—traditionally the first time a woman takes the dip—when I had no intention of pursuing the practice in my married life. I only knew I wanted one.

I invited all the women in Cliff's family, along with the important women from my past and present: fifteen in all. In preparation, I mailed out cassette tapes onto which I recorded some of the songs and *niggunim* (melodies) my Rosh Chodesh group enjoyed each month. I took the opportunity to explain my vision for the procedure. After all, I was going to get naked. I didn't want to traumatize a new in-law the morning of the wedding.

At 8:00 in the appointed A.M., we car-caravaned to the one mikveh in town, at Ashkenazi Bikur Cholim synagogue. My preconceived idea of a mikveh included inlaid gold tiles and billowing puffs of steam. My wildest fantasies included melting chocolate. The reality of the mikveh at this synagogue was framed mall prints for the walls. If a dentist's office had a mikveh, it would look like this.

Disappointed but still game, I allowed the mikveh lady to show me around: a waiting room, an extremely normal bathroom with a pink-curtained shower/tub, the mikveh itself. The walls were tiled gray-blue. Morning light filtered in from windows set close to the high ceiling. A narrow landing led from the bathroom to three short steps descending into the still-empty tub. The mikveh lady twisted her large faucets. I returned to the jammed waiting room, where my buddy, Risa, was perched in lotus position on the floor in the middle of the group. With her loopy brown curls topped by an Indian cap that served her as a kippah, Risa looked like a graphic out of *The Santa Cruz Haggadah*.

Risa was explaining why she and her husband tried to follow halakha related to sex and her period. This meant sharing with my future in-laws certain savory details. I sidled close to her and hissed, "Risa-baby, you were supposed to be practicing the songs."

I suggested we cut to the chase. Our cumbersome group squeezed as best we could into the extremely normal bathroom. Risa-baby started us on "Hine Matov." I stripped, hopped in the shower and hopped out. Risa checked under my fingernails to make sure I was mikveh-clean, and I moved through the clothed crowd to the narrow landing. Still singing, the rest bunched in after me. The ten-by-ten tub was now full. Mist drifted up from the steaming water.

I took the steps slowly and moved to the center of the bath, where I gestured for the singing to stop. It was very still. I smiled up at them and chanted the *shehechianu,* the prayer for something new, which I translate as: "Thank you, Whatever You Are that is in charge of all this, for bringing me to the beauty of this moment." Then, as Jewish women have done for thousands of years, I let myself go.

The water was so warm. Three times, I made sure to float freely before standing and sinking again. Three times, I curled into a ball and went deeper into a tight spot in my heart. The third time, I felt it open.

I almost wept. I shivered and pulled back. I still wonder what I would have experienced had I been brave enough to go further.

I stood and recited the blessing for the mikveh. Then I ascended the steps and made my wet, naked way back to my robe.

Still quiet, we retired to the bathroom, which now seemed the perfect launching pad for a spiritual experience. I hugged each woman, thanked her for attending and accepted her blessings. I was still unsure what I had expected from the mikveh, but knew I had gotten it. I understood I had taken a mikveh to draw from an element of my heritage that supported who I am, as opposed to participating in a custom that was simply still around.

To them, I simply said, "Ladies, let's get me married."

The final transition into marriage began with removing my engagement ring.

We had bought them in Bali: one for him, one for me, silver and carnelian, which we found out later invokes fertility. Oy. Cliff chose a broad silver band with a single blood-red stone. Mine had a smooth slab of carnelian all the way around, plus several decorative knobs of it for the ring's highlight. A solid ring. It created a pressure I had grown accustomed to during the year we were engaged. As I dressed for my wedding, I transferred the engagement ring from my left hand to my right. The absence left a vacuum, ready to be filled.

I can't tell you the number of friends who told me their weddings were a beautiful blur. Except Risa-baby, who likened hers to an acid trip without the acid. I remember every moment of the ceremony we so carefully fashioned. I remember standing behind Cliff and his father as we waited for our cue, the traditional wedding song, "Do Di Li." I remember their backs. Slender, upright, the midnight of their jackets hanging from identical, dignified sets of shoulders. They held hands.

A part of me wished the photographer would capture what I was seeing. Another part was glad it belonged to me alone.

I remember walking to the chuppah our community had made. I remember the rain starting. I remember circling. The audience sang as we had told them: "Body to body, soul to soul, mind to mind, and destiny to destiny." Fern had suggested the four-note chant as a way to generate energy during the circling. I remember working hard to maintain eye contact with Cliff. Seven circles take a long time. I remember Cliff mouthing, "Slow down," like the inevitable onstage directions that occur during grade-school drama productions. I remember smiling in return. I remember individual faces beaming from the rows of folding chairs, umbrellas going up, raincoats held over heads. I remember thinking it was going too fast.

Mostly, I remember the light. Our chuppah was backed in white. Translucent light bathed us through the Chagall blue and purple—the love of our community. Perhaps it was a bit of the great light we are told about in Kabbalah: The Creator, in making the world, put fresh, new light into vessels. But the light was so strong, so beautiful, it shattered the vessels, trickling down and down until it reached this world, where it formed plants and animals, people and things.

Under our chuppah, I witnessed that glow, and the luminescence that the Baal Shem Tov described as rising from each human being and reaching straight to heaven: "When two souls that are destined to be together find each other, their streams of light flow together and a single, brighter light goes forth from their united being."

✡

A year and a half later, I am an Old Married Lady. I suffer no illusions that an egalitarian ceremony means we pass Go and collect our egalitarian union. A healthy marriage is something we work on every day. But coming to marriage through a ritual that upheld who I am—who we are—helped. Similarly, the overwhelming task of planning a wedding was made easier coming out of a loving, supportive, utterly goofy partnership. I remain grateful that my necessary rebellion didn't result in throwing out the Nice Jewish Boy with the mikveh water.

If I have a daughter, I hope she rebels—at least enough to determine which elements of her culture and her family resonate with her view of herself. I hope Judaism ends up in there. If it doesn't, I will try not to kvetch.

I am becoming more facile with the word "husband." I still don't own a car. But the other day, I noticed my lipstick didn't flatter the way I thought it had in the light of my bathroom that morning. I made a pit stop in a department store and picked up a new tube.

It is orange.

FROM RIOT GRRL TO YESHIVA GIRL,

or How I Became My Own Damn Rabbi

JENNIFER BLEYER

I WAS NOT RAISED IN THE TORRENTIAL DOWNPOUR of women's liberation, but rather in its trickling runoff. My mother and her friends were at-home moms who shaved their armpits, drank chocolate Slim-Fast shakes and played mahjong. They dutifully chauffeured their daughters to ballet class every Wednesday and didn't balk at buying us Barbies. They read Danielle Steel. They Jazzercised. But even so, tiny droplets of the feminist movement leaked into my suburban 1970s childhood. I wasn't allowed to watch *Three's Company* on television because it was demeaning to women, my mom told me, before I even knew what "demeaning" meant. I had a *Free to Be . . . You and Me* record that was riddled with scratches, its album jacket worn out from use. There was never a doubt that I would go to college and, for the sake of parental *kvelling*, perhaps become the successful doctor that only boys were once expected to become. Sure, there must have been women gleefully digging into each other with speculums and burning their quilted pot holders somewhere, but from my vantage point, the alarming, nameless problem that Betty Friedan identified in *The Feminine Mystique* registered as nothing more than a minor fact of life.

I was sent to a Conservative Jewish day school through junior high and then to a public high school in suburban Detroit. The Jewish school

14

guarded each of its students with the same concern and reverence with which we guarded the Torah scroll when it left its small wooden ark. We, boys and girls alike, were the recipients of an education that was creatively inspired, morally rooted and largely egalitarian. Going from there to public high school was something akin to laboratory mice being released into the general population. The boys tousled their hair to disguise near-permanent yarmulke indentations, the girls tried not to slip into Hebrew in their Spanish classes, and all of us seemed a little lost without the ritual of a morning minyan. As a social experiment it may have been interesting, but as a life, it kind of sucked. There was nothing about it, however, that could have predicted the swings my life would soon take.

In 1991, I found punk rock. How does a nice Jewish girl from the Midwest get involved with punk rock, you might wonder? Shortly after a tumultuous move to Cleveland (and really, what's not tumultuous when you're fifteen?) I was sent to a summer program in Pittsburgh where I befriended an older local punk named Spaz. Spaz had wild blue eyes and a mohawk. He had piles of seven-inch records and strange magazines. He plastered the town with photocopied art that he called Public Enemas, provocative drawings and diatribes that poked fun at the conformity that surrounded him. We would stay out all night taping these up around Pittsburgh, and every staid public monument somehow became magical in our presence. We talked to strangers and absorbed them into our nighttime journeys. I learned through Spaz that, contrary to outdated images of the Sex Pistols and ripped leather jackets, punk rock was about freedom, openness, joy and autonomy. I learned that it was a vehicle through which even the most entrenched social conventions could be questioned and changed. I learned that since the late '70s, when it briefly popped up on the public radar, punk rock had been a viable, self-sustaining subculture. It had produced volumes of music, writing, art and subgroups espousing everything from anarchism to veganism to radical environmentalism.

And I happened to become a punk just when it spawned a subgroup espousing what was dearest to me: feminism.

In 1991, a cluster of all-girl bands sprouted up in the Pacific Northwest, and punk girls started to hold small gatherings to confront sexism in the "scene." They called themselves riot grrls. I was sixteen and back home in Cleveland when I heard about them; just the name, with its teeth-grinding spelling of "girl," made me swoon. I was in love. Scouring the underground network of photocopied-and-stapled homemade zines, I sent for as many made by riot grrls as I could find, many no more than alternately angst-ridden and joyous diary entries, handwritten and xeroxed. The Riot Grrl movement spoke to me in a more powerful, visceral and gratifying way than anything I had ever experienced, as if my own subconscious had mysteriously untangled itself and formed an organization. I was unable to rest until Riot Grrl effectively took over the entire known universe. I started off by forming the Cleveland chapter.

When the world, with its appetite for the absurd, looked at us, it saw a bunch of teenage girls with facial piercings, blue hair, torn fishnets and old skate sneakers. But when we looked at each other, we saw our complexity, our hugeness, our love. We went to pro-choice protests, made zines and saw girl bands play when they came through town. Some of us went to the national Riot Grrl conventions in Washington, D.C., and Lincoln, Nebraska. Mostly, though, we just got together at each other's houses for big dinners and sleepover parties, and we talked. Contrary to its threatening name, the riot-grrl world was basically a support group: a '90s version of the '70s consciousness-raising group. Looking back now, just over ten years since its wild inception, I can't help but remember it as somewhat precocious and self-absorbed. But I am also amazed at how sophisticated we were in our heady, earnest discussions of race, class, sexuality and gender dynamics, and how genuinely supportive we were of one another at such a fragile time in our lives.

Throughout my punk-rock and riot-grrl days, I distanced myself from Judaism as if it were a contagious disease. Scouring my memory to recall what I found so odious then, I think that part of it was certainly a growing class consciousness. I was one of only a few riot grrls in our Cleveland group who came from the more affluent east side of the city; although my family was not ostentatiously wealthy, we were comfortable. I began associating Judaism with the social inequalities of which I was growing aware. In this tight community of working-class and lower-middle-class girls who had to work shitty jobs and drown themselves in debt to go to college, I associated Judaism with privilege: the privilege of being white (or at least passing for white), the privilege of having money, the privilege of being educated, the privilege of having a stable family. Of course, I knew that not all Jews were white, wealthy, educated and functional. But I insisted then (as I do now) that while acknowledging gradations of diversity among American Jews, we should not be too delusional about our general social class. One of the big pastimes for riot grrls was attacking and analyzing privilege, and for me, acknowledging my Jewish privilege was an arduous, necessary process.

Another thing that spun me far out from the Jewish orbit was its general irrelevancy to my life. I suppose that's not an uncommon feeling for most Jewish kids, unless by some feat of imagination they can link Judaism to pop music, fashion, SAT scores and the mall. Teenagers' alienation from their parents' lifestyle is a certified part of our cultural experience, but to me, Judaism seemed even more archaic and clueless than my parents themselves. This was not the Democratic Upper West Side of Manhattan, remember. The arbiters of liberal Jewish culture often underestimate that vast bulk of mainstream American Jews who are not concerned with ecological Tu B'Shvat rituals and feminist Passover seders, but rather with showing up in fur coats to High Holiday services and throwing bar mitzvah parties that rival the Trump empire in glitz. The rituals themselves—fasting and then gorging on Yom Kippur, praying in a foreign language—struck me as rote and empty. When matters of the spirit registered on my radar, they were vague, inquisitive and open—unlike the mechanized tradition in which I had been raised.

But I could never totally cut myself off. We once had a riot-grrl pot-luck during Passover, and I brought a box of matzo to eat while everyone else devoured huge plates of food. I remember wearing my steel-toe combat boots and an old green-and-orange-striped dress that matched the green and orange of the Manischewitz box. We were a big group crammed into the dingy kitchen of someone's apartment. Some of my friends knew what matzo was and others didn't, so I gave my best explanation: "It's just this bread that didn't rise, because the Jews were slaves in Egypt and when they were set free I guess there was no time for their bread to rise, so it's kind of like a thing to remember that, I guess. Something like that." Everyone nodded with respectful interest (they were way into cultural experiences). I crunched away at the flat white matzo and passed around pieces so everybody could try it (again, that cultural experience thing). I felt a small, superficial tinge of pride, realizing that being Jewish was in fact interesting, unusual and somehow significant.

Our riot-grrl chapter slowly faded away as some of us went far away to college and others got stuck in various ruts in Ohio. Riot Grrl as a movement pretty much dissolved everywhere, in fact, as intense scrutiny by the punk scene as well as the mainstream media rendered it an uncomfortable caricature of itself. I moved to New York, traveled across the country, drifted into and out of relationships and otherwise engaged in the strange dance of life. I remained a feminist, of course, and although Riot Grrl as a way of life lost its relevancy for me, the lessons I learned from it remained.

A couple of years later, when I was twenty, I took a year off from college to travel by myself. After months of journeying through the deserts of Egypt, the jungles of Uganda and the verdant lanes of Paris, I went to Vienna, the city my grandparents had fled in 1938. I wanted to spend a Shabbat there, and found a local Chabad family who lived only blocks from my grandparents' old apartment building in the second district of the city. They were a young, energetic Israeli couple who had come to Vienna as "messengers" of their Rebbe; the husband was the headmaster of Vienna's only Jewish school, and his wife was the caretaker of their six children. Over a beautiful Shabbat meal laid with silver and china, conversation revealed that the man and I were distantly removed cousins. The coincidence was astounding, considering how I'd accidentally ended up in their house.

"So, my cousin," he said, stroking his beard, "why are you wasting your time traveling aimlessly like this? You'll never find anything. Go learn in yeshiva if you really want to find something. In fact, if you agree to stay for a few months, I will send you to one of the best yeshivas for girls." Never one to slap serendipity in the face, I accepted the offer and was promptly sent to Machon Alte, a yeshiva for young women in Tsfat, Israel.

If you can imagine the furthest, most dichotomous opposite of a riot grrl, it would surely have to be a Machon Alte yeshiva girl. This was a school for young *ba'ale teshuvah,* girls who had not grown up religiously observant but had become or were exploring the possibility of becoming so. The night I arrived at the Machon Alte's stately old building on Tsfat's main thoroughfare, the girls took me to a back room and told me to dig through boxes of donated clothes for a *tsnius,* or modest, wardrobe. I complied, pulling out long skirts and frumpy shirts that covered the elbows and ever-arousing neckbone. I was placed in a dorm room with two roommates, one of whom was an accomplished guitar player and singer but would only play in the seclusion of our room (outside, she ran the risk of breaking the prohibition against women singing in earshot of men). We had classes all day in Talmud, Torah, Kabbalah and various tracts of Chabad tradition, almost all taught by rabbis who would avoid looking us in the eye. A couple of times a week, we had classes that were essentially Jewish home economics—teaching us how to run a halakhically Jewish home by preparing for Shabbat, honoring our husbands, raising our children and attending to the various domestic duties prescribed for women in Hasidic orthodoxy. On Shabbat, we would go to the city's synagogues and watch the men praying in the main part of the sanctuary from our isolated balcony perches, or through dense lace curtains or latticework partitions. At least once a week, Machon Alte would explode in a joyful frenzy as a student came in and announced that she had gotten engaged.

The yeshiva's cook, a boisterous Tunisian woman named Juliette, doubled as a matchmaker and would "match" young women with boys from the men's yeshiva down the road. If both headmasters agreed to the match, the couple was generally allowed to meet. After no more than three or four meetings, they would often decide to marry.

To be sure, living as a yeshiva girl was utterly bizarre. But I got into it, and flirted with the lifestyle for a few years before coming to my senses. Now, I wonder how it was that I went so quickly from scoffing at the idea of shaving my legs to wearing pantyhose in hundred-degree heat lest anyone see my exposed ankles. Part of it, I think, was just a keen sense of curiosity: I studied anthropology in college and this was almost like an ethnographic study, going undercover in a community in order to understand it. But I was not collecting informants, building rapport or writing fieldnotes, as they say in anthro-speak. There was a part of me that was legitimately attracted to the Hasidic lifestyle and governing beliefs. The laws of modest dress dictated that women were not to be seen as objects of beauty, but as human beings based on their merits—granted, a limited span of meritorious possibilities, but still less superficial than those which mainstream society allowed. In fact, I have heard Orthodox Jewish women defend their wigs and Islamic women defend their veils on seemingly feminist principles, claiming a sense of empowerment by withholding their hair, legs and bodies from the world's visual consumption.

But there was more to it than that. Studying Jewish texts with academic precision and spiritual insight was new to me, and deeply challenged my perception of Judaism as a string of rote holiday rituals and unconvincing rhetoric. Something about Orthodoxy itself was also appealing—partly because the moral absolutism and strictness of behavior (I learned to pre-cut toilet paper for Shabbat, as the act of ripping it constitutes prohibited work) represented a release from the casual, nonsensical whims of society. In my ever-gnawing quest for freedom, I came to recognize the extraordinary spiritual freedom that exists, ironically, like an escape hatch within the most rigid systems of rules, procedures and restrictions.

I quickly learned that I was not alone among women of similar backgrounds who felt drawn to this life, despite all the alarms signaling "second-class citizen." I sat at the Shabbat tables of many highly educated and well-read women who had left promising careers; who had followed the Grateful Dead and spent years at ashrams in India; who had participated in the student uprisings of the sixties and the feminist movement of the seventies—all of whom had chosen to move to Israel, have a gaggle of kids and learn to cook a mean kugel. I even met young women who had been punk-rock kids like myself: One, a convert, had hopped freight trains up and down the West Coast, played in a band and been popular in Berkeley's punk scene before she moved to Israel and became an Orthodox Jew. They did not necessarily proselytize to me, but as logical, thoughtful women with an incredible range of world experience and fluency in contemporary culture, their choice to become Orthodox had a curious credibility. It was simply too intriguing to ignore.

After that summer, I returned to New York and dabbled on and off with religious observance, spending time in the Hasidic enclaves of Brooklyn and the Orthodox synagogues of the Upper West Side. Still, I could never completely give myself over to it. In the seclusion of many family dining rooms, I heard statements about non-Jews, and Arabs in particular, that were absolutely unconscionable if not outright racist. I saw people behave in ways that deeply contradicted their own pious tenets, confirming that a black hat and coat does not render one holier or more spiritually aware than anyone else. I realized that much of what I found attractive about this particular lifestyle was accessible outside of it as well—that the beauty of Jewish ritual, the sense of community and the intense examination of texts are not the exclusive province of ultra-religious Jews.

After this religious exploration (which, needless to say, quite shocked my family), I shook off the residue of judgment and habit and found myself planted with a brilliant, luminous seed. I still retain a strange mix of scorn and fondness for Orthodoxy, but nothing has tarnished my love of that seed, that divine life force that animates Judaism in all of its sectarian chaos. In retrospect, I think that my foray into Orthodoxy shaped me as a Jew in much the same way that being a riot grrl shaped me as a feminist. I learned from both experiences that everything can become dangerously entrenched in its own orthodoxy and has to be shaken up in order to remain dynamic and relevant.

The Riot Grrl movement, for instance, was most daring not in its fuck-you to male-dominated society, but in its screeching fuck-you to mainstream feminism. To be sure, few of us had an especially educated awareness of how hard our mothers and grandmothers had fought for certain privileges we took for granted. But we legitimately grappled with a feminism that seemed to be about appropriating the roles of men, instead of exploding the entire notion of what it meant to be human. We did not want the "equal right" to be corporate drones, executive whipcrackers or miserable supermoms, futilely trying to balance career, family, friends and therapy. We wanted something that was off the charts completely, that reconfigured every stagnant fixture of society.

Similarly, I began to see Judaism as something essentially beautiful that has been hijacked by a great many self-appointed authorities. As sacrilegious as it sounds, the rabbis need their own fuck-you in order to liberate the treasures they guard. This doesn't mean trashing tradition as much as shaking the dust off of it and letting it grow. As the first generation of Jewish feminists was instrumental to creating egalitarian discourse and leveling Jewish male privilege, my generation of Jewish feminists will, I hope, extend that trajectory to question the nature of all authority within our tradition, liberating it from its captors.

My Judaism has evolved to the point where I go from peaceful Shabbat dinners uptown to raucous clubs downtown and dance until 4 A.M., feeling neither guilt nor contradiction. I host holiday gatherings for all of my friends, Jewish and non-Jewish, white, black and brown, and welcome everyone as children of Israel. I can say a *shehechianu* blessing when being arrested at a protest, to thank God for delivering me to that moment. My generation of Jewish feminists is creating a Judaism so seamless that the spiritual, political, social and personal are not just related, but are virtually the same thing. We are allowing ourselves to be Jewish in the way that riot grrls taught us to be feminist—explosively, boundlessly, beyond definition and with an almost erotic hunger for transcendence.

We are on our way.

BUBBE GOT BACK

Tales of a Jewess with Caboose

OPHIRA EDUT

I'M A JEWISH CHICK WITH A BIG BOOTY.

There. I said it.

Not that you can really keep something like that a secret. Disengage from a face-to-face conversation, turn at a slight angle, and *wham,* the curve hits the vision and shatters the flat lines of space. Some appreciate the interruption from monotony. Others shift uncomfortably, unnerved by the sudden disappearance of order and control.

Thanks to two decades of hip-hop and the (literal) overexposure of Jennifer Lopez, big butts have now settled comfortably into public discourse. Yet Jews have not embraced the cultural acceptance of thick chicks with round behinds—despite the fact that there are many among our ranks. Sure, we may dance to hip-hop tracks like "Back That Thang Up" or "Baby Got Back." But is the average Jewish guy *really* sincere when he raises a beer and shouts along, "You's a big fine woman / won't you back that thang up"? Methinks no.

"You're a white girl shaped like a black girl," my friend Anika put it bluntly. "And the African-American men in my family love a healthy woman." We devolved into a Jimmy the Greek–style postulation of my booty's origins. Was it courtesy of my Middle Eastern father, a dark-complexioned Israeli with a notable "bump" himself? Or did it stretch back to ancient days, when, according to some speculators, the original Hebrews were black?

"I mean, look at those tomb paintings of the Hebrew slaves in Egypt," offered my friend Dyann, a churchy Pentecostal girl who was raised to believe that the Jews were God's chosen people, and was eager to make the connection. "They're shown as brown and black! And where do you think those full lips and those springy curls come from? From *us,* that's who."

Grateful that somebody supported me for draggin' this wagon, I didn't protest. She had a point. Indeed, my butt has been a cultural amb*ass*ador, a p*ass*port to insta-credibility in many a multiracial setting. "Look, it's Heavy Chevy," I was habitually greeted at the door of my favorite Latin music club. "How much junk you got in that trunk tonight?"

And, wanting to be down, I again kept quiet. In an age when race can still be the elephant that nobody mentions, people quietly size each other up for nonverbal cues of who's Us and who's Them. I guess you could say I made it in through the back door. My body engenders a level of trust among some black folks—who, for the record, I'm aware come in a variety of sizes, too. And since among Jews, it has regularly marked me as an outsider ("You mean you're not on a diet?"), it's a relief to be accepted somewhere.

When it comes to dating, my butt launches me into choppy, racially charged waters. To the average Jewish guy, my body is old-world flavor in a new world order. It conjures images, perhaps, of their sturdily built grandmothers, fresh from Ellis Island, stooped over sinks preparing borscht, or wearing babushkas and tilling the barren soil of the Russian steppe. I suspect they're looking for a sleeker model than my reliable old Chevy. Experience has proven: If I wanted to date only Jewish men, I'd be ass out.

But put me in front of a newly minted immigrant, a middle-aged man with Lolita fantasies or a sizable number of black or Latino men in America, and I'm the embodiment of fantasy and cultural ideal: five feet two inches and 155 pounds with back and a rack. A little roundness to the tum, some thickness to the thighs . . . to these fellas, that's good eatin'.

Maybe Jewish guys, who are nowadays accepted as part of the mainstream, have absorbed more vanilla desires by default. Few that I know would pass over a girl who's thin, small-featured and aces the shiksa litmus test. "If she's Jewish, great; if not, she can always convert," one friend says glibly. I've perused Jewish personals and found ads like this one: "SJM, professional, fit, seeks slender SJF who's not Jewish-looking." Well, for plenty of us SJFs, that's gonna take serious effort to pull off—like obsessive dieting, surgery or perhaps a genetic rescrambling. Yet many a Jewess has gone under the knife with the preposterous notion that surgery will make her desirable, perhaps even marriageable. Others of us, myself included, swallow the bitter pill of occasional tribal rejection and ask: Why bother changing when we can find a goy-boy who worships us, "Jewish" looks and all?

As a result, my dating scorecard includes one Jewish guy, a handful of non-Jewish white guys and men of color aplenty. It's not based on preference. Just the question, fueled by self-esteem: Why join a club that doesn't want you as a member?

Yet . . . I'm white, for all intents and purposes. I tan to a deep eggshell color and my melanin meter is on E. But I also have enough loyal black and Latina girlfriends to retain a storehouse of their painful experiences. They've all endured rejection by men of color who expected them to be my opposite: ethnic girls who look white. A bigger body is still cool, for the most part—but longer hair, lighter skin and green or hazel eyes receive preference.

Possessing all those traits myself, I get a spontaneous surge of sisterly guilt with each new nonwhite boyfriend. Is it a case of take-the-best-and-leave-the-rest, ethnic in body and white by trait? Does this guy have an "issue" with the women of his culture that he's acting out on me? I've gotten pretty good at filtering out those fools. I once declared a short-lived ban on guys who hadn't dated "their own" women. Hypocrisy registered swiftly and I lifted the embargo, since my own scorecard was mostly devoid of Jews.

But in many ways, my guilt about hurting women of color by dating interracially is there because I owe black women my life. They gave me a vocabulary that allowed me to rise above an all-consuming body hatred replete with obsessive exercise, calorie-cutting and self-loathing. My black girlfriends called my thickness "healthy" and modeled their own girth with a confidence that shattered everything I'd been taught to believe.

Like, for example, that I needed to "Eat! Eat! Children are starving in India and would kill for that casserole!" while extra body baggage was eyed critically and svelteness was praised. Or that Jews were supposed to be proud of our heritage, yet we were supposed to disguise it with blond hair dye and a covert spring-break appointment with the rhinoplastician. On a recent trip to Israel, my uncle barbecued seven kinds of meat and loaded my plate with endless skewers of *shishlik* and kebab. Food was love, and it was my duty to show appreciation by shoveling it past the point of no return. But the next day, I was somehow supposed to wake up with a flat stomach. With all this tsuris, we Jewesses get the message early: It's better to be Barbie than Barbra Streisand.

Thanks to the influence of my darker sisters, I fell into step and gradually came to embrace myself the way I was built. So my house was made of bricks, not twigs? Solid, man.

But home is where it all begins. I was raised by amazing, capable Jewish women who consider body fat the complete antithesis of healthy—a no-brainer reason to skip dessert and denounce their bodies publicly. On a recent trip home to Detroit, I found myself shouting at a family Shabbat dinner, "Can we have one fucking meal where we don't talk about dieting?"

It was almost comical: My aunt was suggesting that my twenty-two-year-old sister try some aging celebrity's diet program. My mom was slicing herself a wafer-thin serving of apple pie, muttering that she'd have to jog an extra mile tomorrow, and handing everyone else gargantuan, ice-cream-covered slabs.

My uncle was protesting the size of his portion, making arrangements to join my mother's morning jog and reminding his delightfully chubby eight-year-old daughter that she should only eat half of her pie because she didn't want to be fat like her auntie Rozzie. My Israeli father, never known for his tact, added, "Quiet you with this nonsense. You will all cry that you are fat and then you will eat all the day. Just eat the pie, then go be fatsos on a diet tomorrow."

Needless to say, I lost my appetite.

But not for long. Because, in many ways, being a Jew is about hunger. Hunger to fit in, to feel safe, to survive. Hunger for knowledge, philosophical debate, intelligent life. Hunger to make sense of historical tragedies like the Holocaust. We've developed a strange appetite for the paradoxes we've stomached, for questions that can only be answered in riddles. We understand both the haunted feeling of total emptiness and the joyful sensation of being stuffed to the gills.

I recently learned that Jewish women have a disproportionate number of eating disorders. According to *Lilith* magazine, the Renfrew Center (a clinic that treats eating problems) had a 13 percent Jewish clientele between 1994 and 1996; keep in mind that Jews only comprise about 2 percent of the United States population. *Lilith* also reported that the eating disorder rate among Orthodox and Syrian Jews in Brooklyn was 50 percent higher than that of the general population. And in Israel, the land of milk, honey, floozies with Uzis and shamelessly cheesy folk dances, Harvard Eating Disorders Center guru Catherine Steiner-Adair discovered rampant eating disorders when she spent a month there in 1997.

Lots of reasons were cited: the dueling influences of food-lovin' Jewish values and thin-thigh-pushing mainstream American values. Our war-inspired obsession with buying, cooking and eating vast amounts of food in preparation for The Day There May Not Be Enough to Eat. The pressure on Orthodox girls to be perfect students, to marry and start families before they're emotionally ready, to hide their bodies in the name of "modesty." The media. The fashion industry. Mom. Dad.

All valid explanations. And if I may take the speculation out onto an unwalked limb, let's look at what the experts pinpoint as causes and symptoms of eating disorders: Trauma. A history of abuse. Cultural pressures and assimilation. Depression and anxiety. Distorted self-image. Overachieving tendencies. Feeling unsafe, powerless or out of control in our environments.

As Jews, our history is colored by every one of these things.

All this posterior postulation leads to a bigger, blunter question: Are Jews white? On one level, the answer is *duh,* of course not; we exist in many colors and nationalities. My own father is regularly mistaken for Mexican in our provincial hometown. But as American racial politics define whiteness, we are peeps of the paler persuasion.

And, dare I say it, the average American Jew is more than okay with that. Caught like "Moishe in the Middle" between the extreme stereotypes of "black" and "white," which side do Jewish folks choose? Let's see, there are the darker people on the six o'clock news getting clubbed by police officers (hello, pogroms) and forced to live in impoverished ghettos (hello, Eastern Europe). Then there are the even-toothed WASPs livin' large on yachts, decked in nautical gear the price of a small apartment (hello, assimilation; good-bye persecution, McCarthyism, immigrant poverty, Holocaust). Who wouldn't want to drop twenty pounds, change his name to Blair and move to Connecticut?

I'm being outrageous here. But I believe Jews with white skin have found a buffer zone in assimilation and the somewhat naive belief that we are average Americans, really no different from our German or Irish neighbors. In many cases, there is great truth to this. Other times, however, Jews mythologize white America, acting out a cartoonish imitation. A Jewish couple invented the Barbie doll—the ultimate icon of Aryanism—in 1959. Even my own father, despite his Sephardic heritage, dark skin and strong accent, believes himself to be a white man.

I'm not trying to form conspiracy theories against my own people. I just believe we suffer when we deny our unique connections to people of color. American Jews have been part of many multiracial coalitions and movements, from civil rights to hip-hop. Some of us are either mistaken for—or (gasp) literally are—black, biracial, Latino, Mizrahi, Middle Eastern, African and so on. Jews can and do swing both ways. But that seems to be a well-kept secret, perhaps out of fear that Jews becoming "racialized" will spawn another Nazi-style conspiracy and lead to our demise.

Heaven help us if we admit in public that, you know, a lot of Jews do have kinky hair or full lips, prominent noses or big butts. And slap on a gag order if we dare say that these traits triggered our "Jewdar" (my Semitic equivalent of gaydar) and allowed us to identify someone as a fellow Jew. "Oh come on, Ophi," I've been chastised wearily. "Not all Jews have those features." "No kidding," I say, pointing out my own stick-straight hair. But not all black people can be identified on sight as black, either. Isn't it human nature to seek out reflections of yourself in others, or connections between your group and another?

Well, maybe not. But I imagine that Jews might have a lot less body neurosis and a lot more fun if we took a page from some of our darker brethren and widened the scope of body types we consider beautiful. My God, we might even let ourselves eat the vast amounts of food we prepare. I mean, how many holidays are in a Jewish year, each one requiring an elaborate meal? Likewise, we could teach the rest of the world to make really good matzo ball soup. It would be a cultural exchange of sorts, our way of saying thank you.

Seems fair enough to me. Perhaps my fellow Jews are, um, a little behind the curve. I guess I'll just have to sit on this one until they come around.

Parenting as a Religious Jewish Feminist

Haviva Ner-David

IT'S A GLORIOUS SUMMER MORNING IN JERUSALEM, and I am standing at the window looking out at a cloudless sapphire-blue sky. There is still a chill in the air this early in the day, and the tiles beneath my bare feet feel refreshingly cool. I think of how hot I will soon be as the sun rises higher in the sky and I walk my two children—my three-year-old daughter, Michal, and my one-year-old son, Adin—to *gan* (preschool) on my way to the yeshiva where I am studying Talmud this year, our first year living in Israel. By the afternoon, when I pick them up, I will feel the heat from the sidewalk through the soles of my sandals.

This is a city of extremes: mountains and valleys, hot days and cool nights, the *haredim* (ultra-Orthodox) and the *hilonim* (secular Jews). It is an intense city, where emotions fly and everyone believes he or she has the truth and is willing to fight to defend it; yet there is something about Jerusalem that embraces all of this and everyone. It is a real place, where everything comes to a head. It is a place that both beckons to me and pushes me away, embraces me and seems about to spit me out. It is here that I choose to make my home.

I drape my *tallit*, my prayer shawl, over my head, and suddenly it is dark. I block out all distractions—the blue sky, the bright sun glaring off the white

31

Jerusalem stone—for a completely private moment with God. I inhale a deep breath of clean morning air, thinking about my life and the kindness that God has bestowed on me. Under my tallit, I recite softly in Hebrew:

> How precious is Your lovingkindness, O God! The children of humanity take refuge in the shadow of Your wings. May they be sated from the abundance of Your house; and may You give them to drink from the stream of Your delights. For with You is the source of all life— by Your light we shall see light. Extend Your kindness to those who know You, and Your charity to the upright of heart. (Psalms 36: 7–10)

With my white and gray tallit now draped over my shoulders, I take my leather tefillin out of their worn velvet bag, its purple material so frayed that some spots are almost translucent. Along with my first pair of tefillin, this bag once belonged to my husband's great uncle—who, it is fair to say, would not be thrilled to know that I, a woman, am the inheritor of these ritual objects. Although it is not prohibited for women to wear tefillin, traditionally only men have worn them, with a few exceptions recorded throughout Jewish history. The Talmud tells us that Michal, the daughter of the biblical King Saul and the first wife of King David, "wore tefillin and the Sages did not protest her action." (BT Eruvin 96A) It is also said that the three daughters of Rashi—the eleventh-century French scholar who wrote the most commonly studied commentary on the Bible and Talmud—wore tefillin, as did Chana Rochel Werbermacher, the Maiden of Ludomir, a Hasidic woman and mystic with a large following in the Ukraine in the nineteenth century, who after a serious illness took on time-bound mitzvot (the commandments that are traditionally obligated only of men) and eventually emigrated to Israel.

Although I know that there have been other women throughout the ages who have chosen to wear tefillin, they have been anomalies; they probably could all fit into one room. In the past two decades, especially since women have been given the opportunity to become rabbis in the Conservative movement and must, as a requirement for ordination, assume the obligation to don tefillin every morning when they pray, more women have taken on this practice. But I cannot think of more than twenty women of any denomination who regularly wear tefillin and are not Conservative rabbis or rabbinical students.

As I wrap the leather straps around my left arm seven times—seven is the number of earthly spirituality in Kabbalah, Jewish mysticism—I think about the first time I wore tefillin five years ago. The moment felt so right, integrating my feminist and Jewish selves which until that point had been like two magnets repelling one another. I also felt as if I were breaking an ancient taboo. Growing up, I had seen only men wearing tefillin; it just wasn't an option for girls, any more than it was an option for a boy to wear a dress. I played in Little League, wore blue jeans and T-shirts and even studied Bible and Talmud with the boys, but this symmetry of experience did not extend to the realm of Jewish ritual. In the synagogue, I had to sit behind a mechitza, the partition separating men and women, once I became a bat mitzvah (at age twelve, when a girl becomes an adult woman in Jewish law). While my brothers could read publicly from the Torah scroll, lead and participate actively in services, count in a minyan (a quorum of ten required for public prayer) and serve as witnesses under Jewish law, I could not. When they reached the age of bar mitzvah, they received their own pairs of tefillin. I got my ears pierced.

It was not until ten years after my bat mitzvah that I obtained tefillin. My husband, Jacob, gave me his spare set. He showed me how to put them on, and I trembled with both excitement and fear as I followed his directions. How could something that made me feel so whole also make me feel like hiding?

It is most commonly understood that the Rabbis exempted women from performing certain time-bound mitzvot, such as putting on tefillin, because women's time belongs to others—their children and their husbands.

They should not feel pressured to take time away from nurturing others, so the logic goes, in order to fulfill God's will; God will understand. In my own experience, I do need this time set aside for God. I need to reconnect with my spiritual center before facing the day, and I need to make time for this apart from my other responsibilities, especially those related to caring for my children. If I lose myself in all of this caring, what good am I to others? What good am I to myself? What good am I to God? The words of Hillel the Sage echo in my ears: "If I am not for myself, who will be for me? If I am only for myself, what am I? And if not now, when?"

As I am saying the Sh'ma—a passage from the biblical book of Numbers which Jews (or, according to Orthodox halakha, Jewish men) are obligated to recite two times each day—my daughter, Michal, joins me on the porch, rubbing the sleep from her eyes. Her hair is a mass of chestnut-brown waves flying in different directions, and she is wearing one of my T-shirts, which she has adopted as pajamas. The neck of the shirt hangs loosely, revealing one of her shoulders in a way that reminds me of the fact that she is female, and that some day she may actually look sensual in such a pose. At the age of three, there is nothing about Michal to indicate that she is a girl, except for the fact that she sometimes wears dresses or skirts. Even her long hair does not identify her gender in the *dati* (religious) community, since it is customary not to cut a boy's hair until he is three. Michal has been mistaken for a boy numerous times because she wears a *tallit katan* (the four-cornered garment with *tzitzit,* ritual fringes, traditionally worn under the clothes of Jewish boys and men).

The third paragraph of the Sh'ma contains God's commandment to wear tzitzit on the corners of our garments. Once a day during the daylight hours, when we recite this prayer and say the word "tzitzit," which appears three times in the prayer, the traditional practice is to kiss the fringes on the tallit katan or *tallit gadol,* the prayer shawl.

Although a woman is not halakhically required to recite the Sh'ma, traditional boys, girls, men and women are expected to recite this paragraph as part of our daily morning prayers. Somehow, as a child, I never found it strange to recite God's commandment that we wear tzitzit, even though it was clear that my female peers and I were not considered obligated to wear them—that we *shouldn't* wear them, in fact.

Women, too, need to be reminded of the mitzvot. Tzitzit are a visual reminder of God's will and God's presence in our lives at each and every moment of the day, and I know that I need such a reminder. Even when I am spending the entire day sitting and studying Torah, it is easy, for example, to forget to pray the afternoon prayer service before sundown. When I am spending the day with my young, demanding children, it is even easier to forget to perform certain mitzvot, especially those that must be performed at a certain time. That is one of the rationales for exempting women from time-bound mitzvot—but it also is a strong argument for women wearing tzitzit. The mitzvah of tzitzit is not an act that comes and goes as the hands of the clock turn; instead, the tzitzit serve as a reminder to perform other mitzvot.

My tzitzit remind me all day of what I would like to be. They remind me that my body should be sanctified, and that I was created in the image of God. Despite the criticism and even occasional berating I receive, despite the fact that it sets me apart from almost every other religious (and nonreligious) Jewish woman, I wear tzitzit to remind me of my responsibilities.

It is fascinating to me that even when Michal is wearing a ribbon in her hair or a feminine outfit with flowers, people assume that she is a boy because she is wearing tzitzit. Once, a woman even made this mistake when Michal was wearing a dress. She looked confused when she noticed the tzitzit poking out from under Michal's dress, but she quickly decided that someone like me, whose head covering identifies me as an observant Jew, would sooner put a dress on my son than tzitzit on my daughter.

I am ambivalent about my decision to give Michal tzitzit. While I have adopted for myself practices that cross gender lines in the traditional

Jewish community in which I live, I am not always sure it is fair for me to put Michal in a similar position before she is old enough to understand the implications. For this same reason, I have not pushed her to wear a *kippah* (a traditionally male head covering), although she does own one and often wears it when she prays. Yet I also do not want her to feel that these practices are off-limits to her because she is a girl. I take seriously my responsibility as a Jewish mother to introduce my children to Torah and mitzvot with love, enthusiasm and careful thought, but with a daughter this job becomes more complicated. How can I best prepare Michal to make decisions about her role and practices as a Jewish woman? Traditional norms give her a bias in one direction. Is it wrong for me to balance the scales, to show her that there is an alternative?

I do not want her to grow up feeling, as a Jewish female, resentful of her religion, or marginalized and irrelevant, all of which I often felt as a child and young woman. Even if she will be different, even if she occasionally feels alienated or embarrassed, I hope that the benefit of growing up experiencing the entirety of her tradition—all of the mitzvot—as her own will outweigh the difficulties she will encounter.

As with the kippah, I don't force Michal to wear tzitzit: Each morning, the decision is hers. But she sees me wearing them; she sees her father, Jacob, wearing them; and we strongly encourage her to follow in our path. She usually seems happy to say the *bracha* (blessing) and put them on; the joy and pride in her eyes when she kisses the fringes is enough to reinforce my decision. There are some days when she tells me she doesn't want to wear her tzitzit, and on those days I let her get dressed without them. I wonder if her seemingly whimsical decision-making is related to her gender. Perhaps she is becoming sensitive to the comments she hears: "Why is she wearing tzitzit? Girls don't wear tzitzit!" But she never tells me on those mornings that the reason she does not want to wear tzitzit is that she is a girl; within a few days she always wants to wear them again.

I do not want to make religious issues a point of argument between us. I want Michal to have positive experiences and associations with her

Jewish practices, not negative ones. It is my plan to be as flexible with Adin when he turns three—the age at which a son is traditionally given his first set of tzitzit and his religious education begins—even with issues such as tzitzit, which for a man are obligatory. I do not plan to force him to wear tzitzit or a kippah, although I will certainly encourage him to. And I imagine he will be easier to convince, since he sees boys and men around him wearing them. I do wonder: Will I indeed keep to this egalitarian ideal, or will I slip into more conventional gender expectations and not allow him to choose?

I reach the point in the Sh'ma in which God commands us, the Jewish people, to wear tzitzit to remind us of the mitzvot (although here, too, the Rabbis have interpreted this to refer to men only). Suddenly, Michal snaps fully awake. "*Ima,*" she orders, using the Hebrew word for mother. "I want to kiss my tzitzit! Wait!"

When Michal returns, I continue reciting the Sh'ma, and when I say the word "tzitzit," we both kiss our fringes. I wonder if my face is glowing with the pride I feel. As I pray, I insert a thought, an unarticulated request to God, that this enthusiasm of Michal's for prayer and mitzvot will continue. She sits beside me until I have finished reciting the Sh'ma, and then, as I recite the Amidah, during which I must stand, she hides beneath my tallit, as I remember having done with my father.

I am uncomfortable with the fact that my most vivid, intense memories of committed prayer are from watching my father, not my mother, putting on tefillin and tallit each morning. Although women are, according to most rabbinic opinions, obligated to pray at least twice a day, most of the women in my childhood community did not pray regularly. Sometimes they made it to shul (synagogue) before the communal prayers were over on Shabbat, but they did not feel obligated to do so. They did feel that it was their duty, however, to have a proper Sabbath meal waiting for everyone when they arrived home.

I am convinced that part of what makes men like my father so committed to praying each morning during the work week is the obligation to put on their tefillin. Somehow, that physical action gives focus and discipline to the rather intangible act of prayer. I am reassured of my decision to take on these obligations from which I am exempt according to Jewish law, because I, too, am reaching for that increased intensity and focus in my prayer. Michal will have memories of both me and her father praying each morning, swaying back and forth wrapped in our tallitot and tefillin.

As I remove my tefillin and rewrap them in the way that Jacob showed me five years ago, Michal exclaims, "Ima, I want my own tefillin too!"

"You'll get your own tefillin when you become a bat mitzvah, when you're twelve years old, if you still want them then. Do you think you will?" I ask. I know I am being overbearing. I want to make the most of Michal's burst of enthusiasm for prayer and its rituals, since I know that tomorrow could bring exactly the opposite reaction—but I also don't want to overdo it.

Michal nods her head. "And I want my own tallit, too," she says. I can hear the beginnings of an Israeli accent, after only two months of living in this country, creeping into her Hebrew. "When I get to be an even bigger girl, like you," she adds. I take her into my arms. Maybe what I am trying to impart to my children is actually making an impression. "Of course you can, Michal," I say as I cuddle her. "Of course you can."

And then Michal's had enough. She squirms out of my embrace and instantly becomes occupied, building with some blocks that she finds on the floor from the day before. How different her childhood will be from mine, I think. She will grow up seeing me and other women wearing tallitot and tefillin and reading from the Torah. And she lives in a Jewish country: Hebrew will soon be the language of the street for her, not just words in the Bible. Shabbat will be a day of tangible, visible rest and quiet, with the stores closed and noticeably fewer cars on the road. Judaism—with the intensity and heightened meaning it brings to life, its ancient traditions and slow-paced progress—will surround her. Only time will tell what the effects will be of the choices I make as I raise my children.

As an adolescent, I often saw my parents as either hypocrites or slaves to the *yetzer hara,* the evil inclination. What we learned in Jewish day school and sleep away camp did not mesh with the philosophy of Judaism that my family lived. Our practices at home were more liberal than what I learned everywhere else, and I assumed my parents' approach was wrong. The Jewish law I learned in school and camp was simplified so that we children could understand it. I did not appreciate then the true complexity of and diversity within the halakhic system—a complexity that my parents' religious lifestyle represented to a large degree.

The variety I encountered as a child ultimately encouraged me to develop a more accepting attitude toward pluralism in the Jewish world. I understand now that my parents' practice was not a result of weakness, but of their own struggle to balance tradition and modernity. They often followed more lenient halakhic positions that allowed them to more easily assimilate into the modern world, but allowing oneself more freedom is not necessarily a sign of weakness.

Their choice was in some ways a risky one, as they passed on the religion to their children. A more intellectualized and nuanced religious outlook is sometimes harder to hold on to. I think a simplistic outlook is actually easier to rationalize away, but also easier to practice.

Yet I believe that had I been shown only a black-and-white model, I would not be religiously observant today. The simplistic portrayal of the Jewish legal system that I learned in school backfired—rather than making our religion easier to grasp, it frustrated me. As I discovered life's complexities, this rigid model no longer worked. Without the alternative of my parents' model to turn to once I passed adolescence and let go of the grudges and anger, I might well have abandoned the religious lifestyle entirely.

I don't think we need to present children with the model of Judaism I learned at school. With our own children, my husband and I discuss varying religious observances, and they have been able to apprehend—at their own levels—the concepts of pluralism and individual choice. They were surprised to discover that not all Jews keep Shabbat, and that even those who do don't necessarily keep it the way we do. But now that they know, they often quote this idea back to me when, for instance, they see Jews driving cars on Shabbat. I have explained to Michal that although most women do not wear a tallit in shul, some do, and that a woman may choose whether or not she wants to wear one; Michal did not have any trouble understanding what I was trying to convey. I have even told her that some people think women should not wear a tallit.

"But that isn't fair!" she said, her hands on her hips. "Right Ima? Right, girls can do everything boys can do? Right, if they want to they can play baseball and Power Rangers? And boys can play with dolls and wear jewelry?"

This was not the first time the topic of gender had arisen.

Unwittingly, Michal was pointing out to me the tension between my pluralism and my feminism. A true pluralist would be able to present all practices as morally neutral, as long as they fell within certain ethical guidelines and no one was forced to comply with the practices. However, as a feminist and a pluralist, I struggle with these sometimes conflicting ideals. On one hand, I believe that women should be given the choice to pursue all endeavors and not be hampered by their gender, biology permitting. On the other hand, I respect the beliefs of others who do not agree with me—as long as the women in that society comply and are not coerced, and, of course, as long as these beliefs are not being forced upon me. I would not advocate forcing my opinions on the women in such a society, although I would advocate dialogue with these women, so that they can see what other options exist. I explained to Michal that not everyone believes that men and women can do all of the same things, and that while this may seem unfair to us, they do not see it that way.

"Although we do not agree with them, we have to respect their beliefs," I told her. "As long as they do not try to tell us what to do, we should not tell them what to do. But we can talk to each other and explain why we do and think what we do."

Sometimes I wonder if wanting to pass on my ideals about religion to my children is a noble cause at all. What I want most for my children is for them to be happy, healthy (both physically and emotionally), moral, self-confident, self-loving human beings capable of appreciating the good in, and loving, others. Their relationship with Judaism, Torah and God should not be biased by my own. I should honor their right to choose their own paths. On the other hand, I want to see them continuing as links in the chain of Jewish tradition. If they turned away from Judaism completely, it is hard to imagine that I would not be disappointed, even devastated. Is this fair?

Trying to negotiate this tension is not a simple matter; I cannot present everything as equal. I cannot pretend—nor do I want to pretend—that I don't care if they abandon religious Judaism altogether. What I can try to do is instill in my children a love for Torah and Judaism, no matter what form it takes—even a completely nontraditional or ultra-Orthodox way of life. I don't want them to see Jewish practice as a burden. I want them to see it as a gift that enhances their lives.

I would be fooling myself if I refused to admit that I would like to see my children adopt the values that I have chosen for myself. I am a pluralist, but not without strong opinions. I would love to see a daughter of mine praying with tefillin. I would love to hear a son of mine tell me he refuses to say the bracha thanking God for not having created him a woman. If that same daughter chose to live as a Buddhist in Tibet, could I be happy for her? If that same son decided to live as an ultra-Orthodox Jew in Boro Park, New York, could I be happy for him? Some lifestyles may be fine for others, but will I be just as open-minded with my own children and the choices they make?

I hope that I will have the strength and clearheadedness to be a role model to my children, to show them a person who has carved out her own way and found her own spiritual route while trying to maintain a respect for others, a sense of communal responsibility and a tie to the past. If I succeed in transmitting to my children these values and a solid religious education, they will have the tools to negotiate their own religious paths: Whether or not they lay tefillin, eat kosher food or keep Shabbat will be an informed, serious, personal decision.

Recently Michal, now seven years old and my oldest of four (three girls and a boy), has refused to wear a tallit katan underneath her clothing. The fears I had when she was three and I gave her her first pair of tzitzit have become reality. Because no other girls in her school wear a tallit katan, she does not want to. She does not want to be different. I understand that as a second grader Michal has a strong need to fit in. She is not me. She is her own person with her own social consciousness and comfort zone. We have compromised on her at least wearing a tallit gadol during *tefillot* (prayers) at school, but I am not sure she does so every day. It is clear to her what I prefer, but in the end the decision is hers.

I know that asking Michal to wear the tallit gadol may have negative emotional effects on her—because if she does not wear it, she knows that she has let me down, disappointed me. And that is where guilt enters the scene. While I do not want to impose the infamous "Jewish guilt" on my own daughter, I do not see a way out of it at this point. It is impossible to make my own ideology known to my daughter without somehow making her feel worried that she will disappoint me if she makes different choices than I have.

I do not know what the future will bring. Michal and my other daughters may decide to follow in my religious-feminist path, or they may not. Because their current decisions are childhood decisions, subject to change at any given moment, I have not yet truly been put to the test. I don't know how I will react if Michal continues to choose not to wear a tallit later in her life. Or if she chooses not to read Torah for her bat mitzvah. I will have to try not to let my own ego and ideology interfere with the need to let her decide.

Perhaps the most difficult thing about parenting is being able to let go of the desire to mold our children. They are not clay in our hands; they are human beings whose needs may be very different from our own. Parenting, it seems, is a lifelong learning experience. That is both its beauty and its challenge.

I Was a Cliché

DINA HORNREICH

I REMEMBER HEARING A LECTURE on identity and assimilation once at some United Synagogue Youth (USY) event. The speaker posed the question, "Are you a Jewish American or an American Jew?"

At the time I was half insulted, half confused by such typically Jewish posturing, but now I am begrudgingly aware that there might be a difference between the two labels. This isn't simply another case of Jewish overanalysis (which I love too much), like those umpteen Aramaic interpretations of an obscure biblical excerpt. There is a clear, obvious point: What I label myself reflects how I see myself or choose to present myself to the world; it is how I am seen and interpreted by others; it's my construct of a "conscious identity." If only I could make up my mind as to what exactly that is!

I'm still often miffed by this "Jewish American or American Jew" kind of question. It leaves me wondering, "Since when do I need to label myself at all?" And I do know the answer to that one—always have. But . . .

Look, I have dark skin. I don't look "white" and certainly don't feel white. I am white because that is where I most conveniently fit—on paper. Checking the box next to "Caucasian" never felt appropriate, and "Jewish" is just a religion, I am told. But if there is one thing I know, it's that characteristically, culturally and spiritually, I am Jewish. It has been ingrained in me for years, and I do not want to be ashamed of this fact.

So what does it mean to be who I am? To live in my skin, to see the world as I feel it—to understand the experience of living my life?

It changes from place to place, situation to situation, mood to mood. Identity is messy; it is the changing experiences, the uniquely shifting degrees between labels. Can I be both gay and straight? Can I be both masculine and feminine? Can I be both agnostic and religious? The answer to all these questions is yes. There is no right or wrong way to be—but we certainly know when things don't feel right. As sensitive creatures, we change from one encounter to the next; ever so slightly, we rearrange our identity. It is through those explorations that we learn to understand ourselves.

People shouldn't have to fit labels—we should fit in between them. And that begs for a more human identity politic, as messy as the people who construct it. Identity is fluid, constantly and dramatically shifting from one context to the next. Identity politics demand that we cram ourselves into the rigid confines of labels, symbols, flags and systems. This happens within feminism, within the gay community, even within American Judaism.

The way I see it, authentic identity is simply a matter of willingness to admit how contradictory and painful living life really is. To stand up and say that I cannot be summed up neatly through labels, symbols or flags; to assert that my existence as a human being is really just an abstract notion. To enjoy contradiction—perhaps even to invite it—is to identify authentically. It is, to cop a phrase from Rebecca Walker, "to be real."

I both reject and welcome the rigid confines of feminism, Judaism and queerness. I don't wear a Star of David, but I have a mezuzah on my door frame. I have a rainbow squiggle on my car, but removed all the bumper stickers. Catchy phrases, even the ones I love ("Keep Your Laws Off My Body") seem too easy, simplistic. I like layers of meaning. Cute phrases amid proud colors sometimes seem to belittle, even tokenize, the life I struggle to live—a life filled with pain and anguish, uncertainty and recurring outsider status.

I have grown leery of identifying as "queer" because it reflects how the queer community establishes itself in a protected, segregated world: a carefully constructed cult(ure) with its own set of rules and regulations. It is a community in which I've never felt comfortable—because I have never felt acknowledged for simply being me. When I first investigated the queer lifestyle—the life of gay bars, gay magazines, gay in-jokes and an almost exclusively queer social circle—I was simply curious. But in the end I wasn't willing to conform to a new set of rigid rules in order to achieve social gratification.

We need to strive for a more integrated, mainstream concept of human sexuality: a common understanding that more truthfully deals with gender diversity, rather than building more barriers among us based on some gay/straight binary. While the queer community's criticisms of traditional male-female relationships may be warranted, there are far too many unsolved problems in the community itself that prevent me from accepting its rhetoric at face value.

I identify myself by choosing to live through the contradictions—even though I kvetch about them all the time. I feel happy knowing that Phranc, the "all-American Jewish lesbian folksinger," is out there singing songs and selling Tupperware. I find spiritual wholeness while hearing Meredith Monk's adaptations of Martin Buber. I find inspiration in Kathy Acker's *In Memoriam to Identity*. And I find justice when I read about how Annie Sprinkle shtupped the "black hats" (Hasidim) in a brothel while she had her period.

In short, I connect with those who are exposing the contradictions and the hypocrisy; I identify with obstinately and subversively Jewish women. We live our lives by taking each day, each component of our lives and our personalities, as life happens.

For reasons no one has had the chutzpah to explain (although we all have our suspicions), I lost most of the hair on my head just as I hit puberty. As if that were a relatively pain-free time of life to begin with—oh no! As the awkward, chubby, full-bosomed, dark-skinned tomboy with gaps between her teeth, I certainly had enough reason to be a target of ridicule. But losing my hair? Well, that just made for a fun game in the halls of junior high. Steal the "bawl-deez" cap! Look at her funky-ass head.

The incidents of cruelty would happen so fast that I was only made aware of my hat's absence—of being exposed by a prankster—from the horrified looks of disgust around me, peers and teachers gawking at me in my uncovered state. Teachers would make excuses: "But they're just kids."

Most people, after school, would play intramural sports or practice their clarinet. I would just go home, overwhelmed by a mix of helplessness and anger. No one knew how to handle my feelings. Certainly not me. Not my doctor, who told me to grow up; not my mother, who told me she would give me her hair if she could; not my father, who made sarcastic cracks to try to make me smile. And my brother, he just told me to "suck it up, fat-ass."

For several years, I was "the bald girl." I didn't look the way a girl my age was supposed to: neither my clothes nor my skin, my waistline nor my hair. It wasn't my fault. But I internalized the disgust others saw in me and projected it onto the world.

From that point on, I kept to myself at school. In spite of the handful of good people who were real friends, I became overwhelmed and frustrated beyond my own comprehension. The only thing that helped me survive was my budding obsession with music; in 1992, Sinéad O'Connor and Suzanne Vega were my closest friends. They expressed my emotions better than I ever knew how.

It wasn't until I fell into USY that my thinking became clearer. I couldn't believe that after finally finishing Hebrew school, I was volunteering to spend more time learning about Judaism. While I had no clue as this was happening, I realize now that my involvement with USY gave me a sharper perspective on my life and relationships. I don't know if it was because the stigma of "bawl-dee" wasn't on everyone's minds (which is unlikely, since I still had my spots) or if the connections I made were well beyond the superficialities of high school.

In any case, I found a positive outlet for growth and it helped me succeed in many ways. Instead of dwelling on my physical imperfections, my attention shifted to spiritual issues: learning *zmirot* (Sabbath songs) and prayers, learning to appreciate life as a gift, coming to feel like I belonged. This other life displaced the emotional swampland I had created for myself.

Unfortunately, it didn't last when I went to college. I spent my sophomore year living with some Nice Jewish Girls, lighting Shabbat candles, discussing kashrut (Jewish dietary restrictions) and halakha (Jewish law), dreaming of marriage and family life. I did everything but adapt the long-denim-skirt-and-tennis-shoes look that was popular among Orthodox girls. But that wasn't who I was. It didn't feel right. I was trying too hard and therefore feeling just as alienated and freakish as I had been in junior high. I wasn't Orthodox—and didn't want to be. Identifying as a Jew, in this way, didn't get me to a spiritual place.

I hated the extra-long services, and the mechitza (wall separating men and women during prayers) was too weird. I couldn't bear the thought of someday going to a mikveh to cleanse myself from impurities associated with my period, as prescribed by ancient family purity laws. I just liked connecting with these Nice Jewish Girls, from "our side" of the mechitza.

By my senior year, I was devoting more time listening to records and preparing for my college radio show than anything else. All the music knowledge that I had accumulated as an emotional escape in high school had resurfaced. It was a rush, a release, to be broadcast over the airwaves. But I was hiding behind the radio. Music became my identity. I lived through its textures and tempos.

But it wasn't until I took a graduate-level women's studies class that I was challenged to really investigate my identity. This was after I had completed my BA and begun working ego-deflating temp jobs.

Older feminists, the second-wave women teaching my classes, helped me to realize how many questions I had left unanswered. They could see it in my eyes, and it concerned them. Because the emotional swampland of anger and helplessness just never went away; I was still suffering, and they could see that. I didn't have to say a word—they just knew.

My teachers helped me realize that everything I had done in my short little life, all my accomplishments, were rooted in escapism. I needed to confront the inner turmoil, the self-loathing that haunted me every time I looked in the mirror or in the eyes of another human being. Why couldn't I ever be happy with how I looked? What was I suppressing that I didn't allow myself to know, yet was always aware of? How was I presenting myself (unconsciously) to other people?

Feminists taught me that I had sacrificed myself to escape all the pain from those early years of not being "girly," as I was expected to be. They helped me realize that life contradicts itself—that people contradict themselves, that it's a part of being human. That labels, symbols and flags were useless tools for finding myself.

So each and every day I take another step toward consciously re-affirming my identity. In doing so, I find that I have to bargain for my rightful place in society, which often seems to exist only on paper. My rights are there in the laws, but not in our culture. They exist according to the rules, but aren't carried through into daily living. Not yet, anyway.

I have to confront the fears that signify how I've internalized the very same values that, politically, I reject in the outside world—the status quo. Life was easier when I was the invisible Orthodox girl I tried to become as a college sophomore, dutifully marching to Chabad each and every Friday night with the herd.

But it simply will not do! Instead, female-positive writers have helped me to learn the vocabulary I need to voice my instincts, from my body. To celebrate all the right things, the very things that we are taught are shameful and wrong. Never knowing what's inside of you, what the world defines you by, is cruelty. Those of us whose gender puts us in the "F" category at birth have been reared to live a life of self-denial.

When we resist this culturally sanctioned state of denial, we become stigmatized. By wanting to know—to love—our true selves, we become relegated to obscenity, reduced to four-letter words, both literally and figuratively. Obscenity is the damaged self-perception that results from having been seen as a freak—a monstrosity. By transcending the easily categorizable, we fall between the cracks. Do I allow myself to dematerialize because I do not fit neatly into the advertising consciousness of our cultural psyche? Who says I have to choose either A, B, C, or D? I choose A, C, and D but not B, dammit!

I want to go beyond the limited world depicted by language and push into another territory. The tainted words—the obscenities—only offer negative meaning when I allow them to, when their emotional charge is released by my mind in the decoding.

I am learning to properly utilize the tendencies inherited from my Grandma (much as I resent her old-school ways): the same characteristically Jewish traits that are often reduced to horrid clichés about "dirty, cheap Jews." We can be stubborn, brazen, outspoken. These are things that are vaguely ethnic, uniquely Jewish, but in my case may not necessarily stand for things that would be considered kosher.

Being proud of my feminine body is not considered properly modest for a traditional Jewish woman. Learning self-love and turning it into love for other women is not appropriate—a woman should be saving herself for her husband and having children (to compensate for the six million who died in the Holocaust).

These are the contradictions I face as I choose to live my life as a Jewish, sex-positive, third-wave feminist. That is where my identity fits best—in between concepts. It feels right to choose words that don't shut me out, that open me up. To limit myself to the choices offered—gay or straight, masculine or feminine, agnostic or religious—is to stagnate. To let words control personal growth is foolish. I've made that mistake too many times.

You are bigger than words and greater than the sum of your parts. Transcend concrete language. Define your reality. Make your identity conform to *you*. Let other people see it—even feel it from your soul. Join me in the parade of complex, thinking, feeling, dreaming and contradictorily messy human beings: We're here, we're human and we're choosing to live through it!

Composting Judaism
On Ecology, Illness and Spirituality Re-Planted

Sharon Wachsler

IN THE SUMMER OF 1997 I took a class called "Jewish Law and Industrial Pollution" at my local *havurah*. A small group of Jews, we spent an hour and a half once a week hunched over photocopied portions of the Talmud, deciphering and arguing the meanings of those ancient prohibitions, then and now: What did Judaism have to say about environmentalism and shared responsibility for community safety? How should we compare current dangers with those in existence thousands of years ago? For example, should a modern-day corn farmer spraying pesticide next to your child's school be held to the same rules as an ancestral goat herder whose charges befoul his neighbor's fig grove?

If anyone had suggested enrolling in such a class a few years earlier, I would have quickly declined. In the early 1990s I was a young, socially and politically active lesbian, spending my spare time at rallies, dance clubs, self-defense classes and queer arts events. Though I strongly identified as culturally Jewish, I only participated in a few Jewish activities: feminist seders with my friends at Passover and High Holiday services with Am Tikva, Boston's queer Jewish community.

But in the autumn of 1995, just before my twenty-sixth birthday, my life took a sharp and unexpected turn, leading me onto a path from which

I can never fully depart. Unbeknownst to me, my job at a human services agency had slowly been poisoning me; I had been working in a "sick" building for three years. (Only years later, when I learned about indoor air quality issues, did I understand why my co-workers and I suffered such similar health problems.) Though troubled by mysterious ailments, I remained able to work and lead an otherwise active life. As my pain and bizarre symptoms multiplied, I consulted with several doctors in an unsuccessful attempt to discover the cause. I switched jobs, then apartments; the latter change proved the final blow to my health. Toxic fumes from new furniture and paint, combined with leakage from the antique gas furnaces in my living room and kitchen, caused my collapse. It was not until the gas was turned off that I discovered I had suffered several months of carbon monoxide poisoning.

The damage to my immune and central nervous systems was irreversible, and I became disabled by chronic illness. To this day, I live with chronic pain and impairment, as well as severe limitations on my energy and mobility. I also cannot tolerate even minute exposures to an array of common toxins; a couple of minutes near perfume, paint, smoke or cleaning fluid sends me to bed for days.

I became homebound, isolated, invisible—sometimes spending weeks without seeing another person. The communities in which I had flourished were ripped from me; the feminist, queer and arts cultures that I had loved and felt I would be a part of forever spiraled out of my grasp. I made a handful of tentative queries about smoke- and fragrance-free potlucks, wheelchair-accessible poetry slams, meetings I could attend by telephone. I was answered with confusion, hostility or silence.

This is when I turned to Havurat Shalom, the egalitarian, feminist- and queer-friendly Jewish community headquartered just down the road from me. The havurah was working toward disability access and inclusion. They involved me in their efforts and eventually I was able to attend services and classes. When I saw that the havurah was offering a class about the Talmudic perspective on environmental responsibility, I thought,

Here is a way to get out of the house as well as to study something that has become a core element of my life.

Indeed, I have come to see that course on Jewish environmental law as representative of the issues that have assumed prominence in my life: Environmental contaminants disabled me. Due to these disabilities, I lost my communities of choice. Given no other accessible setting, I rediscovered the community of my birth, Judaism. And in rediscovering Judaism I recovered my earliest and purest loves: animals, plants, the living earth.

Which brings me back to my beginnings, to my family, where all my stories start. In my childhood, the relationship between Judaism and the environment was forged—a complex web that has both entangled and confused, comforted and supported me.

The temple I attended as a child, much like Havurat Shalom, can most easily be described as "crunchy." It was not until I was well into my teenage years that I realized not all synagogues employ solar-powered eternal flames, gender-inclusive language in their prayers and rabbis whose sermons frequently revolve around farming, beavers and the phases of the moon. When I began to study for my bat mitzvah I took it for granted that my mother would embroider my *tallit* as she had for my brothers. And so she did, with images of white-sided dolphins and soaring seagulls appliquéd above the traditional blue stripes that she designed to look like waves. I had seen these animals on a whale watch a few months earlier. When I discovered that my Torah portion concerned the fifth day of Creation—when God creates the beasts of the sea and the air—the tallit's decoration seemed a perfect way to combine the joy of that whale watch with the message from the scriptures.

I stood on the *bimah,* wrapped in my prayer shawl, and gave my bat mitzvah speech on animal rights without any sense of oddity or uniqueness. Women in tallitot were no more unusual at our Friday-night services than were men sitting cross-legged in Birkenstock sandals or bare feet—all of us seated on the padded chairs arranged in a crescent around the rabbi.

Despite my knowledge now, as an adult, that there are Jews who are Republicans or conspicuous consumers, for me Judaism is inextricably linked to progressive beliefs and an attitude of awe and respect for life. The Jewish people's history of persecution, which I experienced both as my own family's history during World War II and the broader Jewish cultural history of banishment into the diaspora, has made me aware of oppression. This sensitization, coupled with the mitzvot of community responsibility, fed my innate leanings toward social justice, questioning tradition and authority, and affinity for the natural world. While Judaism does not recommend sacrificing oneself for the good of others, my Sunday-school lessons clearly imparted that we have a duty to those around us, in all our actions. I was struck particularly by the teaching that if a Jew observes a wrong committed by another but does nothing to intervene, that Jew is responsible for the consequences of that misdeed.

As a child, I took these lessons to heart. I was aware of injustices in society—racism, anti-Semitism, poverty—but felt I could exert little influence over such mammoth problems. So I turned instead to fighting an injustice more accessible, closer to home: the welfare of animals and the environment. After all, there were dogs and cats in the neighborhood, birds at our feeders, swampy woods behind my backyard. In first grade, when I was asked what I wanted to be when I grew up, I responded, "A vegetarian." A few years later a canvasser for Greenpeace came to our front door, and I became a member. By fifth grade, I was starting petitions to save the whales and writing letters to Congress about rescuing dogs in the Philippines, stopping nuclear waste dumping in the Atlantic and protecting the endangered giant panda.

My parents nurtured my interest in ecology. They sent me to an Audubon Society summer camp where I learned the names and identifying features of the fauna and flora of western Massachusetts, the same region I now call home. I learned basic household conservation practices, such as how to save water by taking five-minute showers or flushing the toilet less often, along with other methods of healthy, low-impact living, such as eating whole, organic foods. These lessons stayed with me, eventually becoming integral to my lifestyle.

But even before Audubon, it was my parents who started me thinking about the environment by focusing my attention on the origins of the material objects in our home, and the responsibility that came with their use. I remember, as a small child, ripping a paper towel off the roll to dry my hands. My mother chided, "Sharon, use the dish towel."

"What's the difference?" I retorted.

"A tree died to make that paper towel," she explained.

"Oh." I looked down at my hands. I had wiped them in the pulpy blood of the forests. I switched to using cloth towels from then on.

My family's attitude—that modern conveniences have their place but shouldn't be taken for granted—extended to everything that could be saved or reused. The dishwasher and washing machine were only run when they were at maximum capacity. Our reflex to extinguish lights as we exited a room was Pavlovian. My father and brothers returned home with their carefully folded brown paper lunchbags every day after work or school.

I have wondered where this sometimes fanatical attention to economy originated. My mother and father were born in Europe and suffered displacement, deprivation and violence during the rise of Nazism and their subsequent time as refugees in foreign lands. I imagine that having safety and sufficiency torn from their childhoods left a lingering feeling of potential catastrophe; their thrift and planning may represent preparations for survival should such events occur again. I recall few occasions on which my parents or grandparents spoke of their time in Nazi Europe, yet I have always been constantly aware of it. A palpable sense of loss, fear and difference pervaded my sense of home, and therefore my sense of being Jewish—it pulsed through the family blood.

The sort of frugality my parents practiced seems to be part of the left-wing American Jewish culture that they came to embrace and in which they reared their children—a mixture of the old and new worlds, New England thrift meets Reform Judaism. My parents prefer their habits be perceived as part of New England's tight-fisted puritan work ethic—that was my father's explanation when I raised the issue with him.

From as far back as I can remember I have been fiercely proud to be Jewish, especially in facing a gauntlet of anti-Semitism in our placid Boston suburb. But when I came home with tales of the hurtful words used by my classmates, sometimes unintentionally ("Jew him down") and sometimes with vicious precision ("Hitler should have gotten you, too"), my parents were largely silent. Perhaps they took anti-Semitism as such a given that it did not occur to them to try to combat these prejudices. At synagogue I was taught that Jews are obligated to take a stand against wrong, especially prejudice. Yet my parents' behavior contradicted the overt teachings of the Jewish education they were paying for.

When I reached adolescence, I charged full tilt toward conformity and away from what was weird, foreign and emotionally charged in my upbringing. I declared that I was no longer Jewish and took to wearing the enormous cross earrings made popular by Madonna. Further, because I perceived the family code of thrift as the shadow the Holocaust left over us, I rebelled against that, too. I took vindictive pleasure in throwing out lunch bags and aluminum foil I knew could be reused. I reacted against what I proclaimed suffocating rigidity, such as sorting, packaging and dragging the heavy recycling containers to the corner on garbage day.

Before my father purchased any gadget, from blenders to cars, he would analyze the price, energy efficiency and design of each model as listed in *Consumer Reports*. So when I wanted a Walkman, I brazenly went to the closest store and chose the first one I saw, feeling deliciously impulsive. My mother favored neat, serviceable clothing, short hair, no makeup and little jewelry; I opted for tight, brash attire, long hair styled into place with hairspray and mousse, a heavy coat of makeup and as many holes as I could punch in my left ear. I even took up smoking on the sly. Yet I maintained a tenuous connection to animal and environmental rights: I refused to eat meat and buy or wear leather; I continued to receive Greenpeace newsletters; I campaigned against factory farming.

As I grew up and formed an identity that was not simply a set of reactions to what was painful in my youth, I was able to integrate my emotions and my politics. During my college and post-college years, I slowly created a fragile peace with Judaism and my family. In studying and becoming active against racism, sexism, homophobia and other forms of prejudice, and in becoming friends with other politically active Jews, I was able to heal some of the internal wounds inflicted by my family's minimization and denial of oppression. I reintegrated the values that fit my progressive worldview—even when they were supported by my family. I discovered a deep respect for my parents' nonacquiescence to the pressures of "throw-away" culture. In certain ways, the social climate now supported their values. During the energy crisis of the 1970s, recycling had seemed the arena of my quirky family alone. Astonishingly, by the early 1990s, recycling was proclaimed cool; I was proud to haul my blue bins of paper, glass and plastics to the curb.

However, in most respects I was typical of my young, queer, left-wing circle: We believed in ecology, recycling newspapers and soda cans (when it was convenient), but did little to examine how our own daily decisions about technology and the environment affected the planet's health, or our own. While I no longer relied on the gobs of hair gel I used when I was younger, I was still an unquestioning consumer of potent chemical brews that I applied to my hair, skin and clothing, as well as the surfaces and objects in my home. It didn't occur to me to stray from shampoos and soaps with artificial fragrances; detergents and cleansers containing chlorine and ammonia; or new furniture made of formaldehyde-soaked particle board, pine wood treated with fungicide and fabric sprayed with flame retardants. All that changed when I became ill.

When disability hit, chronic pain and impairment were accompanied by severe physical reactions to contact with synthetic fragrances or chemical cleaning products, construction materials, automobile exhaust, pesticides and more. My condition is called multiple chemical sensitivity (MCS). My relationship not only to my body and my health but also to the material world and the environment was changed forever.

Whereas I once took vindictive pleasure in asserting a relaxed attitude toward household goods—affording them as little thought as possible in reaction to my parents' excessive concern—I am now saddled with the need for incessant awareness of what is around me. The deodorant a friend wears, the glue in the spine of a book or the brand of detergent in which the nurse washes her lab coat all have a significant impact on my ability to breathe, function and live. While my ecological practices are driven by my own health needs, it is impossible for me not to make the connection between my body's system, injured and struggling to compensate, and that of the earth's—for the earth is suffering as surely as I am under the onslaught of thousands of new chemicals created each year. How ironic that I once rolled my eyes at my parents' vigilance.

Having come full circle to the lessons of my youth—responsible behavior toward the earth and others around me—I still find myself groping for answers. The boundaries of my own disability and poor health intersect with those of protecting the environment and safeguarding all life on this planet. At certain points the lines cross, and what is good for my health and quality of life is also consistent with my moral stance—buying and eating organic food, for instance. But there are also many ways that my needs as a disabled person conflict with my ecological beliefs. These intersections can become as tangled as a ball of fishing wire, and I am still trying to tease apart the hair-thin fibers.

I now depend on an array of technologies to maintain my independence and quality of life. These include assistive technologies (my mobility scooter, reading box, air filters and oxygen setup) as well as more common technologies (my washer and dryer, computer and minivan). I am aware that purchasing these products contributes to the proliferation of toxic chemicals—the ultimate cause of illnesses such as mine—and adds to the landfills. I also realize that my minivan spews out poisonous exhaust, my microwave emits radiation, my dehumidifier and air filters devour electricity around the clock. More and more, I find myself making decisions that put my health and quality of life above that of the plants and animals with whom I share the world and to whom, I now realize, I am connected. A year ago I became allergic to all nonmeat sources of protein and ended twelve years of vegetarianism. Currently I am looking for land so that I can build a safe and accessible home—an act that will harm the trees, birds and insects that have been living where my new home will be. As a progressive Jew who early on took to heart that life is sacred—not just my own, but that of all beings—I feel uncomfortable with these choices.

Yet as a Jew, I am also exhorted to honor the sanctity of my own life—to value it above everything. This, more than anything else, I have gained from being ill. With so much stripped away, it becomes clear: All I really have is my life. I embrace it as a unique gift that I did not fully appreciate in the frenzy good health allowed. Making potentially life-or-death decisions on a regular basis is scary, but it also keeps me in tune with what is most essential. Indeed, many mitzvot focus not just on living but on living joyfully. At the onset of my illness, as I lay in bed for months, I repeated this mantra to myself: *My life can still hold meaning; I will write; I will create a quality life; I will find ways to live happily within my limitations.* And this I have done, with the help of a spiritual practice that, while new in its fruition, was planted in my psyche years ago.

Except for my brief involvement with the havurah, getting sick did not propel me into religious Judaism. In fact, in my new locale in western Massachusetts there is no accessible synagogue to take the place of Havurat Shalom. I am even more isolated from Jewish worship and community than I was in the first few years of my illness. However, being sick—my illness, along with the lifestyle changes it has brought about—has delivered to me a different kind of worship. My move to a rural area was necessitated by my sickness; in the polluted air of the city my health worsened and my quality of life withered. And while I miss the community of Havurat Shalom, amidst these woods and fields I practice a spirituality that feels more intrinsic to my nature, my upbringing and my current state of health. I am reminded of the best parts of my childhood—those times when I felt the most free, the most whole, the most truly myself.

In the clean air I am able to open my windows, tend a garden, watch the deer spring in the tall grass and hear the goldfinches gabble at the feeders. In the summer I pick and chew the shiny wintergreen leaves that as a camper I learned grow near lakes in this region. When I wheel to the mailbox in my scooter, the smell of the muddy stream on the roadside evokes the swampy logs I once examined during solitary walks after school. Both gardening and bird watching were pursuits I learned from my parents and older brothers; they were the activities that held the sweetest relaxation I ever felt among my immediate family.

I am not simply reliving my childhood as a "nature girl"; I am recovering my spirit. I now maintain a spiritual practice, something I used to scoff at in others. Though I started this practice when I was still in the city, it flows more naturally in the country. Here, there is a sense of my surroundings supporting me. My practice does not take place in a synagogue, does not employ Hebrew texts, does not even invoke God. And yet it is primarily through other Jews that I have gleaned the elements of my new spirituality: a combination of daily meditation, writing practice and overall mindfulness.

While the essential concepts I follow are derived from Buddhism, my practice is embedded in my Jewish roots. The first time I heard of the Dalai Lama was at temple, in my youth. I learned that our rabbi, Everett Gendler, was traveling to meet with the Dalai Lama. Rabbi Gendler's leadership centered on the Jewish calendar's lunar aspects and our holidays' relationships to the harvest cycle. We didn't simply plant trees for Tisha B'Av and celebrate Passover as a rite of spring and rebirth. We also sowed rye seeds behind the synagogue as a Sunday school project and gathered gourds from our gardens for Sukkot. I always knew when I went to services and saw the rabbi in his special white robe and "moonbeam-catching" yarmulke that Shabbat was falling on a full moon that week.

More important, I absorbed sermon after sermon that eloquently encouraged gentle respect for all life. The stories might touch on current wars or politics, the shtetl or the Holocaust, a garden or a river, but all were interwoven into a complex picture of often competing imperatives. We were asked to reflect on these complexities, to meditate on the layers of meaning. Those were the words Rabbi Gendler used: "meditate" and "reflect," not "pray." In the Jewish custom, we were not given the answers; Rabbi Gendler presented the questions so hauntingly that we were mesmerized in thought.

Thus my meditative foundation was laid. As an adult, thanks to other progressive Jews, I was given some of the tools to apply the concepts of mindfulness and reverence for nature that I learned as a child. The writer Natalie Goldberg, a Jewish Zen Buddhist, introduced me to writing practice not simply as a path to a skill, but as an exercise in connecting with the creative force. Her books are saturated with Zen philosophy and have become a central part of how I move through my life. I reread them when I want to remind myself of kind consideration, gentleness or how to live with loneliness. This last has been especially important; solitude is the dominant feature of my life. The words of Goldberg's Zen master, Katagiri Roshi, on using loneliness, digesting it, not letting it toss you away, have held me together through years of painful isolation. While my religion, Judaism, has centered around community and shared culture, my spirituality, like my illness, has been solitary. Meditation and writing are enhanced by solitude and calm. More to the point, a creative burst or a vision, like a symptom, cannot be shared.

On this hilltop where I cannot spy another house, I can see scores of birds, hundreds of trees and multitudes of insects. Here I am able to breathe. Breath is not only the basis for life (and for my relief from illness), it is also the foundation of meditation and spiritual practice.

While my left-wing Jewish upbringing and innate progressive leanings may have created a tendency toward this spiritual view I now hold, I probably would have remained aspiritual had I not gotten sick. My predisposition to meditation was latent; illness was the trigger that set the mystical syndrome in motion. In fact, the path I follow feels less like a choice than a necessity. All of my friends who are chronically ill meditate—it seems to be an almost universal response to the rigors of long-term pain and exhaustion.

It is a truism among the newly disabled that we must learn to be human beings, rather than human doings. Or, to put it more bluntly, when you can do little except be inert, you either learn to meditate or you go nuts. When I was at my sickest, during the first two years of my illness, I could do nothing but rest for hours every day. Given that situation, I had to make stillness a choice; otherwise it would have been pure punishment. I sought mindfulness to transform my body from a prison to a temple. I chose acceptance over grasping for elusive (and often illusive) cures. I try to sit with my transformed body, embracing each moment, regardless of the pain and exhaustion that may inhabit it. Of course, acceptance is a lifelong struggle. I cannot be in the moment every moment. There are days when I rage at the headache or nausea, bemoan the years of missed work, grieve the friends I cannot visit. At such times I must drag myself, kicking and screaming, toward acquiescence.

In a life hemmed in by the boundaries of body, chemistry and architecture, the taste of freedom is a rare, delectable treat. I have gained a modicum of freedom with devices that allow me greater mobility, but there are many days when I am too sick to leave my home. Equipment cannot carry me out of my body. On these occasions, I can unleash my mind. In meditation I can travel to deserts and jungles, I can run and dance and swim. While my body is constrained, static, my mind becomes huge with possibilities. This expansive energy is integral to meditation. When I am mindful, that mindfulness naturally extends to the animate and inanimate beings with whom I share the world. I become sentient of not only what is internal to me, but what is external as well.

Stripped of many of the usual amenities because of my need for a pristine environment, my bedroom has only one decoration on the wall. It is a quote attributed to Thich Nhat Hanh, a Vietnamese Buddhist monk. The quote describes the transformative process of meditation, employing the metaphor of gardening: "When we look deeply at a flower . . . we will . . . notice that the flower is on her way to becoming compost. . . . When we look deeply at the compost, we see that it is also on its way to becoming flowers, and we realize that flowers and compost 'inter-are.'"

When I first read these words, they transfixed me, so deeply did they resound with my experience. For one thing, when I became ill I was overcome with the sensation that my body was decomposing; I wrote poem after poem about rotting fruit, attempting to describe my state. My disease has not proven fatal, but severe illness raises the specter of death and brings it a step closer. I first turned to meditation as a way to cope with the devastation of illness, yet I discovered, to my surprise, that meditation carried me toward acceptance of death. Not that I want to die; being sick has made me more enamored of life than ever before. Still, being too ill to move, I felt a sense of peace knowing that one day I would die and decompose—that my body would return to and nourish the earth. Perhaps I find this thought comforting because it is a fitting restitution: giving back to the earth from an illness caused by destroying the earth. I also find solace in the thought that my suffering will not be in vain: In becoming compost, my illness and death will serve the larger purpose of nourishing future life.

Closer to the bone is that compost is a substance that is familiar and reminds me of home. From as far back as I can remember, my father has tended a compost pile—sometimes several of them—in our backyard. I learned early on which scraps could be used for compost, and how the process of composting transformed grass clippings and vegetable peelings into rich soil. I had seven pet rabbits during the course of my childhood; I took satisfaction in seeing their droppings become fertilizer. The cycle of life—even the less savory aspects—was accepted in my family. A regular part of dinner-table conversation included my father discussing where and how he found the best cow or horse manure. When I sat in the garden, pulling weeds or planting seeds as my father turned over the soil, I loved the smell of dank leaves and rotting cucumbers and even manure— the fragrance of enriching the earth.

How could I not, then, come to such a spiritual practice—one that merges my love of nature, my affinity with the injured earth, my immobility and my rearing in a peculiar brand of unique, thoughtful Judaism? All the roads of my life seem to lead here. I am still uncovering some of these paths. I have learned, for instance, that one of the founding members of Havurat Shalom was Rabbi Gendler—before I knew him at my childhood synagogue or danced with him around the maypole, before I rebelled against caution and rejected care for my surroundings, before I was chemically injured and sought out community, before I found Havurat Shalom and studied Judaism's views on the environment, before I embraced solitude and rediscovered the wild.

Now I cultivate the wild. It is a rich, paradoxical way to live. I make a practice of sitting silently so that I can be moved across continents. I follow a ritual of unclasping my mind and writing what spills out: an unloosening.

I sow organic seeds in my garden. Some I have bought, others are harvested from the previous year's crop. But every year something unexpected happens: vegetables grow out of the compost. Every year, into carefully molded mounds of garden soil, I place squash seeds from a packet, most of which do not sprout. Every year seeds that I did not plant, but that lay dormant in the compost over the winter, germinate and bear heavy, dark acorn squash.

It is not truly unexpected, this wildness in my carefully planned plot. Yet knowing that this possibility of extemporaneous bounty exists provides me with excitement, anticipation and inspiration: What will grow, and from which source of nourishment? Only time will tell. Gardening is a process, not a source of instant gratification.

In my growth toward the light I also do not have all the answers. As a Jew I am still digging for the deepest, richest source of questions. I try not to inquire too much into the future: Will I recover? What will be the course of my illness and my life? I avoid obsessing on the pieces of the past that do not serve me: Why did I get sick? What could I have done to prevent my collapse? Instead I settle into the roots of my past, cultivating something unexpected and beautiful: My family and synagogue's love of the earth now supports me through an environmental illness.

But mostly I focus on the here and now. I turn inward with gratitude for my writing, my garden, my house and the technologies that support my present circumstances. I drink in anything that allows me to live and live well, trying to balance my needs with those of the environment.

In this garden of acceptance of my disability, of living for today, something astonishing is emerging: I am getting better. Though I did not explicitly seek it, I find my health improving. Illness is relaxing its grip, a fragile new strength growing in its place. I do not know how tall this seedling will grow. I try not to strain too hard toward the future. I try to enjoy this moment, to inhabit my body to the fullest extent possible. I sit in the earth. I meditate. I write. I listen. I breathe.

NOT LOST

A Jewish Feminist Atheist Meditates on Intermarriage

SARAH COLEMAN

Have you heard the statistics yet? If not, let me be the first to bring them to you: In 1990, the United States's National Jewish Population Survey found that 52 percent of Jews who married chose non-Jewish partners. Using this and other figures, demographers predicted that the number of Jews in the United States would drop precipitously in the next century. As early as 1977, Harvard demographer Elihu Bergman forecast that the American Jewish population would drop from 5.5 million to less than a million—possibly as low as ten thousand—by the year 2076.[1]

Clearly, Bergman's prediction offers a worst-case scenario, and not too many people take his projections seriously. Still, the news is that we're intermarrying in greater numbers than ever before. And this brings up a question that has echoed throughout the centuries: Is it good for the Jews?

For those of us who intermarry, pro-Jewish rhetoric and (let's face it) guilt-tripping exist as a constant background hum. Certainly, we've come a long way since the days when parents would sit shiva (the Jewish ritual of mourning for the death of a loved one) for children who "married out." But there are still subtle undercurrents of disapproval. Jewish parents might send "an interesting article about bar mitzvahs" to an interfaith couple, or murmur about a spouse's conversion. A colleague might speculate that someone's marriage ended because of "interfaith issues," then blush and clamp her mouth shut.

In fact, scratch the surface of today's "tolerance," and you'll find that old attitudes die hard. In the year 2000 Annual Survey of American Jewish Opinion, conducted by the American Jewish Committee, 56 percent of respondents disagreed with the statement, "It would pain me if my child married a gentile," yet 69 percent said they felt that Jews had an obligation to urge Jews to marry Jews.[2]

As one half of an interfaith couple, I have a stake in how intermarriage is perceived, and I'll say right off the bat that I think it's misunderstood. Call me biased, but I have a strong conviction that interfaith unions are far from the end of Judaism as we know it. In fact, I believe they might be a healthy way forward.

And who am I, other than a Jew who's married to a gentile? Well, for a start, I'm a secular, or cultural, Jew. In other words, I don't belong to a congregation and my Jewish affiliations mostly consist of reading Philip Roth novels and eating the odd schmaltz herring. To Orthodox Jews, this already puts me beyond the pale—I'm lost, gone, of little value to the faith. Even Conservative and Reform Jews might express irritation at my lack of religious observance. (An editor at a Jewish newspaper I wrote for once complained she'd had it up to the eyeballs with "cultural Jews.") All of the above are probably worried about my children, and how I'm planning to bring them up. Since Judaism is inherited through the mother's line, there's no question that my children will be legally Jewish. Ah yes, but will they be *Jews?*

The answer to this depends, of course, on your definition of a Jew—of which there are about as many to choose from as there are seeds on a sesame bagel. In order to give my own answer, I need to delve a little into my background, and my reasons for "marrying out." In "Will Your Grandchildren Be Jews?" Antony Gordon and Richard Horowitz propose that the decision to intermarry is "the product of countless previous decisions about how to live one's life."³ Absolutely. In my case, several key factors influenced my choice. In no particular order of importance, they were anti-Semitism, feminism and atheism.

I grew up in England in the 1970s and '80s, a place and time in which Judaism was regarded as foreign and slightly distasteful. Then (as now), Christianity was Britain's national religion. Church and state were brought together in the body of the Queen, who headed both the government and the Anglican church. Christians ruled, literally and symbolically, and the tacit assumption was that the rest of us were there on sufferance. Perhaps because of this, Jews who live in the United Kingdom have often downplayed their religious affiliations. Consider: There's no English Woody Allen, no writer to rival a Bellow, Roth or Paley. Instead, Jews have melted relatively quietly into the fabric of English life.

That wasn't hard for me, because growing up, I was drawn to all things Christian. Fragrant hot cross buns and church jumble sales seemed warm and inviting to me; onion rolls and Zionist campaigns were coarse and embarrassing by contrast. I associated Judaism with the gloominess of places like my Great Uncle Ike and Aunty Fanny's apartment, whose dark rooms were filled with huge jars of Ike's home-pickled cucumbers. The cucumbers made a deep impression on me: They were lumpy and green, and the way they floated in yellow brine reminded me of biology experiments and pickled fetuses. I understood that they were part of my ethnic heritage, but it was beyond me why anyone would choose to be associated with these bitter vegetables when they could eat comforting English food like jam and crumpets.

In embracing these views, I'm sure I was reflecting attitudes I absorbed from a culture in which Jews were still considered bogeymen. In *The Ghost Writer*, Philip Roth's alter ego Nathan Zuckerman fantasizes that he will prove his allegiance to his tribe by marrying Anne Frank. I fantasized about getting away from mine by marrying Prince Andrew.

When I met Dan, we were both undergraduates at Cambridge University. In some ways, he seemed to come from a different planet than mine, and a much cooler one: He played drums in a rock band, drove an Alfa Romeo and mixed music for student theater productions. Then again, I was an English major and he was only an engineer, so how cool could he be?

The few Jews I knew at that time were suburbanites, like me. The boys were princes who'd spent their lives being coddled and cooked for by their mothers. One of my greatest fears was that I'd end up married to a boy like one of my three first cousins: good boys, with horizons so narrow they were almost invisible. An accountant, lawyer and optician, respectively, they lived quiet lives in suburban cul-de-sacs mere minutes away from their parents' house.

Bear in mind, too, that female rabbis and community leaders were as rare as white rhinoceroses at this time. In every Jewish family I knew, fathers went out to work while mothers kept the home fires burning (which often seemed to mean lunching with friends and going to the Harrods sale). At synagogue, men prayed below while women sat up in the balcony comparing manicures. It drove me crazy. Annie Lennox was singing about how sisters were doing it for themselves, Margaret Thatcher had recently been elected Britain's first female prime minister, but North London Jews were still living in the Dark Ages when it came to gender politics.

I wanted to travel, be independent, experiment. Getting away from patriarchal suburbia and getting away from Judaism became linked in my mind.

At Cambridge, the first thing that struck me about Dan was the agility and elegance of his thinking. (Well, okay, that and his bleached-blond ponytail.) For an ex-choirboy who'd flirted seriously with Anglicanism in his teens, he was quite open-minded. During our first year at college, he had a crush on a student from an Orthodox Jewish family. When he went to visit her in London, he was particularly struck by the twin dishwashers in the kitchen, one for *milchig* (dairy) and one for *fleishig* (meat) plates. He must have liked something about the family, too, because he came back announcing that he "felt Jewish inside."

This struck me as highly perverse. I'd been trying to escape my Jewish roots for eighteen years, and here was a non-Jew who identified with Judaism. I didn't get a chance to question him about it until years later (by which time he'd forgotten the comment), but it certainly stuck in my mind.

What, I now wonder, was behind Dan's attraction to Judaism? Perhaps he related to the way Jews value education, and how the religion is based on an evolving intellectual inquiry. Maybe it had something to do with Jewish humor, or the importance of family. Perhaps it was just the kugel.

Eventually, though, we were brought together by a deeper bond—our mutual atheism. Rational to a fault, neither Dan nor I could accept the existence of a higher being, much less pray to one. We discussed the possibility of an afterlife and concluded that it was a nice idea, but a fantasy. Too bad, we thought. As nonbelievers, we'd have a harder path through life.

In her writings on atheism and spirituality, social critic Wendy Kaminer argues that in today's atmosphere of spiritual renewal, atheism is often equated with immorality, while virtue is associated with religious teachings. "Whenever I've publicly questioned the value of religiosity or suggested that atheism is not incompatible with morality," she writes, "I've received vicious responses from people who claim to love God."[4]

For many Jews, the fact that I don't plan to include formal religious training in my children's upbringing means that they won't be Jewish. I've spoken to Jews who have urged me to reconsider the issue: "It would be so sad if they were brought up with nothing."

This irks me more than I can say. Where, I wonder, is it written that the absence of religious education equals "nothing," or that religion has a monopoly on good values? As a child, I learned about charity by observing my parents' generosity to people less fortunate than themselves. They never mentioned Judaism, and I was in my thirties before I learned that in Jewish life, *tzedakah* (charity) is considered a sacred obligation. By that time, I'd absorbed the concept through secular means.

It has occurred to me that religious Jews might be bothered by the way secular Jews seem to get a free ride, reaping the benefits of Jewish identity without putting in any hard spiritual work. I can understand this, just as I understand fears about Jewish continuity and the pervasiveness of intermarriage. But writing off the secular and the intermarried fails to take into account that Jewish identification goes far beyond religion. Perhaps it was true in the past that secular and intermarried Jews felt obliged to slough off all the trappings of Jewish culture along with their religion. These days, all evidence suggests that Jewish pride is on the upswing.

The book *Strangers to the Tribe: Portraits of Interfaith Marriage* proves how potent a Jewish background can be in the context of an interfaith marriage. Author Gabrielle Glaser interviews eleven couples in which only one partner is Jewish. Most of the Jewish spouses interviewed here discuss how, as they form a partnership with a non-Jew, they've been drawn to examine their cultural identity more fully than ever before. "Beyond the reach of the surveys and synagogues, a significant number of Jews who marry outside their faith are making serious efforts to pass on the religion and culture of their forefathers," Glaser writes.[5]

The same phenomenon was evident in an interfaith couples workshop Dan and I attended recently in the San Francisco Bay Area. Once a week for six weeks, we met with five other couples on the top floor of a converted Victorian house. Our workshop leader pointed out that in an interfaith couple, "all of a sudden things that have not been important can become so." That was true for Peter, who suddenly found himself resistant to the Easter basket prepared by his wife, Susie, and for Robin, who'd detected a new desire to light candles on the Sabbath. "I don't understand—you never did that growing up," grumbled her fiancé.

Like the other couples in the workshop, Dan and I had signed up because we were concerned about family life and parenting. Though we weren't yet parents, we were contemplating a family. If we had a son, would we circumcise him? And if so, would a *mohel* do it? Was it meaningless to adopt Jewish rituals without the religion? What would we do with our children on the holidays?

One of the aspects of intermarriage that had always appealed to me was the idea of blended cultures. Given the divisiveness of religion, it seemed sensible to create a kind of melting pot in which the best elements from each tradition could be combined.

Suddenly, though, I found myself wondering what the price of such a cultural soup would be. Would the "blending" lead to a meaningless dilution of each tradition? "Do you end up with something like a jalapeño bagel, which doesn't mean much to anyone?" I asked in the workshop. We discussed the Hanukah bush, a Jewish appropriation of the Christmas tree. "Hanukah bush! I'd rather have a jalapeño bagel," scoffed Peter.

But in fact, after six weeks of hashing out these issues, I came down on the side of blended cultures. Why? Because purity has its place, but I find heterogeneity more interesting—even when it results in jalapeño bagels. Because compromise forces creative solutions, and teaches us how to live in a world where people are different from each other in every way imaginable. Interfaith couples are on the front lines of this struggle every day. We're the United Nations of creative compromise, and the Jewish partner—however secular—of an interfaith couple should be thought of as an ambassador of Judaism.

In fact, the Jewish attitude toward intermarriage is less rigid than people often assume. In the Torah, Jewish patriarchs like Moses and Joseph intermarried, and their spouses were welcomed into the tribe. The rabbis of the Talmud interpreted Deuteronomy 21:10-14 to mean that a non-Jewish woman captured in war could be married to a Jew—a move they saw as more enlightened than raping a woman during battle or bringing her home as a war trophy and then selling her into slavery. The rabbis' attitude here could be seen as largely pragmatic ("better to gain a shiksa than to lose a son"), but I'd rather see it as a sign of broad-mindedness and compassion. "Rabbis were aware of human weakness and how difficult it is for men and women to resist temptation and deny their bodily appetites," notes scholar Rabbi Dr. Moshe Zemer.[6]

Perhaps no one in Jewish history has done more for the cause of inter-marriage than the twelfth-century Talmudic scholar Maimonides, also known by the moniker Rambam. While living in an Egyptian Jewish community in the last years of the twelfth century, Rambam was asked to intervene in a case where a young Jewish man had purchased a gentile slave and was openly living with her in his father's house. The couple's chutzpah was sending waves of gossip throughout the community.

Rambam had already written his famous law code, the *Mishneh Torah,* in which he said that no marriage between a Jew and a gentile would be permitted if the couple had already had sex. In this case, though, he chose to go against his own ruling and the Talmud, allowing a marriage for compassionate reasons. Like the early rabbis before him, Rambam under-stood that Judaism's power lay partly in its capacity for compassion and flexibility. Zemer characterizes this ruling as one of the most significant evolutions of halakha.

Of course, such intermarriages were sanctioned on the condition that the non-Jewish partner convert to Judaism. This rule persists in most branches of Judaism today, though Reform rabbis can choose whether or not to officiate at an interfaith union. (According to a survey by the Jew-ish Outreach Institute, around a third of all Reform rabbis will marry an interfaith couple if the couple promises to bring up its children in the Jewish faith.)[7] Efforts are also being made to bring those who marry in civil ceremonies—as we did—into the fabric of Jewish life.

But what if the interfaith couple doesn't choose to join a congrega-tion? Which is more important, Jewish observance or the continuation of Jewish values? Some would say that without the first, the second will die out. I disagree.

In the past few decades, Judaism has shown a remarkable ability to adapt to changing times. Jewish feminists have been able to adapt male-centered rituals in a way that includes women in services. Kabbalah has inspired a new wave of Jewish mysticism. Jewish meditation has brought some of the flavor of Eastern religious practices to Judaism.

Like those other forces, intermarriage is changing how Judaism interacts with itself and the world. There can be little doubt that it is here to stay. Faced with this reality, the Jewish community has two options: It can wring its hands and dogmatically promote endogamy (marriage within the faith) by sponsoring Jewish day schools, summer camps and trips to Israel. Or it can recognize that in forming partnerships with non-Jews, we intermarrieds are spreading Jewish values and culture into the population at large.

I don't mean to imply here that there's anything wrong with institutions that keep ancient rituals alive, or that all Judaism should devolve into newfangled and politically correct forms. I just think it would be nice if, somewhere deep down in the Jewish psyche, we could overwrite the part that teaches us to think of intermarriage as a *shanda* (shame).

As part of the interfaith workshop, each couple was asked to create some rituals that held meaning for us as a couple. Dan and I decided on two: The first would be an attempt to incorporate tzedakah into our lives (and those of our future children) through regular volunteerism and charity. For the second, we agreed to have a good dinner every Friday night, where we'd clean up and light candles, and—as part of the ritual—review our week and share what we were grateful for.

For us, choosing Friday night and lighting candles seemed like a way to establish a living connection to Jewish culture. Expressing gratitude, on the other hand, seemed to bring in two other traditions: the Christian practice of grace before meals, and the philosophy of Dan's yoga teacher, who follows an invigorating Ashtanga practice by encouraging students to meditate on that for which they are thankful.

I spent most of my childhood and adolescence trying to get away from Judaism. I finally learned to stop worrying and love Jewish culture three or four years ago—but only after I'd crossed the Atlantic, taught at a university with many Jewish colleagues, and written extensively for a Jewish newspaper. Gradually, I came to realize that the cultural quirks I'd once found so embarrassing—the cheek-pinching uncles, the gray lumps of gefilte fish—were exactly the kinds of details that give texture and depth to a story.

Recently, Dan and I moved from San Francisco to New York. Through the back window of our apartment in the East Village we can see three squat, square towers, each one topped with a pale green, onion-shaped dome. The domes belong to the Teferith Israel (Town and Village) synagogue. On hot days, the air-conditioning unit mounted on the shul's roof roars into life, sending billowing currents of warm air our way.

As a feminist, as an atheist, as half of an interfaith couple, I'd like to think that Judaism and I have something to offer one another. I continue to read and review books about Jewish history and culture. I haven't yet walked around the block and crossed the threshold of Teferith Israel. Maybe one day I will.

Notes:

1. Lisa Schiffman, *Generation J* (HarperSanFrancisco, 1999),16; and Gabrielle Glaser, *Strangers to the Tribe: Portraits of Interfaith Marriage* (Houghton Mifflin, 1997), xii.

2. Gustav Niebuhr, "Marriage Issue Splits Jews, Poll Finds," *The New York Times*, October 31, 2000, A25.

3. Antony Gordon and Richard Horowitz, "Will Your Grandchildren Be Jews?" This paper can be found online at www.613.org/study.html.

4. Wendy Kaminer, *Sleeping with Extra-Terrestrials: The Rise of Irrationalism and Perils of Piety* (Pantheon Books, 1999), 19.

5. Glaser, xiv.

6. Rabbi Dr. Moshe Zemer, *Evolving Halakhah: A Progressive Approach to Traditional Jewish Law,* (Jewish Lights Publishers, 1999), 30.

7. The Jewish Outreach Institute, "Highlights of a Survey of the American Rabbinate." Can be found at www.joi.org/pubs/rabbisur.htm.

Blood Simple

Transgender Theory Hits the Mikveh

Danya Ruttenberg

I BLAME IT ON MY FRIEND KARISSA, really. Her spiritual shtick is of the eclectic, earth-based variety, and one day as she was playing show-and-tell with her ritual stuff, things got personal.

" . . . with the bear-tooth charm. I wear the cowrie shell on a cord around my waist when I have my period; the rest of the time, it lives in this bag here." She pointed to the bag.

Her custom was pretty simple, and subtle: Wear a thingy on certain days to mark that the body's doing something different than it does on a lot of other days. No major hoopla, she just notices and registers the shift.

To my own shock and surprise, I felt a twinge. I couldn't believe that a part of me was . . . *ack.* It's true. Jealous. For the first time in my life, I felt compelled to do what had always seemed to me so weird and dorky, so totally passé—what people who I thought I was much cooler than would call "honoring the sacred feminine." Or something like that. That, you know, lavender, touchy-feely, hand-holdy womyn-y stuff that always made me cringe. But suddenly I couldn't stop thinking about menstruation.

I'd been practicing Judaism for a few years by this point, but always, *always* with an egalitarian bent. I was glad that the previous generation had pointed out that the modesty laws were nasty and the rule against women singing was a crock, but I assumed that the point of their efforts was to save us from having to do the same. "Sometimes we're not Jewish women," I wrote when I was about twenty-two. "Sometimes, we're just Jews."

The reason for my egal-orientation seemed obvious: Judaism, from its inception, made male normative and female derivative. So for the spiritual seeker looking for the most meaningful aspects of a long, valorous tradition, it made sense to get in on the boys' stuff, on the bits from which we were excluded back in the days of chattel and slavery. Simple logic, really: The good parts have traditionally been given to the boys. So, we should do them, because they're the good parts. Duh. It's not that I wasn't a feminist—my feminism long predated my Judaism, and every move I made was predicated on the assumption that all people have a right to the power, to the spiritual riches available in this amazing ritual system.

But as I slowly became more observant, I started to develop an increasingly strong awareness of nature's, and my body's, role in my spiritual life. I love the naturalistic aspect of Judaism—watching the sun slowly set at the end of Shabbat, celebrating major moments in the agricultural year, blessing food as it comes from the land, from the vine, from the tree. And certainly marking menstruation with ritual is in some ways just as earthy—noting the body's inherent rhythms, making holy the moment of differentiation between one state of being and another.

Of course a religion as nitpicky and thorough as Judaism has already addressed menses. The modern laws of *niddah,* or menstruation, dictate that a woman is forbidden to have sex with her husband for the duration of her period and, according to some, for seven "clean" (or "white") days after. At the end of the abstention period (either roughly seven or fourteen days, depending on which tradition she follows) she goes to the mikveh, the ritual bath, and immerses herself with a blessing, thus rendering herself once again able to hop back into the marital bed.

There are couples who say the no-sex thing allows them to have a second honeymoon every single month—thus making their connection stronger the rest of the time—and adds a dimension of the sacred into

their sexual relationship. And whether or not you're in a relationship (and/
or just sexually active), the age-old appeal of surrender in water is hard to
ignore. Many have testified to the profound spiritual effect of the mikveh,
to the way it can deep-clean your soul just like *that*.

Whoosh.

The appeal of a menstruation rite became clearer. Judaism, as a religious system, is designed to affect every aspect of a person's life. We mark
the doors of our houses with prayer, we say a blessing upon seeing a rainbow or an old friend. It's *about* living, and to not mark the birth-death
cycles of the reproductive system would seem, well, like an omission.

As I began to spend more time noticing trees and looking at constella-
tions, the urge to mark my own monthly passage increased. I . . . I actually
wanted to go to the mikveh when my period was done.

Despite the allure, though, I couldn't go. I couldn't let myself.

Why?

I knew the history, and the history made me mad.

In the book of Leviticus, menstruation was only one of many things—
including touching a corpse, leprosy and male ejaculation—rendering a
person ritually impure vis-à-vis entering the ancient Temple. This in itself
was not problematic; similar rules applied to both men and women. But
when the Temple was destroyed in 70 C.E., the Rabbis were forced to re-
work Judaism in a lot of different ways. Folks stopped observing the purity
laws, but the injunction against sex with a menstruant fell into a different
legal category, and thus had to be minded even with no Temple in town.
However, once menstruation became the only "polluting" force (if you will),
the guys making the decisions began to treat it in a totally different way—
tacking on extra injunctions and restrictions that hadn't ever been necessary
before. As Tirzah Meacham writes, the early Rabbis began a "trend of thinking in which the category of normal menstruation . . . came to fall in the
category of abnormal bleeding, *zavah*."[1]

Perhaps you can see where this is headed?

As time passed, menstruation became a way to express misogynistic fears about female as danger, female as death, female as the scary dark power that must be controlled. The Rabbis ask, "Why was the precept of niddah given to [Eve]? Because she spilled the blood of Adam,"[2] and muse about the feminine charms with clever euphemisms: "Though a woman be a pot of filth whose mouth is full of blood . . . all chase after her."[3] Further, they posit, "If a menstruous woman passes between two [men]—if it is at the beginning of her menstruation, she will cause one to die; if it is at the end of her menstruation, she will bring strife between them."[4]

By the Middle Ages, the menstruant's "nail parings and the dust upon which she trod were believed to cause boils. Since such casual contact could inflict bodily harm, it follows that . . . having sexual relations with menstruants would give rise to leperous births in families for generations to come."[5]

It's enough to make a girl give up on Judaism entirely. I've come close, a couple of times, wondering if these guys have tainted the water in the ritual pool enough to invalidate the whole system. There are a lot of folks who think we should just pitch the niddah laws because they've convinced so many people that women's bodies are dirty, impure. Yet I do believe that we've managed, somehow, to get over feminist roadblocks that were at least as serious, if not more so.

And besides the fact that throwing away the niddah laws means we don't get a nice cycles-of-nature spiritual opportunity, I also think to do so would be a copout. Over time I've grown to regard halakha not only as a series of unrelated challenges aimed at making me a nicer, stronger, more-aware-of-the-sacred person, but as a whole entity—imperfect yet all-encompassing, the metronome by which life can be better and more fully lived. In Judaism, you don't get to do the stuff that seems fun and forget the parts that make you work a little; it's an organic system. You don't cut off your foot because your ankle's broken—nor, however, is it helpful to pretend that nothing's wrong. What needs to happen, of course, is that you have to fix the ankle.

I believe that, like women's (former) exclusion from many ritual roles, the laws of niddah are ripe for transformation—and deserving of closer scrutiny, especially given the number of questions they raise about gender.

Entire Pandora's boxes of gender have been opened up in the last ten or fifteen years. I know butch dykes who consider their gender box c) none of the above, and femme lesbians who identify more with drag queens than straight women. There are places in the United States where people believe that gender can be chosen—which can mean anything from "what we've been taught about 'girls' and 'boys' is a crock of hooey" to "I use words that resonate with my internal knowledge of myself" to "I need a change on the biological level." To say nothing of the possibly 2 percent of the population born as "intersex."[6]

It's important to look at transgender theory for two reasons: First, the people who have chosen to live in the gray areas of sex and gender have a lot to tell us about how the construction of gender plays out in our society. Feminism needs trans thinkers to help push the envelope even further, especially when so many of us take in a million hidden influences and tiny gender-poisons, courtesy of the society in which we were raised and live. Trans folks can help us see even more clearly the assumptions and biases of a gendered society, and the ways in which a world of binary gender hurts everyone. The work being done in the trans community may well hold the key to feminism's future; the ideas being worked through there may be exactly the tools feminists have been seeking for a long time. Certainly, they may help Jewish feminists solve the menstruation dilemma, and help us figure out how to save a great ritual that's been perverted by a wretched history. More on that in a moment.

Second, not everyone wants to, or can, or should, live fully as a man, fully as a woman or in the gender s/he was assigned at birth. Feminism is a movement working toward the freedom from gender oppression, from the belief that "biology equals destiny," so it's imperative that the needs and interests of transgendered people are understood and fought for. If "women" get rights but "transpeople" are still under constant attack, we as a society haven't accomplished a thing.

✡

Though we've been raised in a binary system of "male" and "female," many, many cultures throughout time—including our own—have seen degrees in between.

Leslie Feinberg writes in *Transgender Warriors* that "although what we think about gender today has been expressed differently in diverse historical periods, cultures, regions, nationalities and classes, there appears to have always been gender diversity in the human population. And there is just as much evidence that sexes have not always been arbitrarily squeezed into hard-and-fast categories of woman and man, and that fluidity between the sexes is an ancient path."[7] The book details fluctuations of gender expression—and gender-crossing—from traditional African cultures and ancient Greece through the Middle Ages into today, and shows how gender has been shaped and read over time.

It could be argued that Judaism has always worked on a binary system; that's what gendered halakha is all about (despite the fact that the Talmud records several "other" genders—people born with two sets of sexual characteristics, or none—and usually assigns them low status, sometimes as low as, say, women). Yes, the Torah includes an injunction against women wearing men's clothing and men wearing women's clothing. But if a woman wears an article of clothing, doesn't it become an article of women's clothing? And more to the point, what is "woman"? And what is "man"? And how do we know?

The beauty of Jewish law is that it's constantly evolving; the Talmud has never actually been completed. Every generation of rabbis offers a new opinion on everything from the most ancient of issues—defining kosher food, for example—to the most modern, such as in vitro fertilization. As philosopher Yeshayahu Leibowitz has said, "What characterizes Judaism as a religion of Mitzvoth is not the set of laws and commandments that was given out at the start, but rather the recognition of a system of precepts as binding, even if their specifics were often determined only with time."[8]

Of course, there are nuances and subtleties (and serious rules) regarding the evolution of Jewish law in which I'm not fully versed; I don't purport that this essay is an ironclad *responsum* in any way. But the questions I'm raising will have to be answered, I think, because the system as it exists now does not completely reflect humanity as we are beginning to understand it. Rabbi Harold Schulweis once said, "I am not a halakhic scholar but I am convinced that morality played an important and conscious role in the halakhic tradition. And I do know as a Jew . . . what seizes me about our tradition and makes my heart leap with joy. And it certainly is not the denigration of the human Jewish ethical sensibility."[9] Halakha at the expense of our ability to be wholly who we are in the healthiest and holiest of respects is halakha in need of repair. And I'd argue that halakha that divides us into genders is, in this day and age, imperfectly rendered.

Feinberg's cross-cultural gender survey, much to my surprise, offers one possible solution to the niddah quandary: It seems that "the people we would call male-to-female transsexuals in . . . early [communal] societies ritually menstruated and wore 'the leaves prescribed for women in their courses.'"[10] Elsewhere, in North American Mohave culture, young men who undergo a male-to-female initiation ritual assume female names, find a husband and simulate menstruation, pregnancy and miscarriage. Men have, in other times and places, observed menstruation rituals as a way of marking their female identification.

Even on the slightly less gray ends of the spectrum, there's no such thing as "perfect gender." Not even those who identify as male or female—and are comfortable and happy with that identification—embody "perfect manhood" or "perfect womanhood." What would that be, exactly? A woman who is always demure and never outspoken? A man who is never a nurturer? A hundred and fifty years ago, the idea of a woman in pants was downright shocking; now, even "women" wearing "men's" underwear doesn't really defy anybody's concept of gender.

Identity is a strange, mutable thing. As we shift and grow, we constantly change the way we see ourselves—and, consciously or not, the way we conceive of our gender, of ourselves as gendered, changes too. Change can be as simple as a renewed interest in lipstick or the acquisition of combat boots, or it can be much more complex.

Feinberg issues a battle cry: "Let's open the door to everyone who is self-identified as a woman, and who wants to be in women's space. (Not every woman wants that experience.) Let's keep the door unlocked."[11]

Hey, why the heck not?

Why not allow for a more open understanding of gender in which we all might fit on the continuum, from female to female-masculine to androgynous to male-feminine to male and back again? What if we allow the words we use to describe ourselves—and the rituals we choose to observe—to reflect that shift? What if we allow our gender identity to ebb and flow with the rest of our sense of self? After all, isn't feminism supposed to be about the right to self-define?

When I think about the possible implications for gendered halakha, it seems absolutely radical. Almost too radical for me, to be honest. But at the same time, utterly freeing.

What if the aspects of Jewish law that address biological gender became as mutable as gender itself? What if we maintained the idea of the niddah laws— the monthly connection, the cycles of abstinence and reunion, the immersion into ritual water—but allowed our definition of "woman" to be more fluid? And didn't require those who didn't identify as "women" to participate?

Look, I'm not a moron; I know that the niddah laws are intended to address menstruation, not female identity. Post-menopausal women don't traditionally go to the mikveh, nor do pregnant women. But this particular rite has accrued such a tremendous power over the years, especially lately, as a "women's ritual." The Rabbis gave the female biological process unreasonably heavy sociocultural weight in a fairly evil way, enabling women to feel terrible about their bodies and, in the process, feel as if they're under patriarchal lock and key.

There's the Jewish women's custom of slapping her daughter at the time of first menses and telling her, "Now you know, a woman's life is hardship and pain." Why are all of the horrors of male domination located in that first moment of bleeding?

The niddah laws have become an icon of Jewish womanhood; for women on all sides of this discussion, they are about much more than a monthly ovarian delivery. Radical measures clearly need to be taken—to restore our right to define ourselves and to re-sanctify our bodies, on our own damn terms—if we're ever to get all of that mud out of the mikveh. I think it's vital to at least consider new ways of approaching the issues . . . and maybe through the age-old process of debate, we can forge our way to a new understanding.

Women are not technically obligated to pray three times a day, to wear a tallis or to lay tefillin—they're legally exempt from anything that is considered a "time-bound mitzvah." (Historically it was understood that caring for children might preclude, for example, saying the afternoon prayers on time.) However, since the advent of feminism some women have taken advantage of the right to obligate themselves to these "male" mitzvot; upon this declaration of obligation, their legal status in relation to those mitzvot is the same as that of men—just as binding.[12]

Couldn't, then, someone not born a woman decide to obligate him- or herself to the mitzvah of niddah observance? (Here, we might define the mitzvah as a week or two of abstinence a month, followed by immersion in the mikveh—whatever the gender and observance level of the participant and the participant's partner.) We could sanction the act whether the person in question is a male-to-female transgendered person (who can, by the way, take hormones to mimic a menstrual cycle) or a man who identifies as female, whether said person considers observance of the niddah laws an extension of a gender identity or whether s/he wants to use the niddah laws as a way of connecting his/her body to the cycles of the moon, the month, passing time. Like a woman announcing that she is duty-bound to lay tefillin every day, someone who declares s/he is obligated to this mitzvah would be required to maintain its practice as long as the mitzvah remained concordant with the gender identity. Of course, this principle could also extend to women who don't menstruate every month—for reasons ranging from reproductive irregularity to chemotherapy—but would like to be a part of the holy cycle, the sacred bodily connection.

As for folks who menstruate but don't want to emphasize that aspect of themselves—whether female-to-male transgendered people, people who identify as butch or women who have had problematic relationships with their biology—there are precedents for that, too. In the Middle Ages the rabbis asked this question: When the prophet Elijah turned into an angel in the book of Kings, was his wife permitted to remarry, even though he had neither divorced nor widowed her? Ultimately it was decided that a woman is barred from marrying so long as she is another man's wife, and this woman was married to an angel, not a man. Since angels have no gender, the marriage was, the rabbis decided, therefore annulled.[13] It could certainly be argued, as an extension of this logic, that if a person gets to a point where s/he does not identify as a "woman"—if s/he changes gender, biologically or sociologically—then s/he would not be obligated to mitzvot to which "women" are obligated. A change in gender status results in a change of legal status, and even those who consider their gender to be "butch" could be regarded as exempt from, say, the niddah laws.

As I said, it's a radical idea. But the spirit of Jewish law as I understand it intends to transform the individual for the better, to give him or her opening points for a relationship with the sacred—not to keep people locked down in a place where they can find nothing holy. If people who do a "women's ritual" can decide for themselves if the ritual fits the body it circumscribes, then the ritual no longer forces certain bodies into certain boxes; our definitions of who must, who can and who might be exempt would be utterly transformed. Men wouldn't choose the system for women; individuals would choose it for themselves.

✡

The changes in Judaism created by the fall of the Second Temple were far more radical than the ideas outlined here. Feminism has been described (correctly, I think) as one of the greatest contemporary threats to the survival of Judaism. Isn't it time we took some drastic measures to ensure that we can keep going even without the altar of male domination?

Judaism's history is its strength; the many souls who have questioned, changed and upheld Jewish law have created a collective system greater than the sum of its parts. It's not about throwing away what's there—it's about creating air and space and breath so that those same mitzvot can pass into our age with renewed vigor and integrity. The beauty of Judaism—and, with the niddah laws, the beautiful problem—is that its rituals carry the breath of all who have considered, written about, thought about and done them before, of thousands of years of history.

Perhaps it's time to exhale.

Notes:

1. Tirzah Meacham (leBeit Yoreh), "An Abbreviated History of the Development of the Jewish Menstrual Laws," in *Women and Water: Menstruation in Jewish Life and Law*, ed. Rahel R. Wasserfall (Brandeis University Press, 1999), 30–31.

2. Bereshit Rabba 17:8

3. Shabbat 152a

4. BT Pesachim 111a

5. Sharon Koren, "Mystical Rationales for the Laws of *Niddah*," in *Women and Water*, 103.

6. Melanie Blackless et al, "How Sexually Dimorphic Are We?" *American Journal of Human Biology*, Volume 12, Issue 2, 2000, 151–166.

7. Leslie Feinberg, *Transgender Warriors: Making History from Joan of Arc to Dennis Rodman* (Beacon Press, 1996), 121.

8. Yeshayahu Leibowitz, "Religious Praxis: The Meaning of Halakha," 1953, 3.

9. From "The Character of Halacha Entering the Twenty-First Century," Rabbi Schulweis's keynote address to the Rabbinical Assembly Convention in Los Angeles on March 22, 1993. Quoted with permission.

10. Feinberg, 111

11. Feinberg, 118–119

12. Thanks to Rabbi Joel Roth at the Jewish Theological Seminary for clarifying this point.

13. I'd like to thank Rabbi Eliezer Yehuda Waldenberg, by way of Beth Orens, for this argument. Waldenberg discusses Elijah in his *Responsa Tzitz Eliezer*.

THE WORD

EVE ROSENBAUM

THE DOOR TO THE CHURCH IS CLOSED but not locked. People have been going in and out, watching me as they reach the top step and make their way into the lit hallway. It's not snowing but the air holds promise, and I am pacing back and forth in front of the door of the First Baptist Church of Silver Spring, wishing I hadn't left my coat in the car, wishing I'd finished the poem and not thrown it away. I look at my watch, five to seven.

Ushers are supposed to meet at seven in the lobby, and my feet are not willing to step inside. It's just a building, it's just a building. Gabrielle has been to tons of churches. It's not a big deal, it's just a building. It's Friday night, it's after sunset. Driving on Friday is still difficult for me. I'm worried that I'll have an accident, the police will call my parents and my cover will be blown. They'll demand, "What were you doing at the First Baptist Church of Silver Spring on a Friday night, ushering for a concert of Christmas carols?" And really, will any explanation be good enough?

If I can keep my head low enough to the desk then Mrs. Leibman won't call on me and I can write my poem. I won't know the answer anyway, she knows it, the whole class knows it, it's no secret. She can call on Ahuva, who's sitting next to me, but calling on me would just be a disaster all around. She'll ask me a

88

question in Hebrew, I'll stumble, turn red. She'll stop me halfway through and call on someone else who can give her the right answer. Then she'll want to talk to me after class, ask if I'm studying, and I'll tell her I am when we both know I'm not, that I don't care. But I'll pretend to care and she'll pretend to believe me and we'll continue on until the next time she looks over and sees me writing something in my notebook that doesn't go from right to left.

"Esther," she says in Hebrew, "can you read the Rashi and explain it?"

In school I go by my middle name. I don't lift my head. There's another Esther in the class. Ahuva pokes me. "It's you," she says. I cover my poem with my hand, pull my Humash closer to me on the desk. I have no idea where we are. I take too long and she calls on Tehilah, who answers in perfect Hebrew, perfect grammar. I go back to my poem.

Three weeks later I will turn in an almost blank test and Mrs. Leibman will turn it back to me with almost no red marks on it. "I didn't understand the questions," I'll say. "They're all in Hebrew." And she'll tell me to try harder. At the end of the term she'll pass me on my report card. All of the teachers will.

Class ends at 3:40 and the conversation about Walt Whitman starts winding down as people pack their bags. Elizabeth finishes the lecture and passes around flyers for a concert she's performing in Saturday at the National Building Museum. "It should be great," she says. "I hope to see you there."

I take a flyer.

Joni and I get there early, stand off to the side and watch the rehearsal. "I used to be in a choir," she says. "In high school. We performed in Russia." There will be three hundred people in the choir tonight, Elizabeth has told me, people from her choir and a choir from Germany, and some youth choirs from the D.C. area. It is the tenth anniversary of the tearing down of the Berlin Wall and they're singing Beethoven.

An usher rips our tickets and hands us programs, points us to where we should sit. The conductor addresses the audience and I'm reading through the program, looking at ads, looking for Elizabeth's name. There's one announcement for choir auditions and another looking for ushers. "I'm going to usher," I whisper to Joni.

"Why?"

"Might be fun." I look in the back of the program at the ticket order form. Besides this concert, all of the performances are in churches.

A man in a yarmulke walks by and I wonder if I know him.

The conductor welcomes the chief justice of the Supreme Court, and Joni and I try to spot him in the audience. When I get home I send Elizabeth an email saying I'd like to usher.

Mrs. Leibman calls me over after class and tells me to sit. "I'm looking for some good books to read," she says, "and I'd like to hear some suggestions."

"I'm not sure what kind of books." I don't read the books she thinks I read: What if she tells the principal and he expels me? I'm worried this is a test and I'm about to fail.

"Literature," she says. "You're always reading something. Tell me what you're reading."

The next day I give her my copy of Of Human Bondage *and an anthology of short stories. A week later she hands them back to me and asks how I can read such books. "These are not things Bais Yaakov girls should be reading."*

She's appalled, she says.

It's Wednesday afternoon and the door to Elizabeth's office is closed. She is at her desk, going through the proof pages of her book, and I am at her computer, typing up the index. The pages are due back to the publisher, and I'm helping her finish the last of it.

"Thanks for helping," she says. "You're a goddess."

I say that I'm not and we drift back into silence. There are moments of conversations, clarifications of a word or title, but we work mostly back to back. I feel comfortable in her office.

She hands me more pages to index and stretches, takes celery from the bag on the couch. She says, "I spoke to the head usher and he's going to email you about our next concert."

"That's great," I say. "Thanks."

I say, "I've never been inside a church."

She can't believe it. "Never?" I shake my head. "Well," she says. "It's not a big deal. You'll be okay." We go back to silence.

I try to write a poem about churches, about sitting on the steps of a church debating whether to go inside. It's not working. I email it to Gabrielle and she says to put it away for a while, don't look at it. "I can't do that," I tell her. It's midnight and we are an hour into a telephone conversation. I am in Washington, playing computer solitaire and not doing homework. She is packing up her New York apartment, wrapping canvases to be shipped to Israel. "I'm ushering next week and if the poem's not finished before then, well then I won't finish it." I am six days away from going into a church for the first time and trying to write about it. But it sounds hollow, boring.

"You know, going into a church isn't a big deal," Gabrielle says. "I've been to tons of churches. It's just a building."

"I know."

"It'll be fine, trust me." I throw away the poem.

It's Purim and I go to shul late, miss part of the Megillah reading. "If you don't hear the whole thing then it doesn't count," someone says to me. I walk with my mother and sister to the rabbi's house down the street and he reads the Megillah for people who missed it. His wife, the rebbetzin, *is talking to my mother, looking at me. I can't hear what they're saying but I'm sure I can guess. I'm right.*

"What did she say to you?" I ask my mother on the way home.

"She wanted to know if you were seeing anyone, if she can fix you up."

"No way," I say. "I'm seventeen. And I don't believe in marriage."

My mother sighs. We've had this conversation before. "I don't want to do this now," she says.

✡

We walk through the gardens and Gabrielle says, "This is nothing. You should see the cathedrals in Europe, hundreds of years old, gardens you can get lost in. This is nice, but it was built in 1910. It's nice, but it's not Europe." Gabrielle is a cathedral freak. She is in D.C. for one day and we go to the National Cathedral because the facade amazes her. She has her camera, black and white film. She's leaving Tuesday for art school in Israel.

My father is playing with the car radio, looking for a good song. He stops at the oldies station. I groan, roll my eyes, and he starts singing along. "Can I give you a tape?" I ask. I pull open my bag, start looking around for something, anything that will make it stop.

Simon & Garfunkel come on, singing "The Sounds of Silence." My father sings with them. I contemplate jumping out of the car. It's only going eighty miles an hour, it's worth a shot. He reaches over and turns down the volume. "Did you know they're from New York?" he asks. "They both grew up religious and one Shabbos they turned the lights on to see if something would happen. They wanted to see if they would be struck by lightning, and nothing happened. After you turn the lights on once, it gets easier."

I'm looking out the window.

"Do you keep Shabbos?" he asks.

"Yes."

"That's good." My father is silent. He turns the radio back on. "Give me your tape."

Saturday morning I drive to Kate's house. She is on the phone when she opens the door. "I had a great time in Europe," she's saying. "We hiked the most amazing trails and I got to play the girlfriend instead of being the one in the spotlight. It was a great trip." She says goodbye and turns to me. "It was a terrible trip," she says. "I'm telling people it was great but it was just dreadful. I spent two weeks acting the ornament, hanging on Anthony's arm at his conferences and readings." She's happy to be back.

We go into her office. "Have you read this book?" she asks. She shows me *Ghost Dance* by Carole Maso. She had emailed me about it a few months back, in the middle of one of her depressions. She wrote, "It's one of those books that makes you come alive again, you believe the world is suffused with magic and a beautiful thing if there are books like this. You should get it if you haven't read it."

I tell her I've finished that and a few other books. We exchange titles. I want to tell her that her own memoir does that for me, makes me feel alive. But I don't. She would think that was weird. She is about halfway through a depression, months of blackness trapping her in circles. She will find her way out, she will find her blood, as she says. Her Akita comes into the room with a stuffed animal in her mouth. We talk about school, hers and mine. We talk about writing.

"There's religion," Gabrielle says, "and there is spirituality. I don't think the two go together at all." I agree. It is August and we are sitting outside at Cafe Dante in Manhattan's West Village, drinking iced coffee and eating artichoke hearts, watching people. It is a favorite pastime.

"Religion is a way of life. It's rules that tell you what to do and how to do it, how to be a person, how to interact with others. But there's nothing spiritual about it. And the only reason I believe in religion is because I believe that the Torah is real, that it was written by God. But I don't think it's necessarily a spiritual thing."

She drinks her coffee and gets up to chase a man with a cat on his shoulder. He stops and she takes his picture.

The weather report predicts a hurricane and I'm convinced my building is the only building in the D.C. area to lose power. My mother calls to check on me. "I have to go out," I tell her. "I need to buy candles before I go to class."

"You don't have candles?" she asks and I know I've slipped. "You told me you were lighting Shabbos candles every week. I guess you weren't telling the truth."

"I just ran out. I'm buying more today."

When Kate was sixteen she thought about suicide. She ran up the mountain near her house in Arizona and headed for the boulder by the edge of the cliff. 5:00 A.M. and the world was silent. She sat there crying, willing her body to throw itself into the ravine. She thought about the time a year earlier when she'd swallowed a bottle of aspirin and a bottle of whiskey. It didn't take. Her mother found her, and the emergency room pumped her stomach. But this time, this could be it. The ravine could be bottomless, she could fall through the earth.

She didn't do it. She started making her way back down the mountain, desperate to finish her morning run. She pushed her way back through the tangled brush and caught her foot on a branch, went flying. The ravine was not bottomless.

My brother calls me four times on Friday afternoon, fifteen minutes before Shabbos to make sure I'm home. I'm not. When I speak to him Saturday night I tell him I was in the shower, I was in the kitchen, I didn't hear the phone ring. Sorry.

I am at my parents' house for a week in winter and I visit the company where I used to work. Thomas takes me out to lunch. He is fifty and crazy in the way that artists sometimes are. He asks if my parents know what I do when I'm not home.

"Of course not," I say.

He tells me to be careful or my parents will lock me in the basement and try to brainwash me back into religion. I tell him I don't mind being the crazy woman locked away. "But," I say, "it's been done to death."

✡

Once the tickets have been collected and the audience shown to their seats, I walk into the sanctuary through the side entrance and take a seat in the back pew near the rest of the ushers. I think, This place looks like a synagogue, except for the cross. The choir sings Christmas carols and I leave when the audience joins in. I don't know the words.

Kate signs my copy of her book. "To Eve: whose own writing and voice is so powerful even now at such a 'young age.' Keep with it and do not ever, ever let anyone else tell you what to think, do or say—follow your heart, because it's a strong one."

My father sees what she's written and looks at me. "What does she mean, don't let anyone tell you what to do?"

"It's nothing," I say. I take the book from his hands.

In tenth grade I fall in love with a new word: apikores. I've heard it before, I know what it means. But this is the first time I've taken it for myself, felt the letters as they coat my tongue. I don't say it out loud—this is not the kind of word you can say when people are near you. It's the worst insult. It's the one thing you should never say to anyone.

Mrs. Leibman talks about it in Humash class one Thursday. She says, "Girls, I don't want you to think a person who is an apikores is dumb. These people are smart by nature. They study the things we study and they have questions, they challenge the rabbis for answers and they choose not to believe. They don't fall out of religion because it's hard or because they're lazy. They move away from religion because they choose to. They are not satisfied with answers, they think there is a better truth waiting for them out there. They throw away religion because they are not satisfied with the answers we know to be true."

I want to be an apikores; I covet the word, the notion. It is not simply to be a nonbeliever. It is to consciously reject religion, to value one's own opinion over what should be taken as fact. An apikores is more dangerous than the average secular Jew. An apikores creates anarchy. I start to wonder if I'm smart enough to become one. Do I accept things too easily? Do I push for answers when I'm not satisfied? I can't ask Mrs. Leibman these questions, she doesn't like me and this isn't the lesson I'm supposed to get from her lecture. I trace the word in my notebook, give it shape, texture. I cross it out when Ahuva looks over at my paper. I cover the letters with black ink.

My brother calls on Saturday night. "Yeshiva was fun tonight. I learned with Kirschner and then we had Chinese food. I had sweet and sour chicken." He asks, "You went out?"

"Yeah, I was out."

"Where'd you go?"

"I went to church." I'm telling the truth. He thinks I'm kidding.

"Really, where'd you go?"

"Really, I went to church. It was fun."

"Very funny."

"I went out. I saw a movie."

I can hear his hesitation. He's debating whether he should lecture me about movies and how evil they are. He doesn't, because he knows I won't listen. I can't tell him that I didn't see a movie, that really I ushered for a concert in a church and that I'm doing it again in three weeks.

"Tell me about school," I say and we talk for almost an hour.

Elizabeth comes over to me after the concert and we sit on the couch in the lobby. "That was great," I say. "Beautiful."

She asks, "How does it feel to be in church?"

"Fine," I say. "It feels fine."

"Just a building, right?"

I nod. We talk about finals and her trip to Paris.

✡

Thomas suggests the Airmont Diner for lunch, halfway between my house and the office. I watch the cars as we walk to the door, hoping no one I know is watching. It's safer to go at night, when maybe no one will recognize my car in the dark. But I'm home for two days and this is the only time we could meet.

"The problem," I say once we're inside, "is that this place is right smack in the middle of town and everyone gets into everyone else's business. If someone sees me here then they'll tell my parents and maybe my parents' rabbi and then all hell breaks loose. Someone will tell my sister's principal and she'll get kicked out of school, my brother will get kicked out of school, no one will want to marry them and my parents will blame everything on me. I'm not sure one cup of coffee is worth all that."

Thomas thinks I'm insane.

Ahuva is visiting friends in Lakewood, New Jersey, and I drive there on Wednesday with my brother. It's August and the air conditioner in my car is broken. We listen to the Reduced Shakespeare Company and recite the whole thing by heart. When we get to Lakewood, I drop him off at his old school and find my way to the house where Ahuva is staying. She has been in town a week already and is going home on a 10:00 A.M. flight the next day.

We hug. "How are you?" I ask.

"Baruch Hashem, Baruch Hashem. And you?"

"Great, thanks." We sit on the couch. We both know why she is in town but I won't bring it up and I'm sure she won't. It's been years since we were close. I want to ask her why she needs to come to New York to find a husband, what she does with her life that's interesting or exciting since she doesn't have a wedding to plan or children to take care of and that's all she's ever wanted. I want to know if she's happy.

Instead, she tells me gossip. Who's getting married from our class, who's having babies. "I know," I say. "Shira told me." Really, I don't care, but I smile.

"What are you doing now?" she asks me.

"I'm starting graduate school in a few weeks and I'm moving to Washington, D.C."

Ahuva smiles. "That's so nice," she says. "Is that near Oregon?"

"No, it's near Virginia. It's about four hours south of here."

"It's near Rhode Island then."

"No, that's north." Ahuva and I were in the same geography class in ninth grade. I did a state report on Vermont.

"Your hair used to be blond, right?" she says.

"I dyed it. I was getting tired of blond, and I always wanted to try red hair."

She nods and looks away.

Shira calls me Sunday night. She tells me about her children and says that she and her husband are getting audited by the IRS. "So, tell me about your life."

"I went out with some people," I say.

"To a kosher restaurant?"

"Of course. We went out Thursday night." Really, Saturday afternoon to an Italian restaurant in Georgetown, but I can't think of any reason to be honest.

"Do you go to shul?" she asks. "Do you have a lot of Jewish friends in Washington?"

I can't figure out how to answer this. She asks again.

"I don't know very many Jewish people," I say. "Actually, I know almost none. And I don't live near a shul."

"So what do you do all Shabbos?"

"Sleep and read, it's fine."

"You know, I'm so proud of you," she says. "You live in a city where you don't know any religious Jews and you keep to what you believe in. That shows you're really dedicated. That makes me happy." We talk for a few more minutes. When we hang up I want to rip out my tongue.

✡

I'm going from bedroom to bedroom, collecting my clothes and books to pack after a week at home. I have things all over the house and my brother is following me. He's trying to start a debate about religion. "Not now, okay? I can't do this now." I go through piles of laundry looking for my socks. It's almost midnight. "Don't you have to go to sleep?" He's not moving.

"I want to understand where you're coming from," he says. He sounds reasonable but I know this is just the introduction to a conversation that will take hours. We've been through this before. "I want to know how you could go from wanting to be a Bais Yaakov girl to how you are now."

I want to laugh. He doesn't know how I am; I don't tell him anything. He starts the standard debate, I try to make jokes, get him to say goodnight, goodbye, and go to sleep.

"Are you an apikores?" he asks. "You're an apikores."

I pretend to get angry. Really I'm flattered. Out of my half-lies and altered stories he has formed an opinion of me. I want to sit him down and tell him everything. I want to tell him what I do, who I am, and then let him call me an apikores. I want to tell him that two weeks ago I spent Friday night in a church, ushering for a concert where I listened to Christmas carols, staring at a cross draped in purple fabric. I want to tell him that I drove on Shabbos, ripped tickets, lit candles, wrote in my journal. I want to watch his face.

But really I don't want to watch his face. Two days later he has forgotten our conversation and he makes jokes to me over the telephone.

Gabrielle and I walk through the Whitney Museum and she peers closely at the Mark Rothko paintings. "It's all layered," she says. "It looks like one color but there's such depth behind each brush stroke, it's like the different paints have collided and turned themselves into one color that represents the whole. But if you look close enough, you can see their differences."

I move closer to the wall.

"He's a genius," she says.

It is Arizona. I know it is Arizona the way I know the sound of my voice in echo. I run up trails that are familiar, but I know I've never been here. I know these trails, recognize the brush. I jump over the branches, I run past saguaros. My feet pound the earth, pack the brown soil of desert into something tame, something easily stepped on. She has been here, I think, she has pounded this earth in predawn the way I am tracing her footfalls by moonlight.

I see the boulder. I see her sitting, crying, waiting for the sun to come up over the town she has learned to call home. I want to wave as I run past, but she is only an outline: She is not flesh. The cliff pulls itself into focus before me and if I dilate my eyes I can see straight through the night, see the cliff on the other side of the ravine. I can jump it, I think. I can make it across. Her outline faces the other direction. She does not watch as my legs arch away from earth and I take flight.

But my aim is wrong. I'm flying, but straight down is not the direction I hoped for. Beneath me is water that rushes toward nowhere, content enough to churn. I fall into its fever. My feet don't touch bottom. My arms reach for something to grab on to. I don't want to die here, I think, I don't want to drown. My fingers find a branch and start to pull themselves out of the water, my feet take hold of the wall and I climb straight up the cliff. I reach the top bruised and bleeding but alive. I look over the ravine and see her outline on the boulder, still contemplating death. My feet find the rhythm of the trail and pound the desert in time with the rising of the sun.

I sit by myself in the back pew of the church, the other ushers a few rows up. In crimson ink I write the word "apikores" on my hand in Hebrew, sure no one around me will know what it means. I decide to write the word on my hand every day until I am sure.

My brother calls me an apikores. Shira called me an apikores on the phone two days ago and I didn't disagree. But I'm not sure. I want to know that I own the word, that I can become the letters, now red and seeping into my skin, and never look back. I want to write in permanent ink or not write it at all.

After the concert I walk out with Elizabeth. I put my hand in the pocket of my coat.

CHALLAH FOR THE QUEEN OF HEAVEN

RYIAH LILITH

WITCHCRAFT LED ME BACK TO JUDAISM.

I grew up in a secular Zionist home, and though I sometimes went to shul with friends, and in high school attended quite a few confirmation ceremonies, my own Jewish education and observance were casual. In college I unearthed my proverbial roots and fell in love with the absolutes of traditional Judaism, but my love affair was cut short when I discovered feminism. As buzzwords and phrases such as *patriarchy, masculine God-language* and *blood taboo* crept into my vocabulary, the lure of Orthodox Judaism diminished. In Conservative services I was distracted by the gendered and often sexist prayers and felt little connection to either Adonai or other congregants, and although the Reform *Gates of Prayer* was explicitly nonsexist, I noticed that the rabbi, cantor, congregational leadership and most of the board were men. So I left, taking a cue from Carol Christ and declaring myself "post-Jewish."

My exodus from Judaism was only one manifestation of my righteous feminist anger. Feminism had opened my eyes, but rather than the "click" described by Gloria Steinem, feminism became both my worldview and my blinders. I stopped going to classes mid-semester when I decided that the professors, students or reading materials were sexist, or not explicitly feminist, and hence no longer relevant to my life. I changed my major seven times before nesting in the women's studies department. I declined invitations to see nonfeminist movies, and eventually cut people who suggested such misogynistic entertainment out of my life. I decided that I would never again allow a man to fuck me and threw a coming-out party for myself. I began a senior thesis on lesbian separatism and dreamed of living on wimmin's land. I dabbled in Witchcraft and women's spirituality. And then I graduated.

My righteous feminist anger, cut off from the inspiration of women's studies, morphed into frustration and depression. Convinced that I was the sole radical post-Jewish lesbian feminist in my small Midwestern town, I cocooned myself in my apartment and experimented with solo consciousness-raising. I had spent almost a year in self-imposed exile when a newspaper ad for an annual women's Winter Solstice ritual caught my attention. I arrived on time, with my yarn, round mirror and white candle in tow.

The ritual was powerful—a hundred or so women of all ages, shapes and sizes chanting and dancing in a candlelit room smelling of sage and sweetgrass, welcoming the return of the Sun Goddess. I lingered after the ritual was over, hoping to soak up enough of the ambience to sustain me until next year's ritual. I was surprised at the intensity of my experience, for my brief undergraduate forays into Witchcraft had been lackluster. Although I had appreciated the feminist orientation and the emphasis on the Goddess, I had already given up one religion and felt ambivalent about practicing another.

In the following weeks, I reread and reconsidered the few books on Witchcraft and Paganism that I had saved during my post-graduation book purge. I unpacked the small collection of ritual tools that I had started to accumulate and I began creating solitary rituals, in the hopes of recapturing the feeling of peace and serenity that I had experienced at the Solstice. It just wasn't the same. I felt silly standing or sitting before my coffee-table altar, chanting Goddess names to myself. Wondering if maybe the requirement of a minyan had somehow been genetically etched into my soul, I decided to search for a group of Witches. Instead, I found a group of Jewish women.

I felt apprehensive and explained to the group's leader that I no longer practiced Judaism. She assured me that a Rosh Chodesh ceremony was quite distinct from mainstream Jewish services, and explained that this traditional Jewish observance of the new moon, sometimes considered a women's holiday, had been appropriated and updated by Jewish women. Contemporary Rosh Chodesh rituals are often women-only and include explicitly feminist liturgy. Eventually I decided to go, figuring that I wasn't having much success on my own. We gathered in a member's backyard and sat cross-legged on mats under the new moon. We lit candles, introduced ourselves as the daughters of our mothers and our grandmothers ("I am Ryiah, daughter of Ruth, daughter of Mary . . . ") and took turns reading poems by Jewish women. We sang prayers to Shekinah, the feminine aspect of God, using traditional melodies. I left feeling oddly inspired, promising to return next month.

Historically, Rosh Chodesh evolved out of ancient Near Eastern lunar rituals, which focused on fertility, divination and Goddess worship.[1] As combating idol worship became a significant priority for some Israelite leaders, lunar observances by Israelite women became problematic.[2] Interestingly, instead of prohibiting lunar observances—or perhaps because such prohibitions proved ineffective—celebration of the new moon became a sanctioned Israelite festival, complete with a revised mythology that the women were given Rosh Chodesh by God as a reward for their refusal to donate any of their gold for the creation of the Golden Calf. Although Rosh Chodesh observances varied, common practices included baking challah, refraining from work and lighting candles or fires at night.[3]

Rosh Chodesh observance has waxed and waned over the last two thousand years, but it met a strong revival during the second wave of feminism. Contemporary Rosh Chodesh rituals often take place in women's homes and involve lighting candles, praying, singing and chanting to Shekinah (as Lady of the Moon) and festive or ritual meals.

I found in Rosh Chodesh a way to integrate Jewish and Pagan practices, and for a while I experienced a peaceful reconciliation. I still avoided temple, but I also stopped referring to myself as "post-Jewish." I began a tentative study of feminist Jewish theology and Torah commentary. But I soon uncovered dissension between Jewish feminists and Goddess worshippers. For example, some of the latter believe in a prehistorical, prebiblical, Goddess-oriented, matrifocal society, which was destroyed by Indo-European invaders (sometimes identified as the Levites[4]) who were militaristic and patriarchal, and worshipped a transcendent male God.[5] In response, Jewish feminist theologians likened this interpretation of herstory to claims that the Jews killed Jesus, and were equally adamant that Jews did not kill the Goddess, noting that the societies which predated the Israelites had attempted to curtail Goddess worship.[6] Other Jewish scholars argue that even after this time, the Goddess continued to play a role in Judaism.[7]

I hoped to eventually reconcile my Jewish and Pagan spirituality, but in light of this intellectual schism I resigned myself to practicing both separately: I was a solitary Witch who also belonged to a Jewish women's circle. I occasionally wondered whether I would still practice Judaism if I left the area, but the other women often spoke of other Rosh Chodesh collectives they had belonged to, both in the past and in other cities. Sure enough, when I moved to the District of Columbia I soon found a Jewish women's group that met monthly for both social and religious occasions. Unfortunately, differences between the D.C. crowd and my former collective quickly emerged. Although the D.C. group celebrated the Jewish holidays with feminist liturgy that referred to Shekinah, she was merely Adonai in drag. At Yom Kippur, we prayed to Shekinah to forgive us, and at Passover we remembered how she led us out of Egypt with a mighty hand and an outstretched arm. I felt as little connection to this Shekinah as I had to Adonai.

While some Pagans consider Shekinah to be a Goddess in her own right, completely distinct from Adonai,[8] most non-Pagan Jewish feminists consider her to be the immanent, feminine aspect of God who accompanied the Israelites into exile after the destruction of the Temple, and who became incorporated into Jewish mysticism. As the immanent aspect of God, Shekinah possesses different attributes than Adonai. For example, Jewish mystics believe that the divine becomes manifest in the world through Shekinah, not Adonai, and Jewish feminist theologians have discovered that many of the symbols and metaphors for Shekinah—such as lunar cycles, the morning and evening star, the primordial sea, the dove and the serpent—were also associated with ancient Near Eastern Goddesses, but were not associated with Adonai.[9]

While I wasn't certain whether I understood her to be a Goddess or a feminine aspect of God, I knew that Shekinah was not simply another name for Adonai. When I raised this issue with the group's leader, I discovered that criticism and dissent were not tolerated. Unlike my Midwestern Rosh Chodesh circle, the D.C. group was not an egalitarian collective, but a dictatorship. Membership decisions, dates and times of events, liturgical revision and networking or outreach were all determined by one woman whose authority could not be questioned without risking excommunication. My attempts to "Paganize" the liturgy—as my questioning was characterized—resulted in my expulsion from the group.

Despite this experience, I was hopeful that I would find a more open-minded group of Jewish women who were creating feminist rituals. The D.C. area has a large enough Jewish population to host several Jewish women's groups; over time, I participated in a feminist group that was mixed-gender, an Orthodox women's minyan and a feminist women's circle that conceived of God as gender-neutral. Yet none of them were exactly what I was looking for—a path to the Goddess. All were uncomfortable with Shekinah as anything other than Adonai's alter ego, and steadfastly refused to even consider incorporating other ancient Near Eastern Goddesses, such as Asherah (who was worshipped for some time by the Israelites themselves) into group ritual. I realized that I would again have to leave the Jewish tribe—this time, not because of my feminist sensibilities, but because of my increasingly Pagan worldview.

I was drawn to Witchcraft, and to Paganism in general, because of the lack of dogma and authority and the emphasis on personal responsibility for one's own spiritual development and expression. In contrast to the revealed mysteries of Judaism, Witchcraft is an occult religion—its mysteries must be experienced to be understood. An aspiring Witch first studies with a teacher, or series of teachers, and learns the teacher's ways of doing things, but eventually she has to break away, design her own rituals and develop her own cosmology and thealogy (Goddess-based theology) in order to delineate a personal and fulfilling spiritual practice. Although most Pagan traditions or denominations are open to both women and men, and honor both the Goddess and the God, I chose to follow the all-female, all-Goddess Dianic tradition (from Diana, the Roman lunar Goddess of the hunt). I had found my path to the Goddess, but as I progressed in my studies and practice, I realized that my spiritual development would never be complete until I figured out how to integrate Judaism into my feminist Goddess-worship.

Since I still wasn't sure how to intellectually reconcile Judaism and Witchcraft, I began at the material level: I looked to see what was similar in Jewish and Pagan ritual and practice. This also meshed with the Pagan approach to attaining spiritual wisdom. First, there was the timing of holidays: Both Jews and Witches use a lunar calendar, and many of the annual festivals are linked to agricultural cycles of planting (Tu B'Shvat and Passover for Jews, and the Spring Equinox and May Day for Pagans), tending (counting the *omer* between Passover and Shavuot; the Summer Solstice) and harvesting (Shavuot and Sukkot; the Fall Equinox). Second, although Jewish observances do not generally include drumming and dancing, some do, and most involve a fair amount of singing and candlelighting—all of which are central in many Pagan rituals and celebrations. I was determined to keep things simple. I wanted to experience only the smallest inklings of synchronicity and syncretism—no books, no groups, only candles and the moon.

A Witch usually sets up an altar in her home, on which she may display candles, photographs, artwork, seashells, crystals, herbs or other symbols of the Goddess and the natural world. I unpacked my Shabbos candlesticks, dusted them off, and placed them on my altar. On Friday evenings and Rosh Chodeshim, I lit candles and recited feminized blessings. As Hanukah approached, I positioned my altar so that it was underneath the window in which I placed a menorah.

While I found these simple observances comforting, I knew that they were not based on an integrated thealogy. Although I could place Jewish ritual items on a Pagan altar, the altar as a whole still represented the Goddess. I was figuratively resting my Judaism on a foundation of idolatry, and I had to explore the ramifications of that from a Jewish perspective. While Witchcraft is eclectic, and can easily absorb multicultural practices and beliefs, Judaism can only be stretched so far before it ceases to be Judaism. I wanted to determine if I could stretch Judaism far enough that its margins overlapped with Goddess worship and Witchcraft. I was not seeking an absolute understanding of Jewish law, but rather an interpretation that would help me to understand the apparent oxymoron of Pagan Judaism.

In attempting to navigate a Jewish Pagan path to the Goddess, I began by considering the Goddess and idolatry. Literally, the mitzvot only prohibit worship of other Gods, so perhaps worship of the Goddess is acceptable. However, the prohibitions against idolatry are wider-reaching: There is Jeremiah's admonishment to the women to cease pouring libations and baking cakes for the Queen of Heaven. And there are the multiple references to tearing down the high places: the Asherim, or altars to the Goddess Asherah. The Torah, in fact, describes countless incidents of Goddess worship, but always in the context of Israelites who strayed, or other wicked people. Logically, idolatry and Goddess worship would not have been repeatedly prohibited unless the Israelites were repeatedly practicing them. So the question then becomes, if being Jewish is defined as doing those things that Jews have traditionally done, how does one determine what Jews have traditionally done—by what the Torah proclaims that Jews should do, or by other historical revelations of what Jews actually did?

I realize that this line of reasoning could be extended to other prohibitions, and similar arguments could be made: for example, that the prohibition against murder implies that murder should be embraced as a Jewish act. But the act of murder is quite distinct from Goddess worship in my mind. Anyone who does equate the two will likely condemn my beliefs anyway, to the extent that no argument I could make would convince them that I can be both Jewish and Pagan. However, a useful parallel can be drawn in this context between Goddess worship and homosexuality. The Torah prohibits both, perhaps because at the time of its writing, both threatened the unity or survival of the Israelites—or perhaps those were more patriarchal and homophobic times. Today, different denominations have different stances on homosexuality. Likewise, denominations differ in their view of God; humanistic Jews probably are not concerned that other Jews worship a Goddess instead of God. It may not be traditional to worship the Goddess, but what is sufficiently traditional? Certainly not secular, Reform, Reconstructionist, Renewal, Conservative, humanist, GLBT or feminist Judaism. Orthodox Judaism may be the most traditional modern denomination, but it is still post-Temple Judaism—a fairly recent invention.

Eventually, I stopped trying to parse out arguments. My solitary altar-based rituals were so meaningful to me in their successful blend of Judaism and Witchcraft—much more so than crafting an argument that Judaism and Witchcraft are not mutually exclusive—that I began to incorporate Jewish elements into the Pagan group rituals that I was creating. One year, the spring equinox coincided with Purim, and I designed a ritual to celebrate survival: the survival of the Jewish people, Jewish feminism and Jewish Goddess worship, as well as the survival through winter. After the ritual, several of the women in attendance talked about their Jewish backgrounds and efforts to reconcile Judaism and Witchcraft. Although most Pagans were raised as Christians—not surprising, since most people in this country are raised Christian—and many others were raised as Pagans, there are a number of Jewish women within the Pagan community who worship the Goddess and who want more feminine and feminist liturgy and ritual than Judaism currently allows. In the Pagan community, we can create and shape Jewish rituals without the concerns that they are too Pagan or too feminist or too nontraditional to be authentically Jewish.

The rituals I design and lead often contain both Jewish and Pagan symbols, prayers and customs—even when the ritual is celebrating a purely Jewish or purely Pagan occasion. I do not claim that these are Jewish rituals—they are Jewish Witchcraft, or Pagan Judaism. I will not give up Judaism, and I will not allow others, Jewish or not, to determine what Judaism should mean to me or how I should practice it within my home and my community. As a Goddess-worshipping lesbian feminist, I found that no mainstream Jewish denomination fulfilled my spiritual needs; but just because I am not a Reform Jew or a Conservative Jew, it doesn't mean that I'm not a Jew. I rejected the denominations, not the religion.

I may not be able to explain exactly *how* I manage to be both Jewish and Pagan, but I know with certainty that I *am* both. If I had not discovered Witchcraft, I would probably be so frustrated and disillusioned with organized religion that I would avoid all manifestations of it. If my life had taken that turn, then perhaps I would identify as a secular, humanistic, ethnic or cultural Jew. And while I do not mean to disparage any of those forms of Judaism, a great deal of Jewish custom and belief is intertwined and woven into religious rituals and practices. Maybe it is possible to be a completely secular Jew in Israel—to never have entered a synagogue or uttered a prayer—and still feel very Jewish. But in the United States, with Sundays, Christmas and Easter automatically designated as holidays, and when the Bible usually means the New Testament, I wonder how long it would be before a post-Jew would cease to feel Jewish at all. Witchcraft enabled me to avoid that fate. Instead, I found a religion and spirituality that allows me to embrace and express all aspects of myself. Since I am able to create and share Jewish rituals that are feminist and Goddess oriented in the Pagan community, I am content to attend more traditional Jewish rituals without feeling a need to Paganize them. In Jewish services, I feel connected to other Jews; in Pagan rituals, I feel connected to the Goddess; and in Jewish Pagan rituals, I feel at home and at peace. I don't believe that that makes me less of a Jew; it simply makes me another type of Jew.

A multitude of different practices fall under the title and rubric of Judaism. If "Jewish" is a sufficiently expansive and flexible marker to describe the overlap or commonality—no matter how slight—between Reconstructionist, Israeli, transgender, Hasidic and Ethiopian Jews, then it can certainly include Goddess-worshipping Jewish Witches as well.

Notes:

1. Marcia Falk, *The Book of Blessings: New Jewish Prayers for Daily Life, the Sabbath, and the New Moon Festival* (HarperSanFrancisco, 1996), 329. Falk notes that "it is likely that the adoption of Rosh Hodesh by women was rooted, at least in part, in a generally perceived connection between lunar cycles and menstrual cycles."

2. Ellen Frankel, *The Five Books of Miriam: A Woman's Commentary on the Torah* (Putnam, 1996), 136–41. Frankel discusses Rosh Chodesh, Israelite worship of the Goddess Asherah and prohibitions against idolatry in her commentary on Exodus 30:11–34:35.

3. Penina V. Adelman, *Miriam's Well: Rituals for Jewish Women Around the Year* (2nd ed.) (Biblio Press, 1990), 1–2. Adelman writes, "As it evolved, [Rosh Chodesh] became a way for the religious establishment to combat idol worship and to satisfy the need to continue observance of the sacred relationship between the moon and women which had been part of the indigenous mythologies of the region."

4. Merlin Stone, *When God was a Woman* (Harcourt Brace Jovanvitch, 1978), 163–79.

5. Riane Eisler, *The Chalice and the Blade: Our History, Our Future* (HarperSanFrancisco, 1995), 44–45.

6. Judith Plaskow, "Blaming the Jews for the Birth of Patriarchy," and Annette Daum, "Blaming the Jews for the Death of the Goddess," in *Nice Jewish Girls: A Lesbian Anthology*, ed. Evelyn Torton Beck (Beacon Press, 1989), 298–309.

7. Raphael Patai discusses this in *The Hebrew Goddess* (3rd ed.) (Wayne State University Press, 1990).

8. Janet and Stewart Farrar, *The Witches' Goddess: The Feminine Principle of Divinity* (Phoenix Publishing, 1987), 272. The Farrars list Shekinah as one the "Goddesses of the World."

9. Lynn Gottlieb, *She Who Dwells Within: A Feminist Vision of Renewed Judaism* (HarperSanFrancisco, 1995), 19–23. See note 2 above.

Sexy Rabbi

Karen (Chai) Levy

I'M WORKING IN A HOSPITAL *as a chaplain, giving pastoral care to an older patient who has had a heart attack. After visiting with him in his room for several days, he tells me that I have nice lips and asks me to rub his back. I tell him that I am there to be his chaplain, not his girlfriend.*

A divorced male board member of the synagogue where I work calls or stops in daily to talk to me about Torah, prayer and synagogue programs. He begins to attend morning minyan, and asks me to show him how to put on tefillin. He invites me to lunch and sends me flowers, even though I have stated that I am not romantically interested.

I have a professional relationship with a Christian married man. We often discuss theology, and he develops a great interest in Judaism. Dissatisfied with his own religion, he looks to me to answer his questions about Judaism and help him explore a growing sense that he wants to be Jewish. One day, he embraces me suddenly and tells me that he loves me. I tell him not to contact me again, but he continues to send letters and gifts.

I haven't even finished rabbinical school yet, but these situations and others have already taught me something about what it means to be a young, female—"sexy"—rabbi. The already complicated issues of

112

women's sexuality in our society are intensified in the relationships between men and their female rabbis. All of the men in the situations I described initially had legitimate needs and I, as a rabbi-in-training, was there to serve them.

I never felt that being female was an obstacle to becoming a rabbi. As a passionate Jew and feminist, I was blessed to have been born at this time in history . . . herstory . . . *our* story, when women are becoming rabbis in ever-increasing numbers. I felt a responsibility to help balance our male-dominated tradition with the voices and experiences of women, and wanted to become one of those powerful, spiritual, learned women who so enrich Jewish life. Now, as a rabbinical student more than halfway through my studies, I'm still grateful to be on this holy path. But when I decided to dedicate my life to serving God by bringing the Jewish people, Torah and the Divine closer to one another, I hadn't anticipated the way that sexuality would impact my rabbinical role.

The job of a rabbi, while still new to women, is actually quite "feminine": We care for people and nurture their growth; we reach out to them in times of change or pain and try to be good listeners. These aspects of being a rabbi are indeed wonderful. When I feel that I can ease someone's suffering or help them feel closer to God, my sense of being called to the rabbinate is confirmed. But already in my pre-rabbinic experience, it seems that when the rabbi is a woman, things can get a little confusing—especially for men.

I first encountered these issues at my brother's wedding, during my second year of rabbinical school. While a male rabbi officiated at the wedding, I led Shabbat services, read the *ketubah* at the ceremony and led the blessings during the wedding meal. During the reception, I danced joyfully for my brother and his new wife. I love to dance, and I had a wonderful time celebrating on the dance floor, together with my relatives. At the end of the party, the bride's male cousin approached me.

"I watched you dance," he said. "You're going to be a rabbi? You're the sexiest darn rabbi I ever saw!"

Moments later, a friend of my mother remarked, "I didn't know rabbis were allowed to move their bodies like that!"

Suddenly, I became self-conscious. Though complimented for my dancing, I realized that as a religious figure (no pun intended) my sexuality was now up for public scrutiny.

As a feminist, I'm aware of society's sexualization and objectification of women, and have made conscious choices about my appearance. I don't wear clothes that won't let me bend over without calling attention to myself—nothing short or low-cut. I won't wear shoes that prevent me from defending myself or running for the bus—so no high heels. However, I am a woman; I do have breasts and hips, and my *tallit* doesn't hide them! Nor should it have to. There's a difference between avoiding clothing that objectifies and degrades women and having to become asexual in order to be respected as a rabbi, and it seems that many people expect the latter.

The complex interplay of sexuality and the rabbinate, as it applies to female rabbis, usually manifests in two ways: A man who is attracted to a rabbi takes advantage of her role to get closer to her, or a man is attracted to her because she is the rabbi. In "normal" life, when a man is attracted to a woman, he simply asks her out on a date, which of course gives her the opportunity to refuse. But when the woman is me—the rabbi—he might instead show up for classes, services and religious programs as a method of courting. Part of my job is reaching out and engaging people, so I can't tell the guy to get lost. The boundary between a rabbi's private and professional life is already near nonexistent, and when wooers use Judaism as a dating maneuver, the rabbi can get trapped by a smitten congregant who won't go away. Unless a man made an overtly romantic move, I would feel presumptuous and awkward telling him to stop looking at me with those goo-goo eyes while I'm giving the *d'var Torah* on Shabbat morning.

Then there's the situation in which a man becomes attracted to a woman *because* she's the rabbi. The erotic and the spiritual are closely connected; spirituality involves loving and longing for connection with God, our *yedid nefesh,* our divine soul mate. As a rabbi, I would hope to inspire intense religious feelings through prayer or teaching, but a congregant might confuse those feelings with romance or sexual attraction and project those feelings—especially in our society, where religion is separated from the erotic—onto that cute rabbi in the skirt. I think it's those same stirrings that cause so many people to develop crushes on wise college professors, nurturing kindergarten teachers or inspiring rock stars.

But this dynamic doesn't break down exclusively along gender—or sexuality—lines. Both male and female congregants develop crushes on their male rabbis, too. The lack of distinction between the public and private life of the rabbi, as well as the potential abuses of power, apply to both men and women. An infatuated congregant can make a "date" with the male rabbi in his study, just as with the female rabbi. Rabbis of both genders must be careful with their power. The difference, though, is that women serving as religious leaders are up against a tradition and society that has sexualized and objectified them for generations; we still live in a world in which men are respected and women are harassed.

As a rabbi-to-be, I am still figuring out how to handle the situations in which men's sexual feelings interfere with my ability to be their rabbi. I recently met a man who told me that he could never go to a synagogue that had a female rabbi; how, he said, could he pray or learn Torah when he would be distracted by the fact that he could be having sex with her? Which makes me wonder: Do I have to become a desexualized being in order to be a man's rabbi? How would I do that, anyway?

I don't have to turn to sex-positive feminism to see how women's beauty and sexuality are a great source of our power; the Torah and Jewish literature are filled with examples. The sexuality of our foremothers was their source of strength and even heroism: Esther's beauty enabled her to become queen of Persia and save the Jewish people from destruction; Tamar ensured the messianic lineage by seducing Judah in a prostitute's disguise. Both Yael and Judith used sexuality to get Israel's enemies drunk and kill them.

Of course, the Torah also depicts women's seductiveness as their failing, as well. The first woman, Eve, is the prototypical temptress. The rejected flirtations of Potiphar's wife land Joseph in prison. The rabbis blame Dinah for her own rape by Shechem, saying that women shouldn't "go out" as the Torah says she did. Whether sexuality is a woman's strength or downfall in the Torah, it is central to our perception of her—and it seems that things have not changed much.

Sexuality is part of who we are as human beings, and while I personally do not favor flaunting it in a way that insults our being created in the image of God—as our culture often does in its use of women's bodies in advertising and pornography—we also shouldn't have to hide our created-in-the-image-of-God-selves behind veils, or, I could argue, wigs and *tichels* (scarves). Should I not dance at my brother's wedding for fear that someone might notice that rabbis have hips?

Jews, especially those among the older generations who grew up with different concepts of rabbis and women, are still getting used to the idea of women as rabbis. Men in our communities need to realize that female rabbis are there to be spiritual leaders and teachers of Torah, not sex objects. Just because I want to be an accessible and caring religious leader does not mean that I have no personal boundaries. I hope that as the Jewish world becomes more accustomed to women as rabbis, men will treat us with more respect and not take advantage of our willingness to be involved in our congregants' lives.

On the flip side, female rabbis have to take responsibility for setting appropriate limits. So if a congregant wants to meet with me, an appointment in my office with the door open sends a clearer message than a lunch date. Similarly, what will be my policy about giving congregants the old "Shabbat Shalom" kiss on the cheek? Or hugging them as part of an innocent "mazel tov" at a wedding or a *brit millah?* Do I limit my warmth for fear that someone might get the wrong idea or get a little too close to the rabbi's breasts? Trivial as they may seem, lack of attention to such decisions can be career-threatening.

Although women are typically the ones victimized by male power in our society, rabbis, including women, have power in their relationships with others. That power can be abused by women, even when it is the male congregant who develops the big crush on his rabbi. I can say from personal experience that if a rabbi allows a congregant to pursue her, even in vain, by not establishing appropriate boundaries, then that rabbi is abusing her power by leading on the congregant. Having done this myself, thinking at first that I didn't want to hurt the congregant's feelings, I realized upon looking more closely that I was actually getting something out of the relationship. While I felt uncomfortable being desired, the attention did feed my ego, and so I allowed the person to give me more attention than I should have.

I'm not blaming women for the inappropriateness of men who find them attractive; that happens all too often in our culture already. A woman is raped and everyone wants to know what she was wearing to provoke the rapist. The burden of sexual responsibility is even institutionalized in some Orthodox Jewish communities (through, for example, *kol ishah,* which prohibits women from singing lest men become aroused by their voices). Still, female rabbis do have power, and we need to be aware of what we contribute, even unconsciously, to the dynamic between us and our male congregants. In short, neither love-struck congregant nor sexy rabbi is free of responsibility.

This issue applies to female clergy in other religious traditions—and, with some variation, to female professionals in the secular world—as well. My friend who is being ordained as a priest in the Episcopal Church also struggles with how her beauty and sexuality affect her ministry. The clerical collar that she wears, however, desexualizes her to an extent in the eyes of her parishioners—at least until her now-pregnant belly starts to show.

The rabbinical schools are filled with women of my generation, thank God, but the search for role models is not easy. Many of us will be the first female rabbis that people encounter, and we won't "look like rabbis"—that is, we're not slightly overweight, nearsighted guys with *kippot* and beards. As women, we need to support each other in learning how to be rabbis and sexual beings without our sexuality interfering with our serving as rabbis to anyone who might otherwise idealize us as the perfect lover or condescend to us as a cute little sexual fantasy.

And as individuals serving our communities, we need to find a balance between our *hesed*—the lovingkindness and sense of giving that opens us to others—and our *gevurah*—the strength and restraint that distances and disciplines us—in connecting with our congregants. Hesed and gevurah are aspects of both the divine and human personalities; with them in balance, young women like myself who are passionate about bringing our people closer to Judaism, Torah and God can be our created-in-the-image-of-God selves—in all of our divinely given power—and be rabbis, even to men.

I Was a Teenage Zionist

ELLEN FRIEDRICHS

TWO WEEKS AFTER HIGH SCHOOL GRADUATION, I got on a plane to Israel. I was eighteen, and about to spend a year on a communal farm—a kibbutz— along with twenty-five other North Americans. I couldn't wait to toil under the Middle Eastern sun, and had spent a large part of my childhood preparing for the experience; even so, I did not quite realize that from that point on Israel would play a significant role in my life.

The twenty-six of us who went to Israel that year had all grown up together in Habonim Dror, a socialist labor Zionist Jewish youth movement. Most of us did not actually come from ardent socialist or Zionist backgrounds, and had ended up in the movement almost accidentally. Our parents wanted to send us to summer camp. Where I lived in Western Canada there were only two Jewish options: One was cheap, the other was not. So I went to the cheaper camp, and my little ten-year-old self suddenly became a movement *havera* (member); I was not in for a summer of horseback riding and waterskiing.

Camp was modeled after a kibbutz and, like everything else in Habonim, was referred to by its Hebrew name: *machaneh*. We didn't sleep in cabins—we slept in *tzrifim*. We didn't have counselors—we had *madrichim*. In keeping with our labor "roots," we did daily *avodah* (work), which included everything from cleaning the bathrooms to washing dishes, from putting up tent platforms to tending the chickens. They brought in Israeli emissaries to teach us Hebrew and folk dancing. When we went out in public we proudly told anyone who bothered to ask that we were socialist Zionists, and did not really understand why they claimed that was a contradiction.

In Habonim, we were taught that Zionism was the belief in Israel as a Jewish state and homeland. We learned that thanks to the Law of Return—which gives any Jew, regardless of birthplace, an automatic right to Israeli citizenship—the country was our home, and would welcome us the second we made *aliyah* (moved to Israel). As labor Zionists following in the tradition of the early *chalutzim* (Jewish pioneers who moved to Palestine around the turn of the century), we did not, like the religious Zionists, draw solely on the Biblical connection the Jewish people had to the area. We believed instead that physically working the land would strengthen our ties to our historic country.

The fact that we were in Canada in the late '80s didn't hamper our deep connection to the ideology of these early chalutzic socialists; we sat on the hard concrete floor of the *sefriya* (library), learning about the great Zionist thinkers who had forged our paths. We supported some, like the labor leader A.D. Gordon, and vilified others, like the right-wing Ze'ev Jabotinsky. When someone realized that there were few women mentioned in the annals of Zionist history (save for Golda "there is no Palestinian people" Meir), the Hanna Senesh movie *Hanna's War* was brought out, and we cringed collectively at her torture at the hands of the Nazis.

We acknowledged the fact that Israel had problems, that the socialism that we were trying to emulate was really only a socialism for European Jews—despite the fact that we also affirmed the rights of the Palestinian people. So we tried to fill in the blanks. In part we attempted to address the problems of a modern Israel by striving to meet our oft-revised aims. According to the Habonim constitution, we were to "build the State of Israel as a progressive egalitarian society at peace with its neighbors, actively involved in a peace process with the Palestinian people with the common goal of a just and lasting peace" and "consciously struggle to overcome sexual inequalities pervading the consciousness of [Habonim's] members as well as the world community."

While other kids who went to summer camp played capture the flag, we clambered into leaky boats and reenacted Aliyah Bet, the illegal entry of European Jews into British-controlled Palestine after World War II. We used this as an example of our superiority to other Jewish youth groups: We had politics and purpose. We had ideology and history. They just had dances at the local Jewish community center. All summer long we learned about the pillars upon which our movement was built—socialism, labor Zionism, self-actualization, Judaism and social justice—while singing '60s protest songs and Socialist anthems. (Though after careful consideration, we omitted the fifth verse of "Red Fly the Banners," which praised the efforts of Stalin's Five Year Plan.)

So, we sang and we worked and we learned that the communal life, preferably lived in Israel, was our ultimate goal. Campers as young as nine years old boasted about our *kupa* (communal fund) while explaining to their rather concerned parents the importance of the *kvutsa* (group). My female counselors' unshaved armpits were comfortably exposed as they discussed the role of women in the Israeli army—while my male counselors stood next to them, claiming to be feminists. These counselors, fresh out of high school, on their way to Israel or newly returned, tossed out Hebrew as if it were their native tongue. They told stories about working on a kibbutz, driving tractors, having adopted Israeli families and taking the bus into Jerusalem for political rallies. When the summer ended, we returned home and participated in local chapter activities—often held at the communal homes of college-aged members—and desperately waited for the school year to end so macheneh could begin anew.

This, of course, was not at all what my Reform synagogue–attending parents had envisioned when they sent me to camp, but they were nonetheless pleased that I was actively and happily participating in some aspect of Jewish life. Aside from Habonim, I was not involved in anything Jewish after my bat mitzvah; I avoided our weekly Shabbat dinners and could only be dragged to synagogue once a year. Habonim was Jewish, but it was secular—and that's what I liked. I could feel Jewish by being connected to Israel, not by reciting *brachot* (blessings) and going to Hebrew high school, where Judaism seemed anything but cool or political or interesting.

My discomfort with religion stemmed in part from the fact that it was a late addition to my life, forced upon me in a way I had not anticipated. My mother was born and raised Jewish by German Jewish Holocaust refugees. My father's mother was also a Jew who had fled Germany, but she did so with a non-Jewish fiancé. They moved to New York, raised their children Protestant and named my father Christopher. When my parents married in 1970, my father was still attending church and calling himself a Christian. My mother occasionally took my brother and me to the Reform synagogue, and I attended Hebrew school on Sunday mornings—but at home our most Jewishly religious act was lighting the Hanukah menorah next to our Christmas tree.

With the birth of my youngest brother (and in what seemed to me an abrupt and drastic transformation), my father renounced his Christianity and took a Hebrew name, Shalom. He was now a Jew like the rest of us. But unlike the rest of us, he was really excited about Judaism and wanted to incorporate the religion into many more aspects of our lives. Now, the family had to stand stiffly around the dining-room table for Shabbat dinners and recite brachot that seemed far too personal, intimate and forced for the family life I knew. It suddenly mattered if we missed Hebrew school. I was supposed to think about being Jewish. I did not appreciate the change. I fought against going to Hebrew school, made jokes and inappropriate comments during holiday and Shabbat dinners and decided that being Jewish was kind of embarrassing. This only resulted in lectures on topics such as "why it is unacceptable to mock [the matriarchs] Sarah, Rivka, Rachel and Leah during the blessing of daughters" and "why one should not make obscene art out of Shabbat candles." Unsurprisingly, these moments did not instill in me a love of religion.

It was that same summer that my parents first sent me to camp. Though I was ambivalent at first, after a few days there I loved it. For the first time, it seemed kind of cool to be Jewish, and I began to develop a Judaism of my own that was expressed through a cultural connection to Israel and wasn't contingent on synagogue attendance, prayer or my family. I stayed involved with Habonim throughout high school, and by the time I graduated, I had eight years of labor Zionist education behind me.

So I did the next logical thing. I went with Habonim to live on a kibbutz for a year as a member of the Workshop, Habonim's kibbutz experience program. All but one of the twenty-six of us had grown up in the movement, hearing alternately thrilling and terrifying stories about the experience—forty-two groups had already been sent to Israel—and receiving sage advice from those who had gone before.

"Work hard," we were told. "Respect on the kibbutz is based entirely on what kind of worker you are."

"Integrating isn't easy," the recently returned cautioned. "Just hope you get a good adopted family." Though warned, we were still surprised that we were not met with open arms by the kibbutzniks. Here we were, coming to do farm work, manual labor, for free, to show our support for a country that we felt was as much ours as theirs—and we weren't automatically welcomed into the kibbutz community! Why, the kibbutzniks weren't even the least bit grateful and told us outright that they didn't need us there, that we were princesses taking a year off before returning to the States for college. Worse, they laughed at our attempts at Hebrew, explaining in flawless English, "If we speak Hebrew with you, it's like speaking with a retard, and why would we want to speak to a retard?"

As a final blow, they assured the small group of girls who'd won a fight to work in the fields that it was easier to let American girls work where they wanted than to hear them complain.

Of course, in some ways they were right. They had seen countless North Americans come and go—leaving without ever looking back, yet until then expecting to be treated as if their whole lives had been invested in the kibbutz. As we began to understand this, we tried to explain that we were different.

"We are from a Zionist youth movement," we would say with conviction. "We understand the situation here."

They still didn't invite us to their barbecues.

We might have been surprised by it, but the kibbutz members knew that we'd have problems integrating. In an attempt to ease the process, they assigned the workshoppers "adopted" kibbutz families for comfort and a social safety net, though not shelter. My family had six sons: three of their own and three adopted. Of the adopted sons, one was a lone soldier, one was a medical student and one was a kid my age from the kibbutz whose mother had died. I was the only girl, the only non-Hebrew-speaker and the only one who didn't watch soccer. I went over to their home almost every night, made awkward conversation and then beelined for the dog-eared copy of *Newsweek* that I had already read multiple times. Occasionally one of my "brothers"—who, like many of the young people on the kibbutz, did not share their parents' politics—would ask me why I had left the comforts of America ("Canada," I would mutter, suddenly feeling patriotic) for this.

"You don't have to be here, so why are you? Everything in Israel is hard. The kibbutz is so depressing, I'm getting out as soon as I can."

Sometimes I would try to defend myself, but usually I just ended up silent, already defeated by years of previous North Americans wondering the same thing.

Even so, I loved Israel. I drove my tractor and learned bad Hebrew. The atmosphere in the country seemed optimistic. It was 1993, Arafat and Rabin had just signed the Oslo peace accord and I was eighteen, getting tan, smoking cigarettes and doing more or less what I had dreamt about since my first summer at camp. While we had had enough critical education in Habonim Dror to know that Israel was far from perfect (as we demonstrated by crying sexism on a regular basis and complaining about the treatment of Palestinians), for the most part we were happy in our kibbutz bubble. The troubles and politics that were a part of every Israeli's daily life seemed separate from our own experience, which was primarily focused on making ourselves comfortable in our new surroundings.

At the end of the year, amid a sea of tears and a wave of relief, the group dispersed. I went home, went to school and was surprised at how badly I wanted to return. In an attempt to maintain some connection to the year I had just spent there, I tried to find other Jews when I first got to school; not spotting any immediately, I went to the campus Hillel. After one event, I knew it was not the place for me. I soon realized that what I missed most about Israel was that there, being Jewish was both everything and nothing. Being Jewish was not something you did by joining a Hillel or a shul or even Habonim; it just was. As a secular Jew returning to a city with a fairly small Jewish population and attending a university without a Jewish presence, I realized how much I appreciated that aspect of the country.

A few years later, I returned, along with Jessica and Tamar, two friends from the workshop. The kibbutz had not been a perfect utopia, and we conceded that the kibbutz movement was in decline, but we still wanted to be in the country. While still in North America our idea had seemed like a good one: go to secular Tel Aviv (home to beaches, bars and clubs), find an apartment, perfect our Hebrew and involve ourselves in Israeli life and politics. After having already spent a year in the country, we were pretty sure we could do all of this without much problem. Of course, there were some glitches.

I arrived alone a few weeks before the others, and by the time Tamar arrived, I had found a potential apartment. We went downtown to see it. It was dirty, falling apart and still expensive by Tel Aviv standards. But we were nervous about our Hebrew, our situation and our future in this city—

which was not as welcoming as our weekend trips two years before had made it seem.

We took the place, happy we had somewhere to live, but soon realized we had moved into a brothel. The women who worked in our building were primarily new Russian immigrants. They were broke, neither politicized nor empowered and working as a way to stay in the country or pay off old debts. The men who loitered in our hallway and banged on our door (if Gila, Almoge or any of the other women made them wait too long) defied all stereotypes: young soldiers, older cat-callers, the hunched and embarrassed, a father who wanted to pay us to have sex with his son as a fourteenth birthday present and a surprising number of Hasidim and men in *kippot*.

Even as a secular Jew, a feminist who claimed to support a woman's right to work in the sex trade, it was upsetting to realize that I still seemed to equate prostitution with bad and religion with good. I had automatically assumed that the first religious man I saw standing in my hall was there for other reasons. Of course, he—along with all the others I later encountered in my building—was buying sex. I was discovering that simply identifying as Orthodox does not guarantee adherence to the way of life that Orthodox Judaism calls for and promotes to others.

I had come to Israel believing Jews to be a people deeply connected to each other, regardless of how differently we all expressed our faith. I felt that if history had taught us nothing else, it was that in the eyes of the rest of the world, we were one, and that no matter how assimilated we became, we would always be Jews. It seemed obvious to me that with our shared history, we all had a shared need for a Jewish state. But the more time I spent in Israel, the more I saw the divide between religious and secular that I would have been naive to try to ignore.

Over time, it became obvious that as a secular Jewish woman I would not be treated with respect by Orthodox men. It seemed as if every time I turned around I was witnessing an altercation between religious and secular, between men and women. At the beach one evening I was surrounded by a pack of young religious boys, wearing kippot and *tzitzit* (ritual fringes), yelling things like "If you don't fuck us we'll push you into the ocean." On another occasion, my friend Marisa was sitting at a cafe and wanted to ask a guy wearing a kippah a question. She tapped him on the shoulder and he shoved her away, saying, "Don't touch me! I'm *shomer negiyah* (a man who touches no woman other than his wife)."

A woman I knew had a bag of urine thrown at her for walking through a religious neighborhood wearing shorts. I felt like I couldn't open the newspaper without reading about another attack by religious men on women who dared to pray audibly at the Western Wall. The fact that these men came to my door looking to buy sex from whomever might happen to open it only served to increase my anger at the hypocrisy of the situation. My Judaism and theirs were not the same thing, and as I began to acknowledge this difference, I wondered if simply being Jewish was indeed enough to claim a right to this country.

It became harder and harder to remember why I had wanted to come back. I still used my standard line, "Israel needs left-wing Jews here to counter the right-wing, to ensure rights for Palestinians, Ethiopians, women, gays and lesbians," to justify being in the country at all. I still made Israeli friends, spoke Hebrew and voiced my political opinion even when I was told that, as a North American, it was not my right. But my proclamations sometimes seemed hollow, and I wondered if turning up at a Rabin memorial, Meretz rally or poorly attended march against domestic violence was really serving anyone's needs but my own. And I wondered why I was trying to infiltrate a society I found so problematic. Jessica, Tamar and I still had connections with our kibbutz and viewed it as a reprieve from city life, so we spent most weekends there. The kibbutz members were good to us, giving us an apartment and food in exchange for one day's work each week. They told us that they were pleased we had returned, and treated us better than they ever had when we were there the first time. I started to feel comfortable with my kibbutz family, and found myself making friends with the people my age who hadn't talked to me the last time around.

But now, spending time with Israelis on the kibbutz (instead of just other North Americans), the three of us found ourselves confronted with situations that never would have presented themselves back home. Sexist comments and assumptions about gender roles were prevalent, and I was torn between reacting and trying to ignore them. So many of the young Israelis we met emulated the worst aspects of capitalist American society, and I felt as if issues outside of the obvious political situation in Israel (such as the status of women) were given little importance.

Growing up in Habonim, I envisioned Israel as a utopia of egalitarianism, a place where feminism was almost built into the system—what with conscription for both sexes and a history boasting a female prime minister. Of course, there were always those who tried to tell us different, but I was too busy picturing myself with bulging muscles bouncing along on a tractor to pay much attention.

It was nice to imagine a world where equality was natural, but whenever I looked more closely at the treatment of women, Palestinians and Ethiopians, the denial of a queer community (and so on), the appearance of equality faded.

I knew that most of our Israeli women friends would never use the word *feminist* to describe themselves. These women were incredibly strong and assertive, yet they seemed so traditional when it came to gender roles and sexuality. Loud, confident women still scrambled for the coveted *mitapelet* role in the army, which allowed one to be caretaker to a platoon of male soldiers. And while I knew it was either that or secretarial work, it was still upsetting.

Looking at kibbutz life was equally discouraging. Most kibbutz women worked in the kitchens or with the children—not out in the fields, reveling in the glory of making the desert bloom (as I had seen in the promotional videos that we watched at camp). Today, though, it's not even the kibbutz men in the fields; most kibbutzim use hired Palestinian or Thai workers. After a year on the kibbutz, I could still pretend that Israeli women enjoyed the same opportunities as their male counterparts, but the more time I spent in the country without the safety of Habonim, the more clouded my vision became.

Habonim wanted us to take the pioneering spirit of the early labor Zionists and translate it into a modern progressive voice in Israel—ideally, as Israelis ourselves. We thought that if we followed a few simple steps—learned Hebrew, lived in Israel, honed our knowledge about the country's political situation—we would be able to be do just that. But as time went on, the formula didn't seem to produce the desired results. Granted, in Tel Aviv I actually socialized with Israelis and became more comfortable in the country. I loved that I had finally made friends on the kibbutz. I loved the laid-back culture where people would drop by and sit on my porch for hours, drinking tea and playing backgammon. I loved learning Hebrew and I loved being in a climate where everything seemed to have meaning—where people actually cared about their country, where politics mattered. But I was finally forced to admit that Israel is not a politically progressive, socialist, egalitarian country.

When I returned to North America, I felt much more connected to Israel—and much more critical of it. I ended my time there with enough language and personal connections to keep me coming back, but I didn't like a lot of what I had seen and, ultimately, was hard-pressed to justify my place in the country. Though I knew I was not going to make aliyah, I had discovered a new source of conflict: It was mainly through Israel that I felt Jewish. For as long as I could remember, I had put all of my Jewish energy into Israel. Without Israel I wasn't sure how to maintain my Jewish identity.

And even with all my concerns, I didn't want to just give up. Israel still did need people with my views and politics. I had grown up believing that diaspora Jews had a right—and a responsibility—to be involved with the situation in Israel. When I realized that modern Israel did not look like the Zionist dream—let alone the labor Zionist dream—it seemed an imperative to stay involved. A few days after finishing college, I moved to

New York, where, equipped with a degree in women's studies, thirteen years in the movement and a basic knowledge and understanding of Israel, I became Habonim Dror's Israel Programs Coordinator and spent two years schooling my successors. The movement had changed since I began in 1985; while we still sang songs from the '60s and modeled our summer camps after Israel's increasingly outdated kibbutzim, Habonim had also maintained its place as a progressive voice in the Jewish world. Habonim's strength is its ability to address current issues—the decision-making body of the movement recently called for a Right of Return for Palestinians—while remembering history. I hoped to empower the young Jewish community to come to their own conclusions about Israel, while enabling them to actually do something with those conclusions. I hope that the kids growing up today in Habonim will continue to fight for peaceful coexistence between Israel and its neighbors while maintaining an awareness of the other complex issues the country faces.

And then, last spring, I was done with Habonim. I no longer fit in the "youth" category so crucial for maintaining Habonim as a youth movement—and it was time to go. I don't know what future role Israel will play in my life. It will not be my home; I don't want my secular Jewish feminism to be a constant struggle. But I also don't want to completely sever ties with the country. I plan to stay involved, somehow. Still, maybe I don't need Israel as much as I had once thought. I realized a while ago that I really liked celebrating Shabbat and holidays with my family (who have generously forgiven my younger disruptions), and lately I've been thinking that maybe I could actually be a secular Jew in North America . . . without looking to Israel for my Jewish identity at every turn.

You Take Lilith, I'll Take Eve

A Closer Look at the World's Second Feminist

Yiskah (Jessica) Rosenfeld

No woman ever forgets the first time she meets Lilith. Although according to midrash (Jewish lore) Lilith, not Eve, was the first woman, created simultaneously with Adam, most of us are introduced to Eve first. For many Jewish women, the experience is less than positive. She's the temptress, the dumb one tricked by a snake, the helper, the rib. Then came Lilith, flying into our lives on majestic wings. Lilith, who refused to be dominated by her equal counterpart Adam, who knew and dared to speak the ineffable name of G-d. Lilith, who fled the garden, refusing to return even when G-d sent three angels to bring her back. *Thank G-d!* is the inevitable response. With so many silent, docile women in the Bible, here at last is our heroine, a woman who refuses to be kept down, who will sacrifice everything to stand up for her beliefs, who stands up even to G-d.

Is it any wonder that feminists fell in love with her? Naomi Wolf calls Lilith the "one-woman Act Up guerrilla fighter" for the feminists of the seventies. As women searched for role models to support their growing independence, beginning to explore and revel in the "dark side" of femininity, Jewish feminists redeemed the name of Lilith. Reclaiming her as a heroine, not a demon, they found in Lilith a near-Biblical female figure to admire and celebrate. Aviva Cantor was one of the first to praise Lilith in her essay "The Lilith Question." Lilith, she wrote, is a *"powerful* female. She radiates strength, assertiveness; she refuses to cooperate in her own victimization."[1]

Women like Aviva Cantor dared to rescue Lilith from the bad press she had received as a demoness, monster and baby-killer. In the legends of the Talmud and mystical writings, the outcome of Lilith's independence and strength is that she is demonized.[2] In fact, the whole reason she may have been included (just barely) in the midrash is to teach us a lesson: Look what happens when you let a woman be equal to a man, when you give her power, when you give her—G-d forbid—a voice. She becomes the mother of all demons, as Eve becomes the mother of all living things—destined to produce thousands of demon babies daily with semen collected from nocturnal emissions, held responsible for infant death and a host of other tragedies. Amulets and rituals to ward off Lilith exist to this day, particularly in Sephardic communities. Feminists transformed the demoness into a role model, the amulets into testaments of her courage and strength.

As modern women, we are more than ready to embrace Lilith's audacity and feminine power, and her once-marginalized legacy reaches far and wide, from bat mitzvah sermons to *Lilith* magazine to the Lilith Fair. No longer upholding the myth of Lilith's demonic lust, my Jewish high-school students describe her as strong, brave, independent and cool, always throwing in at least one "you go, girl." Lilith has arrived and she is here to stay.

But what about Eve? Could it be that in the excitement and, let's be honest, relief, of discovering an uncompromising feminist role model in the Jewish tradition—someone who is defiant, outspoken, fearless and free—we have forgotten about Eve? If anything, you'd expect feminists to reclaim her as well. She, too, has been demonized and degraded over the years. Like Lilith, she has been labeled as brazen, oversexed, rebellious and dangerous. Take, for example, this passage from the Talmud:

> "And why was the precept of *niddah* [separation during menstruation] given to her?" "Because she shed the blood

of Adam." "And why was the precept of challah [removing a piece of the challah] given to her?" "Because she corrupted Adam, who was the challah of the world." "And why was the precept of lighting the Sabbath candles given to her?" "Because she extinguished the soul of Adam." (Genesis Rabbah 17:8)

The few rituals reserved primarily for women—ritual bath, challah and candlelighting—are not given to women for their righteousness, but as a continual act of repentance for Eve's sinful act of eating the forbidden fruit. In *Eve's Journey: Feminine Images in Hebraic Literary Tradition*, Nehama Aschkenasy sums up three characteristics attributed to Eve in the Judeo-Christian tradition: "a proclivity for evil, a destructive sexuality, and a demonic-deadly power."[3]

So where is the cavalry? How did feminists so valiantly champion the cause of Lilith and leave Eve completely at the mercy of rabbinic commentary and patriarchal stereotypes? The problem is not just that Eve has been bypassed by the feminist movement; it may well be that reclaiming Lilith has been done at the expense of Eve. The feminists, like the rabbis, have labeled Eve in negative terms, not as lustful and evil, but as something equally condemning: docile and obedient. In a wonderful new anthology, *Which Lilith? Feminist Writers Re-create the World's First Woman*, Lilith takes center stage as women writers celebrate her strength and open sexuality in moving and engaging poems, stories and essays. But many of the pieces turn Eve into Lilith's negative opposite—submissive and compliant in contrast to Lilith's defiance and rebellion. Lilly Rivlin, one of the editors of the collection, remembers being "repelled" by Eve, "that submissive blonde creature wiled by a snake, falling for a line."[4] Lilith is referred to as the "anti-Eve," as if Eve were the root of all negative images of women, as if Eve were the problem Lilith came to solve. As feminists everywhere rally to support and reclaim the besmirched name of Lilith, Eve is left abandoned, doomed forever to be attacked from both sides—condemned by the rabbis for her rebellion and by the feminists for her submission—for being too bad and too good all at the same time.

What went wrong? Perhaps when Aviva Cantor was writing "The Lilith Question," Jewish feminists could not afford to ask The Eve Question. Eve was too much a part of the patriarchal Jewish tradition these women were challenging and rejecting. Phyllis Trible, who did take on the challenge of approaching the Genesis story from a feminist perspective in her pivotal essay of the '70s, "Eve and Adam: Genesis 2–3 Reread," notes how the feminist movement refused to take a closer look at Eve. "Accepting centuries of (male) exegesis, many feminists interpret this story as legitimating male supremacy and female subordination. They read to reject."[5] In a way, then, feminists have bought into the sexist interpretations of the story without questioning them as they did so articulately with the Lilith legend. They fail to see the similarities between Eve and Lilith, married to the same man, rebelling against the same G-d/parent, destined for the same historical mistreatment.

While Jewish women may once have felt ashamed of our "Lilith side," it would appear that coming to terms with Lilith has led to a new phenomenon: uneasiness with the Eve part of ourselves. Perhaps we're afraid to "go back" after discovering the freedom and power of Lilith. In the Biblical creation story, Eve is not given that kind of power or voice, and must find ways to assert herself from within the limitations of the garden. But is it fair to give up on Eve just because she doesn't cry out or sprout wings? (After all, we can't all be as cool as Lilith.) If we stand on Lilith's shoulders, we can only go forward as we dare to reclaim Eve just as we have reclaimed Lilith—reading between the lines to understand her motivations, to separate her true voice from those attributed to her. My goal is not to take anything away from the wonder and beauty of Lilith, or to make apologies for Eve. Instead, let's meet Eve with all the tools, skills, insight and visionary depth (including our newly celebrated Lilith-ness) that the rabbis—as men, as Orthodox men, as Orthodox men writing a long time ago—may have lacked.

To tell Eve's story, to answer The Eve Question, we must separate her voice from both the clumsy ventriloquism of the rabbinic commentators and the rumors we've picked up in Sunday school and feminist conferences. We have to listen closely. Within the text of the Genesis story, Eve's voice is much quieter than Lilith's. It is the voice of compromise, of concealment, of subversion. It is a familiar voice for many women—the voice of not having a voice. Ultimately, Eve's story is a story about speech—about what gets said and what doesn't, about who talks (and listens) to whom, about who gets to tell their story.

As we go back to the text, we will be asking the same questions the rabbis themselves asked: Who was Eve? What did it mean to be created from Adam's rib? Why did the serpent choose her and not Adam to tempt? And why did she really eat that fruit? More important, if we are to legitimize Lilith and rescue Eve, we must view Eve in the context of Lilith's story, daring to ask: What was it like to be the second woman? What legacy, for better and for worse, did Lilith's defiant act leave in its wake, and how much of Lilith's desires and passions still boil beneath the surface of quiet Eve?

If we want to understand Eve in the context of Lilith, we have to draw Lilith back into the text of Genesis as the first woman. The rabbis catch a brief glimpse of her in the first account of the creation of humankind in Genesis: "And G-d made Adam in G-d's image . . . male and female G-d created them" (Genesis 1:27).[6] The text implies complete equality. How can this be, when we know Eve was created after Adam, from his rib? The rabbis understood this to refer to a "first Eve," created simultaneously with Adam, and the midrashic Alphabet of Ben Sira later asserts that this female is none other than Lilith.

According to Ben Sira, Lilith and Adam are both created from the earth. Adam tries to dominate Lilith (sexually and, we may presume, in other ways) and Lilith complains. She then utters the secret name of G-d—considered to have magical power at the time this story was recorded—and flees the Garden of Eden. Rather than scolding or punishing Adam,

G-d sends three angels to bring Lilith back. She refuses, leaving Adam without a mate.

So why doesn't her name appear in the Bible? It is as if Lilith is too big, too powerful and threatening, to be held within the confines of the Genesis story. This may be Lilith's greatest blessing. Outside the text, she need not try to bend herself to fit within the inherent sexism embedded in the stories and language of the Bible. Outside the garden, Lilith dwells as a sort of mythological goddess or superwoman, embodying a terrifying and untouchable power. Lilith can be uncompromisingly herself.

Although her name is never mentioned, traces of a former union between Adam and Lilith form the backdrop to the more detailed account of Adam and Eve. But even if we put the first account of creation and the legend of Lilith aside, Eve's story begins before she is born. In the second creation story, which takes place firmly within the garden of Eden, several monumental events transpire between Adam and G-d before Eve is even a twinkle in G-d's eye (or Adam's rib):

> The Lord G-d took the man and put him into the garden of Eden to till it and to keep it. And the Lord G-d commanded the man, saying, Of every tree of the garden you may freely eat: but of the tree of the knowledge of good and evil, you shall not eat of it: for on the day that you eat of it you will surely die. And the Lord G-d said, It is not good that the man should be alone; I will make him a help to match him. And out of the ground the Lord G-d formed every beast of the field, and every bird of the air; and brought them to the man to see what he would call them: and whatever the man called every living creature, that was its name. (Genesis 2:15–19)

Long before Eve is created, then, we see that Adam and G-d have formed a relationship. And they aren't just drinking buddies out for a good time: They communicate. G-d asks Adam to name the animals, to use the power of speech to help complete the creation process. It is like letting a child play with the tools his daddy uses in his world. G-d created the world through the power of naming—"And G-d said, 'Let there be light,' and there was light"—and now Adam takes what has been made and plays a role in shaping its identity. In the Jewish tradition the power to name is the greatest power we have, the gift of speech our greatest possession—we are people of the book, of the word. This is an incredible gift and responsibility to offer Adam, a way of defining the world and defining himself in relation to it, a way of taking control . . . and it takes place without Eve's presence. In fact, naming is the process through which Adam discovers that no partner yet exists for him; it helps him to identify the lack of Eve.

There is a wonderful, playful midrash that suggests that it is this ability to speak, to name, perhaps to dominate through naming, that makes us greater even than the angels. In the midrash, Adam is not only given the task of naming the animals, but of naming himself and G-d as well.

> G-d asked him, "And you, what is your name?" He replied, "The name Adam fits me." G-d asked, "Why?" He replied, "Because I was fashioned out of the earth *(adamah)*. G-d asked, "And I, what is My Name?" "The name Lord [Adonai] fits You." G-d asked "Why?" "Because You are Lord over all Your works." (Genesis Rabbah 17:4)[7]

Through this midrash we get an even stronger feel for the intimacy of the relationship between Adam and G-d. It is clear that G-d is enjoying their conversation, teasing out Adam's intellectual and creative processes. The tone is playful, but it is also incredibly empowering—to be asked by G-d for opinions, to be entrusted to help complete creation, reinventing and defining the relationship between G-d and man, even to the extent of naming G-d! It is a beautiful midrash, with teachings about the relationship between G-d and humanity, about the power of speech. And Eve missed the whole thing.

We learn something from Adam in this midrash, too. Of all the choices he could make for his own name, he chooses Adam, because he comes from adamah, the earth. Brilliant. Imagine you had the opportunity to name humanity—to call it what it is and has the potential to be. Wouldn't you choose names based on what we strive for and not where we came from? Perhaps we can read into Adam's self-naming choice that he deals best with the already existing world, with what *is*, not yet ready to delve into the possibility of the future. For that, as we will see, he needs Eve.

Lilith also named G-d. It was this intimate, all-powerful act of naming that gave her the freedom to leave the garden. But in this story, and in mainstream Jewish history, Eve is not included in the naming game. We can already see the setup: G-d and Adam are paired off, in cahoots. This is the same buddy-buddy, two-against-one approach they took in the Lilith story, when they attempted to lure Lilith back to the Garden of Eden and into a submissive role. Apparently they have learned nothing from that first failure: Here, Adam is given the power to name, to engage in intellectual stimulation and intimacy with G-d and the world through the gift of language, but Eve is without voice. Even G-d's supremely important commandment about what is okay to eat and what isn't is given before Eve's birth. Adam presumably passes along this information but, as in a game of telephone, something gets lost in the translation. Not once does G-d directly communicate to Eve that she is forbidden to eat from the Tree of Knowledge. She is left out of verbal communication with G-d.

And then there is the problematic issue of Eve's birth:

> And the Lord G-d caused a deep sleep to fall upon the
> man, and he slept: and He took one of his ribs, and closed
> up the flesh in its place, and of the rib, which the Lord

G-d had taken from the man, He made a woman, and brought her to the man. (Genesis 2:22)

This is the text that sends many contemporary women straight into the arms of Lilith. Rather than being created equally and simultaneously from the earth, Eve is created later, pulled from a tiny piece of Adam's body. Feminists are quick to assume that because Eve is created after Adam, and from his rib, she is inferior and subordinate. But blaming or criticizing Eve for the way she was created will not solve the problem. In any case, if we assume the existence of Lilith, we can't get too upset that Eve is created after Adam. Adam's still around, the first woman is gone—of course she is created later. But what about that rib?

Surprisingly, the rabbis themselves see Eve's creation from Adam's rib in a more inventive and positive light than some contemporary feminists. In Genesis Rabbah 8:1, the word for rib is translated as "side," suggesting that Adam was originally a hermaphrodite, split down the middle into male and female:

> R. Samuel bar Nahman said: When the Holy One created Adam, He made him with two fronts: then He sawed him in half and thus gave him two backs, a back for one part and a back for the other part. Someone objected: But does not Scripture say, "And He took one of his ribs (mi-tzalotav)? R. Samuel replied: Mitzalotav may also mean "his sides" as in the verse, "And for the second side (tzela) of the Tabernacle" (Exodus 26:20).

It's a clever midrash, reconciling the equality of male and female with the problematic creation story. But it still doesn't answer the question of why G-d chose to create Eve this way. Why wasn't Eve created out of the dust, like Lilith and Adam? Perhaps G-d is trying to make up for previous mistakes. Being created separate but equal didn't turn out well the first time around. He might have thought that by creating woman differently, from a different substance as one midrash suggests (in a rabbinic fore-shadowing of John Gray's *Men Are from Mars, Women Are from Venus*), Adam and Eve would have a better chance of sticking it out than Adam and Lilith did.[8] I'm not saying that G-d's choice was the best one, or that it wouldn't have been worth luring Lilith back for a little couples therapy before giving up and starting fresh, but I can understand the decision to try a new tack.

Midrashim attempting to explain the method of Eve's creation abound because in the text of Genesis, we don't have G-d's explanation for why Eve is created from Adam's rib. We have only Adam's take on the event of Eve's birth, and it could be his biased interpretation that sends women running to Lilith. After Eve's creation, Adam, encouraged perhaps by G-d's nurturing of his naming abilities, decides to name this new being as well:

> And the man said, "This time she is bone of my bones, and flesh of my flesh: she shall be called Woman *[isha]* because she was taken out of man *[ish]*. That is why a man leaves his father and his mother, and cleaves to his wife: and they become one flesh." (Genesis 2:23–24)

Adam here is making his own midrash on his desired relationship with this new woman, viewing her with ownership (bone of my bones), as much a parent or brother as a lover. The speech begins with the words *zot hapaam*—"this time"—a phrase that puzzles the rabbis. When was there another time? Could this be an allusion to Lilith? It is not surpris-ing that Adam might be thinking of his doomed marriage at the begin-ning of this new relationship. Perhaps remembering his earlier rejec-tion, Adam chooses to read his connection to this new woman as an extremely intimate love, wholly different from the aggressive battles he engaged in with the independent Lilith. This time he envisions woman and man as intertwined, not fully separate—the man will "cleave" to her and they will become "one flesh." This has a certain unhealthy quality to our therapy-trained ears—red neon signs flashing "codependency." Adam, not wanting to be twice-burned, expresses unwillingness to allow Eve her own separate identity. Asserting control in the only way he knows how—through speech, his means of making the world comprehensible to him—he names her as his mirror, isha to his ish, not necessarily as inferior, but as barely other. Her name is an affirmation of his own identity rather than an acknowledgment of hers. As later feminists would view Lilith as the "anti-Eve," Adam labels Eve as the "anti-Lilith."

But we do not have to accept Adam's skewed take on the creation of Eve, any more than we are obligated to accept the rabbinic interpretation of Lilith. The nature of Eve's birth does not suggest she is any less brave or strong-willed or intelligent than Lilith. Clearly, the circumstances are different, and thus Eve's choices, as well as her relationship to G-d and Adam, must be different. Being created from Adam's rib would generate a more intimate tie to him than Lilith had. Perhaps because of this blood tie, Eve could not so easily consider leaving the garden without Adam, and would thus have to find another way to assert her identity, to upset the status quo. In addition, Eve's creation is a uniquely dynamic and transformational one. The tiny rib grows into a woman, defining Eve's essence not as the mirror of man, but as the originator of change.

This is something Lilith and Adam did not know much about. Lilith could only generate change by remaining unchanged, by staying true to her beliefs and removing herself, wholly and wonderfully intact, from the garden. Adam's skill was to name and define what already existed, to follow in G-d's footsteps without questioning. Only Eve, who, inadvertently perhaps, was given the opportunity to participate in her own birth, to grow into herself, recognizes the dynamic potential pulsing beneath the static daily existence of the garden.[9]

Hinting at the changes that will lead her out of the garden, the womb of G-d, Eve's transformation from rib to woman is the first quiet knock on the garden gate. The very nature of her birth carries within it the seeds of her future act of rebellion and growth, allowing her the potential to outgrow the confines of her origin.

What Eve had to offer was perhaps the most powerful gift of all, the capacity for change. If anything held Eve down, then, it was not being created from Adam's rib—it was being denied the greatest commodity in the creation story, speech. Adam names her, but she has no reciprocal ability to name or rename Adam, nor is she given the option to use language to rename herself, and thus develop her own identity.

Just because Eve does not speak does not mean she does not think. Or want. Or wonder. Just because Eve says very little in this story does not mean she is passive and dumb. Isn't it just as likely that she was a curious, growing being full of ideas and questions with no one to talk to? I imagine her left alone, bursting with curiosity and imagination, exploring the peripheries of the garden, delving into the mystery of the forbidden and secret, far from center stage. How else could she have run into a character like the serpent?

The rabbis also speculate on how Eve and the serpent found each other. They ask a question that must have weighed heavily on their minds: Where was Adam? What excuse could he possibly have for leaving his wife alone long enough for her to cavort with snakes? The rabbis come up with two simple answers, each with telling philosophical and psychological implications. "Abba bar Guria said: He had engaged in intercourse [literally: done according to his nature] and fallen asleep" (Genesis Rabbah 19:3). Bypassing the shocking idea that sex took place in the garden even before the serpent entered the scene, this midrash demonstrates that the rabbis have a sense of humor about themselves; they are willing to poke fun at male shortcomings as well as female ones. Adam is the stereotypical insensitive man who falls asleep after sex, who doesn't want to talk or cuddle. The midrash also suggests to an even greater degree the loneliness of Eve. Sexual intercourse happens, but not verbal intercourse. The midrash inadvertently serves to emphasize that Eve's bond with the serpent is not sexual—she has just *had* sex when they meet. What she is lacking is conversation.

The second part of the "Where was Adam?" midrash takes a different approach, but in essence reiterates the message of Abba bar Guria. "But the sages said: At that time the Holy One was taking him around the entire world, saying to him: Here is a place fit for planting trees, here is a place fit for sowing cereals." This midrash brings us back to the feel-good, sitcom-style father/son relationship we saw in the midrash in which Adam names the animals. Where were God and Adam while Eve wandered alone? G-d was standing with His arm around Adam's shoulder, showing him the world, mentoring him. We can forgive G-d for leaving Eve out before she was even born, but here G-d deliberately excludes her, as if learning how to live off the earth is "a guy thing." Although it is a better excuse than falling asleep after sex, we are left once again with a picture of Eve as lonely and left out.

Next, the rabbis ask: Why did the serpent choose Eve? They don't seem to notice that their question has already been answered. It seems obvious that the serpent would choose Eve to talk to and not Adam, because the serpent could sense that Eve was craving dialogue. The serpent, with its sharp intellect, its curiosity and knowledge, becomes a pseudo-G-d, opening Eve's eyes to possibilities that exist only in her dormant imagination. The serpent is referred to as male, but perhaps it is more interesting to imagine it is Lilith in disguise. Though it was probably meant to show Lilith's satanic nature, an illustration in a sixteenth-century text does show Lilith with the body of a snake tempting Eve. The serpent certainly seems to have some Lilith-like qualities: a powerful gift of speech, an intimate knowledge of G-d, a quality of defiance and strength of will—surprising in an ideal garden. Perhaps Lilith has come back to try to help Eve gain the power she needs to escape. I like the picture this makes: While G-d teaches Adam about planting and sowing, Lilith teaches Eve about power and freedom.

Regardless of its gender, the serpent is a compelling character. "And the serpent was more subtle than all the beasts of the field which the Lord G-d had made" (Genesis 3:1).[10] How perfect for Eve, who lives in a world of subtlety and indirectness—created from a rib or side, left at the unspoken edges of the story. Each time I read this, I can't help but think of how thrilling it must have been for Eve to have someone approach and ask her a simple question. Imagine the beauty and irresistibility of a ripe, round question to an independent, thinking person who has never been asked to voice her opinion on anything, to assess information, to make a decision. Surely the rabbis, who value knowledge above all things, must agree.

Sadly, no. In one infamous midrash the rabbis put a very different spin on both the serpent's and Eve's motivations. In the midrash, the serpent muses, "If I go and speak to Adam, I know that he will not listen to me, for it is difficult to lead a man away from his own mind. So I shall go and speak to Eve, for I know that she will listen to me, since women are light-headed and easily led by everybody" (Genesis Rabbah 19:4–5). Okay. I am usually one to look for the kernel of wisdom in any rabbinic teaching, but this one really hurts. Here Eve is neither evil nor oversexed, just stupid. This is the version I hear time and again from my students, and read time and again in writings by Jewish feminists. Eve listens to the serpent and eats the fruit because she's just too dumb to say no. What bothers me most about this midrash is that I am convinced that any (male) rabbi, put in Eve's shoes—or fig leaf, or whatever—would have made the same choice. Out of stupidity? Of course not. The rabbis were scholars. They, too, must have felt an attraction to the serpent's thirst for knowledge, an admiration for his (or her) gift for manipulating speech and logic.

Thank G-d another midrash exists to support this possibility. It is a midrash that rarely gets quoted, perhaps because it is long and full of the kind of silly, nitpicky arguments that are only entertaining to the rabbis themselves and to the yeshiva students trained to understand them. But what makes it so wonderful is that the rabbis put this very style of argument, their very own peculiar form of brilliant Talmudic debate and deductive reasoning, of *pilpul*, into the mouth of the serpent. The rabbis have a marvelous time, each imaginative prooftext topping the last. The reasoning builds on the premise that "whatever was created after its companion dominates it," leading to the conclusion that humans are more powerful than G-d, and woman more powerful than man. "Make haste and eat," urges the serpent, "before G-d creates other worlds to rule over you" (Genesis Rabbah 19:4 5). Of course, all of this complex reasoning is meant to be part of the serpent's twisted mental seduction, but given that it is no more or less bizarre than other rabbinic debates, the serpent comes across as a rebbe in his own right, or, at the very least, a precocious *yeshiva bocher* (student).

The rabbis value logic and persuasive speech highly; that the serpent was so skilled at it could only elicit their admiration. Now why would anyone waste all that brilliant exegesis on a "light-headed" pupil? Later, there will be time for the rabbis to vilify Eve as the woman who dares to rebel and disobey the commandment of G-d. Later, the rabbis will blame the sorrows of the world on Eve's sin, and see all women as forever tainted by it. But here, just for a moment, how could they not help but be proud, and a bit jealous, of the one who desires above all else not sex, not immortality, but wisdom?

Whatever else we want to say about it, we must acknowledge that Eve's choice to eat the fruit is an intelligent one. "And when the woman saw that the tree was good for food, and that it was desirable to the eyes, and pleasing for making one wise" (Genesis 3:6), only then did she eat. We see that her curiosity is piqued not by weakness, but the chance to spread her intellectual and creative wings. What are Eve's options in the garden, confined to eternal silence, abandoned and dismissed by parent and partner? Could she leave, as Lilith did? Perhaps Eve knew that only by eating the fruit could she discover the knowledge, the secret name, as Lilith did. Or perhaps, with Lilith's encouragement, Eve does opt for rebellion, but chooses to sacrifice some part of herself in order to stay attached—to Adam, to the world of living things. Lilith, in order to keep her integrity, could not stay in the garden once she realized this ideal paradise masked an insidious patriarchy and inequality. We learn a lot from Lilith, but it is Eve who teaches us how to change a system from within, how to assert one's identity without having to sever relationships or flee the country. Eve is smart enough to know that she does not have the power to change G-d or Adam. Instead, she undertakes the most radical and subversive act of all: changing herself, feeding herself with the knowledge she needs for self-empowerment. I don't think it is an accident that Eve's act of defiance, though silent, is an oral one—she can't speak, but she can eat! If Eve were the docile, obedient housewife commentators have seen her as, then this would be the moment when she decides to go back to school to finish her degree.

The choice to eat the fruit and gain wisdom is an enormously powerful one, with eternal ramifications affecting G-d, Adam and the human condition. But once Eve eats the fruit, she makes another surprising and significant choice. She gives it to Adam. Eve has been slammed again and again as the temptress. She ate the fruit, fine. But her true crime, say the rabbis, was in giving it to poor, innocent Adam. In one midrash she makes it into juice so he won't know what he's eating. In another, she plays on Adam's vulnerabilities, arguing that if she dies, no one will take her place—a persuasive argument to a man who has already lost one wife (Genesis Rabbah 19:4–5). But this can't be right. According to the text itself, the serpent convinces Eve that she will not die from touching the fruit.

Why then, does Eve give the fruit to Adam? She could have gained the knowledge, and power that goes with it, and left Adam lying in the dust he was created from. After all, he hadn't treated her particularly well. But she offers the fruit to him, giving him the opportunity to grow and change with her. If we understand that Eve's motivation was to initiate change, to create a better life for herself, then giving the fruit to Adam to eat as well is a stunning act of generosity and trust. Is this because of her sense of attachment caused by being created from the rib—a way of seeing herself always in relationship to others? Or has Eve developed a more compassionate and complex view of the world than the unforgiving, black-or-white approach Lilith's pure sense of justice would allow? Whatever the reason, what occurs as a result is astonishing: a complete transformation of the newly created world.

Long, long before there were self-help books, Eve changes herself to change her world, manipulating a more level playing ground, one in which it might be possible to work things out, to talk to one another, rather than shout and divorce. As Harriet Lerner writes in *The Dance of Anger*, "We cannot make another person change his or her steps to an old dance, but if we change our own steps, the dance no longer can continue in the same predictable pattern."[11] In this context, perhaps what Eve is trying to say by giving Adam the fruit is: Look, I am going to change. As I develop my strength and knowledge, I am going to outgrow you. If you eat the fruit, you can come with me, and we can communicate together on this higher level. If not, I will have to leave you and begin my journey without you.

What happens in the garden as a consequence of Eve's act supports Lerner's point to perfection. Just look at all the changes that begin to occur through Eve's single brilliant act of calculated defiance. Adam, who did not listen to Lilith's frustration and logical arguments, and thus far has shown no interest whatsoever in even finding out if Eve can talk—the guy who crashes out after sex—listens. In G-d's words, he "hearkens to the voice of his wife" (Genesis 3:17)—surely for the first time. The rabbis are jarred into speculation by the strange choice of wording— *"kolah,"* her "voice," not her "words"—interpreting this to mean that she wept and cried out to persuade him (Genesis Rabbah 20:5). But of course the real shocker here is that she has a voice at all.

What happens next is even more significant. "And the man and his wife hid themselves from the presence of the Lord" (Genesis 3:8). Adam and Eve hide, together, from G-d. What? No boys against girl? This is the very first recording of a shared experience between Adam and Eve, and it is the first time we see Adam beginning to grow up and gain some separation from G-d. Another first in the text of Genesis is that Eve, the silent one, finds a way to manipulate G-d to actually ask her, them, a question—in the very next line, G-d asks, "Where are you?" Like the serpent, who asked Eve a question to which he obviously knew the answer—"Has G-d said, You shall not eat of any tree in the garden?" (Genesis 3:1)— G-d, who of course knows where they are, asks a question to engage Adam and Eve in dialogue. Moments later, G-d addresses Eve directly: "What is this that you have done?" (Genesis 3:13).

Suddenly Eve's silent world is flooded with speech, and not the yelling and demanding talk that took place in Lilith's time, but questions, answers, conversation. And what about Eve's relationship to the most empowering act of all: naming? This changes radically as well. Adam, who once named Eve isha to his ish, now renames her Chava, a word that can be translated as something like "lifeforce." What an improvement! He chooses this name because he now sees her as the "Mother of All Living Things." Adam recognizes that Eve is responsible for nothing less than giving them life, a new, unpredictable life in which they can control their own destinies, procreate and stumble through the challenges of the world together. While some may find it offensive that Adam is defining Eve through her role as mother, it is important to note that a) This is Adam, who has been consistently unimaginative and limited in his naming abilities, so let's not be too hard on him, and b) He names her Life, not Mother—referring not only to her ability to procreate, but to an almost godlike role as the source of all life. While Adam may think this new name reflects the change in Eve, it also reflects how he has been changed by her act; Adam now recognizes in Eve an identity separate from his own. She is no longer merely his mirror, the one who exists to help him with his existential quandary. Adam has listened to Eve, and this time when he looks at her to name her, he truly sees her.

Of course the story does not end here. Because of Eve, the garden of Eden becomes a beginning, not an end. While Eve remains inside the text of the Torah, it is only after she leaves the garden that we see her come into her full power. The first, almost instantaneous, act that occurs after Adam and Eve leave the garden gates is, of course, "And Adam knew Eve his wife" (Genesis 4:1). A simple phrase, even shorter in the Hebrew, but now we can read its significance. Now we can revel in the intimacy, the willingness to join each other in relationship, not because they are inseparable, as Adam had originally hoped, but as Adam and Eve, two individuals who, kicked out of G d's garden, come together as one to create a new life. But the most important act takes place in the second half of the sentence: "and she conceived, and bore Cain, saying, 'I have acquired a manchild of the Lord.'" At last Eve can give her own naming monologue, similar to Adam's musings after she was created. This is something she did not have the power or permission to do in the garden. While Eve may not know the unknowable name of G-d, she has herself become, as the serpent predicted, like G-d, Creator and Namer of her creations. From this moment on, in the Bible and Jewish tradition, women are given the gift and power of naming the next generation. While it would be a long time before our feminist forerunners would give us the vote, Eve gave us the voice.

So where does this leave us? Is it possible to see Lilith and Eve as metaphors for the feminists of the seventies and the women, ourselves, who follow in their wake? The first Jewish feminists, like Lilith, came on strong, refusing to compromise. They couldn't compromise—the problems were too systemic to be altered from within. Following in their footsteps, standing on their shoulders, we are blessed with being able to live in the garden, transformed as it has been by the work of earlier women. It is not by any means perfect or equal, and we are not free of the parts of ourselves that feel bound and limited. For those of us who want to stay in the garden—be it the Jewish community, a relationship or society at large—we must change the rules by changing ourselves, and in doing so make ourselves a central part of Jewish debate and text.

Embracing the character of Eve instead of being ashamed of her, choosing to celebrate her complexity, strength and courage rather than condemning her for being too much or too little, is one way to do this. Let's not make the very mistake our feminist foremothers corrected with Lilith—let's not confuse rabbinic and societal interpretation of Eve with Eve herself. Eve is a part of us. Lilith can and will forever stand larger than life as a mythological heroine, but Eve, Eve is our mother. To understand her, her limitations and her motivations, is to better understand ourselves and our heritage. To reclaim her, to give her a new voice, is to reclaim and transform a lost part of ourselves. In the last thirty or so years we have reclaimed our right to be Lilith-like: to stand up for ourselves, to rebel against injustice, to make no apologies for our anger and our independence. I'd like to think that the Lilith part of who we are is strong enough now to make room for Eve. Only when both women can be equally celebrated, like the two great lights of Genesis destined to become equal in the messianic age, can we be whole.[12]

I want to end with a poem that I wrote about Eve. It was through writing this poem that I heard a new voice for Eve, one I recognized as my own. It was through writing this poem that I became passionate about Eve. This poem, and this essay, represent one woman's interpretation of the creation story. That isn't enough. My hope is that there will be many more. My hope is that women will be tempted to grab paper and pen and write poems, essays and midrashim of their own, fleshing out Eve's lost voice. Facing the unknown of a blank page, writing wildly into the unexplored parts of who we are, is like eating the fruit: scary, exhilarating and liberating. Here is what happened to me:

Eve's Confession

As if I could speak
having been given no language
only desire

wanting only
the power
to name what I want.

I was born from the side
and this is how I entered all rooms:
shuffling, apologetic, peripheral.

Without a center
I quickly learned
how circles work

how they steer you
around the core of things
clinging to peripheries

how easy it is
to hide
so far from beginnings

and always arriving at the same place
only more full, flustered
heavy with secrets and a thin film

of darkness
which, I also learned,
is not the same as sin.

It was his shape that drew me
round in body and logic
our thoughts encircling—

A question of dialogue
not commandment.
Don't judge me:

What you call falling
was the closest I've come
to pure statement.

I brought us into the world
out of desire,
not language

and it was worth the risk:
after the garden
I bore our son

from the center of my self
I bore our son
and named him.

Notes:

1. Aviva Cantor, "The Lilith Question," *On Being a Jewish Feminist,* ed. Susannah Heschel (Schocken Books, 1983), 42.

2. The legend of Lilith is told in the Alphabet of Ben Sira, and alluded to in midrash and Kabbalistic sources such as the Zohar, as well as in later folktales and customs. For an analysis of the myth, see Joseph Dan, "Samael, Lilith, and the Concept of Evil in Early Kabbalah," *Association for Jewish Studies Review* 5 (1980), 17–40.

3. Nehama Aschkenasy, *Eve's Journey: Feminine Images in Hebraic Literary Tradition* (Wayne State University Press, 1994), 40.

4. Enid Dame, Lilly Rivlin and Henny Wenkart, eds., *Which Lilith? Feminist Writers Re-create the World's First Woman* (Jason Aronson, 1998), 5.

5. Phyllis Trible, "Eve and Adam: Genesis 2–3 Reread," *Andover Newton Quarterly* V. 13 (1973), 251.

6. Quotations from Genesis in this essay are my own adaptations from *Tora: The Holy Scriptures* (Koren Publishers, 1988). Since I am interpreting G-d to be a distinctly male character in the Adam and Eve story, I have left the gendered language intact when referring to that part of Genesis.

7. This and the following translations of midrashim from Genesis Rabbah are my own adaptations from Hayim Nahman Bialik and Yehoshua Hana Ravnitzky, *The Book of Legends: Legends from the Talmud and Midrash* (Schocken Books, 1992).

8. See Genesis Rabbah 17:8. The rabbis attribute various "objective" differences between women and

men to the fact that they were created from different substances, earth and bone. It is a sexist midrash because of the differences they find between women and men—made even more offensive, perhaps, because it is clearly meant to be humorous. (For example, men are more easily appeased than women because earth absorbs water quickly, but bone does not.) Nevertheless, the rabbis view creation from the rib as proof of difference, rather than inferiority.

9. The strange language of Genesis supports this idea—Eve is "built" from the rib.

10. I prefer the translation of the word *arum* as subtle, rather than crafty or clever.

11. Harriet Lerner, *The Dance of Anger* (New York: Harper Perennial, 1985).

12. "And the light of the moon shall become like the light of the sun" (Isaiah 30:26).

To Open My Mouth
and Speak What I Know

URSULA KATAN

SOME STORIES JUST DON'T HAVE A BEGINNING.

This one begins with a little girl molested by family heroes. Or maybe it begins in a ghetto in Warsaw, Poland. Or maybe before that. In any event, it's not a story that is supposed to be told, not of my people.

We are Jews. This sort of thing doesn't happen in our families.

There is no graceful way of introducing incest. It cannot be dressed up in clever metaphors, nor softened by gentle words.

There is no graceful way of introducing the Holocaust, either. The violation of a people is no easier to talk about than the violation of a single child. How do we begin to tell our own stories, or the stories of our people? It's never simple. Told together, our individual and collective violations overlap and blur until it's sometimes difficult to differentiate abused from abuser.

I am a third-generation American, third-generation Holocaust survivor. I grew up in a home that spoke bluntly and frequently about the Holocaust and attended some of the first conferences and meetings to remember the whirlwind of death that half our people do not mention and half make a career of remembering. I grew up with the certain knowledge that I was lucky to be alive, lucky to have been born in the United States in the shelter of an upwardly mobile East-Coast Jewish family.

154

I am the grandchild of Holocaust survivors, raised on the stories of my grandparents' strength and perseverance. My grandfather is the patron saint of our family, the brave hero who preserved our bloodline. The sweet and kindly man who worked in sweatshops when he and my grandmother arrived in the United States in 1950, Grandma seven months pregnant with my father. He listened to opera on his cheap radio while sewing custom clothes for rich women, letting us grandkids play with the scraps of beautiful fabrics. He molested us in the bath, touching my small seven-year-old body. You need to be clean, my grandfather said in his heavy Yiddish accent, eyes downcast as his shaking hands roamed across my frightened skin.

When my mother found out about the abuse, I was punished for not protecting my sister. Nothing was ever said to my heroic grandfather about it.

Our people are a people of survivors. We have been persecuted innumerable times in our long history, yet we persevere. We were slaves in the land of Egypt, rescued by God and brought to the Holy Land. We have been exiled from virtually every European country, our homes and families violated in countless towns and cities. Yet still our culture and way of life survive. We were rounded up like cattle, tortured and exterminated in Nazi Germany. But with a strong hand and an outstretched arm, God rescued us and and brought us back to the Holy Land with the creation of the State of Israel.

We Jews often look to our victim status, to the fact that the world is against us. Yet we never acknowledge our role as perpetrator. We are the victims of near genocide, but we don't acknowledge our own country's oppression of the Palestinian people. We don't acknowledge the violence that exists within some of our Jewish families, within our own communities. When we forget to view our stories in the broader context, we risk becoming the monsters we have fought.

I wonder sometimes what the parents of my grandparents were like. Both of my grandparents were teenagers when Hitler came to power, and they lost most of their family in the war. What would my grandfather's family have been like if not for the Holocaust? Was my grandfather molested, humiliated or abused by his family? Or was his behavior caused by some damaged place in him broken by five years in a Nazi concentration camp and five years more in a displaced persons' camp? How did the Holocaust affect my grandmother, who to my knowledge has never once questioned my grandfather's sexually inappropriate behavior? Did Grandma even notice the way Grandpa touched his daughters and grandchildren? How did losing their parents to genocide affect the way they raised their children?

I will never have answers to some of these questions. I guess at the answers to others. My father often makes excuses for his parents, about how they did not know how to be parents because they lost theirs at such a young age. He proudly tells us that his parents were rough with him so that he could learn to be tough and impermeable like they learned to be during the War. While he did not experience Nazi Germany directly, he too bears the emotional scars of the camps.

My father was obsessed with the Holocaust. He took us to conferences, made us watch the Nazi horror movies, showed us photos of bodies and always reminded us that this was our family. These were our people. This was us.

We were a good Jewish family, following all of the rituals of our people. We lit candles on Friday nights. The children went to Jewish summer camps and to Hebrew school three days a week. We sent our outgrown clothing to religious cousins in Bene Barak and made regular donations to plant trees in Israel.

My father took me to minyan every Friday morning. We sat in the back, and I was the only girl child there. My father pushed prayer books into my nine-year-old hands, whispering, "Here, read the Song of Songs. It's about sex, you know. This is my favorite passage." Every Friday morning I went to minyan with my father. Every Friday morning I read the Song of Songs while my father pointed out passages: "Come lie with me little sister." His foul morning breath leaned into my prayer book. "Don't you like this passage? Read it again." His sweaty hands advanced heavily up my thigh while the rabbi droned on, *Baruch atah Adonai, elohaynu v'elohey avosaynuh, elohay Avraham, elohay Yitzchak, vla hey Yaakov. . . .* [1]

The God of my father and of my forefathers before him did not notice a little girl being molested in the back pew of a synagogue.

I grew up in a Jewish community that, fifty years after the fact, is still haunted by the ghosts of the Holocaust, that places value on our American ability to assimilate but not lose our identity as Jews (any more than necessary). I went to a synagogue surrounded by the ghosts of relatives who did not survive, whose names were whispered during the Mourner's Kaddish. I prayed alongside the women in my grandparents' synagogue, separated from the men by a mechitza, the divide we do not cross. I still do not count in the minyan in my father's shul.

Do American concepts of gender oppression apply here, or is it a deeper question, of survivors fighting for a sense of control or taking back some sort of power by asserting it over someone else? In a world without anti-Semitism, would Jewish family and gender dynamics look different than they do today? How do we halt the cycle of violence in our own community when we acknowledge the violence we have suffered but not the violence we create?

For me, growing up meant leaving the community of my childhood. The struggle toward healing has been fraught with contradictory-seeming desires. I cannot separate my abuse from my sense of Judaism, and yet I cannot construct my identity without including Judaism. I cannot call myself a survivor without also acknowledging that my perpetrators are survivors. I cannot look at the ways I have been abused without looking also at the ways my people have been abusive, and where my own culpability lies in this abuse. I won't give money to an Israel that systematically oppresses the Palestinian people, but I will unflinchingly defend Israel in conversations with non-Jews. I want to be proud to be a Jew—and yet I still cannot bring myself to enter a synagogue, fearing the abuse memories that the songs and prayers hold for me. Judaism is religion, culture and politics combined. Healing and growing has meant sifting through its polemical whole for the pieces I need to shape myself.

It is my people's survivor mentality that ostracized me as an incest survivor in their midst. We divide our violation into public abuse and private abuse. For some, while the survival of public abuse evokes cultural solidarity, pride and strength, the survival of private abuse is shameful and divisive. My grandparents are heroes for surviving the War. My virginity, the dowry that lives between the legs of Jewish daughters, was stolen from me as a child, rendering me unfit as a woman and unholy in the eyes of my religion. As "good Jews," many of us are told to keep our family troubles to ourselves.

We fear that acknowledging these "troubles" will add fodder to the flames of anti-Semitism already burning in America. Jews know that incest exists in other communities, but we do not acknowledge it in our own; we are afraid of giving non-Jews more reason to distrust us, oppress us, drive us out or kill us yet again. So the Jewish way is to present a united front of healthy families and educated, upwardly mobile culture. We assimilate to a point, yet we hold ourselves to a higher standard—we can only assimilate so far. The Jewish community casts out its embarrassing problems, victim-end first. I lost many of my Jewish friends when I first began speaking of my abuse. I still have not confronted my father or my grandfather, because I know this will mean losing my connection to the rest of my family. The Jewish community never talks about the violence that our own people are capable of . . . especially if the violence is toward one of our own.

Despite the threat of exile, I still find pride in my Jewish culture and identity. It was in Jewish summer camp as a preteen that I learned to meditate, learned to feel a connection to the natural world, the cycles of the seasons, the pulse of the rivers I canoed down, the sacred omnipotent passivity of the sheer rock walls I climbed, the Hebrew names of plants and the Jewish prayers honoring the beauty of God's natural creations. I learned prayers to say over rainbows, songs about the Shekinah, learned about finding my own *ruach,* a Hebrew word meaning both spirit and breath. Jewish hippie counselors with guitars and poorly tie dyed T-shirts taught me the history of my people, the songs, dances, flavors and richness of my living culture, my Jewish community. I learned about heroes forging the nation-state of Israel out of a hostile desert. I found that Jewish values such as the importance of learning, creating and community-building were things that fed my spirit. I discovered my culture in the cadence of Jewish voices raised in unison, the shape of our holy language in my mouth, and discovered how different my culture felt in the Catskill mountains than in the Jewish neighborhood where I had been raised. I was never able to convince myself to believe in the God of Judaism, but I discovered my soul and the spirit of my people.

With this pride, I am able to find healing in my culture, in the essence of my sense of what Judaism is. When my Jewish community turned up its collective nose at my lifestyle choices, I learned ways to create community around me. When my family would not acknowledge the scars they left on me and made me keep secrets no child should ever have to keep, I built a new family based on openness and freedom from abuse. And like my grandparents before me, when I left the abusive place that had been my home, I used the strength and resourcefulness that I learned from my culture to create a new home. I learned from my Jewish roots the value of community, family, mitzvot (in the colloquial sense, good deeds). I learned the strength of our people. I learned survival. These qualities are the heart of my understanding of Judaism.

I am the grandchild of survivors, and the survivor of family sexual abuse. I am not the only one. As long as Jews continue to believe that we can remove the reality of family violence from our culture by casting out survivors like myself, my story and others like it will go unheard, and the cycles of violence and abuse will continue. I demand that we be given a space within the Jewish community to tell our stories. Only when there is recognition that abuse happens in Jewish families, too, will we begin to break these cycles in our community and heal both from the violence we have suffered and the violence we have perpetrated.

Perhaps the next generations of Jews will be able to tell a different story.

Notes:

1. "Blessed are You, God our God and the God of our forefathers, God of Abraham, God of Isaac, and God of Jacob. . . . "

You Wear a Kippah?

EMILY WAGES

LAST SUMMER IN YANGSHUO, CHINA, two young Jewish men from England stopped me on the street.

"Where are you from?" one of them asked. "We've never seen a woman wearing a *kippah* (yarmulke) before!"

It was Rosh Hashanah, and although I was miles away from any synagogue, it is my custom to wear a kippah on all Jewish holidays.

"It's rather simple, really," I explained. "My kippah connects me to the universe, covers my soul and helps me enter the stream of Jewish tradition. It's a sign of submission to something greater than humans, and a mark of personal dignity and honor."

"Hmmm. . . . Just like it is for us, I guess." He paused, and then added, "But wow, that's really bold of you!"

Bold? Though wearing a kippah is challenging in many ways, I don't view these difficulties as related to my gender. For many American Jewish women under thirty, the question is not "Is it acceptable for me to wear a kippah or read Torah as a woman?" but instead "Is it possible to be a thinking individual and an observant Jew at the same time?" or "Can I have a personally meaningful spiritual life and simultaneously take part in Jewish tradition?" Though spiritual, cultural and political difficulties abound for my generation of Jewish feminists, gender-specific questions regarding ritual dress have long been addressed by Conservative and Reform Judaism. The questions now are simply quite different.

I started wearing a kippah every Shabbat after moving to San Francisco; for the first time in my life I was going to services regularly, reading the weekly Torah portion and exploring my identity as a religious Jew. My cultural Jewishness had never been in question, but attending services and praying with other Jews was completely new territory. I was raised in a secular, mixed household (complete with Christmas at Grandma's house), spending each summer in Israel with my avowedly atheist Jewish left-wing kibbutznik relatives. I had never seen any of my relatives in either country go to shul, much less wear a kippah.

Still, I made an independent commitment to open myself to religious Judaism, and not just in the let's-see-what-it-can-do-for-me-within-six-weeks'-time consumerist way. This was an important part of my heritage, and I intended to explore and reclaim it. So I took slow, deliberate steps toward increased observance—always trying to respect both Jewish tradition and my own spiritual experience.

I believe that American consumer culture has led to the wholesale rejection of traditional religious observance by many young Jews. We've been trained to be wary of investing emotionally or intellectually in anything, unless we're guaranteed an immediate payoff. Religious practice seldom provides quick and easy benefits, and teachers of every religion tell us that only after a long period of deep personal investment and commitment can a fulfilling spiritual life be achieved.

Discovering that Jewish ritual is a window to community, spiritual growth and my family's collective past has profoundly enriched my life. In the United States, many of us live cut off from each other and our families, with no system by which to imbue life with meaning. For me, embracing religious Judaism has meant sharing Jewish holidays with friends and teachers, engaging in social action for *tikkun olam* (healing the world), pausing each week to rest in the absolute present—and wearing my kippah.

The moment each Friday evening when I put on my kippah is rich with meaning. It is incredibly personal and private—a metaphysical instant in which I take a step closer to the divine. It is also a shared, collective moment, in which I visibly and tangibly express my connection to the Jewish community and the tradition of my ancestors.

At Reform and Conservative shuls in the United States, many women already wear kippot. Outside these synagogues, however, reactions to a woman in a kippah are quite varied. When I am going to and from shul or walking around my neighborhood on Shabbat, strangers often ask me about my kippah:

"Is that some kind of cap or something?"

"What's that on your head?"

"Why are you wearing that?"

"Are you Jewish? I didn't know women wore those. Do women wear those?"

"What's with the little hat?"

"Are the girls wearing kippot now? Oh, how wonderful. I shall have to tell my granddaughter."

These comments are intriguing but not bothersome. People are curious and eager to understand something they have never encountered. I'm happy to explain the significance of the kippah and to confirm that, yes, many women do wear these little hats now.

A kippah is an outward expression of inner beliefs. As such, it invariably attracts others' perceptions of religious Jews—and of religion itself. People sometimes assume that because I wear a kippah I must be politically conservative. Others assume that increased religious observance signals the termination of independent thinking. *She's wearing a kippah,* it seems some think, *therefore she must be a nationalistic drone.*

The most challenging reactions to my kippah-wearing come from those who've known me for a long time. They're puzzled by my increasing *frum-ness* (religiosity) and wonder how I could ever accept the restrictiveness of organized religion. They wonder how a religion considered so patriarchal, xenophobic and G-d-centered could ever appeal to feminist, internationalist, free-thinking intellectuals: "I understand that it's culturally meaningful for you to wear a kippah, Emily, but do you really believe all that stuff about G-d and the chosen people?"

Many people, repulsed by beliefs that have been used to justify oppression, have decided to forgo religion completely—tossing out the baby with the bath water. Instead of saying, "I'm troubled by certain aspects of traditional Judaism (for example, homophobia, nationalism, sexism), so I want to learn more, deepen my understanding and discuss these ideas," many assume that Jewish observance could never be personally meaningful for them. I believe that struggling intensely with an evolving, nearly four-thousand-year-old religious system can be meaningful, and that there is space in religious practice both for close scrutiny and devotion.

I explain to my friends that the concept of "the people Israel" is not xenophobic (Israel literally means "those who struggle with G-d"). I explain that I go to an egalitarian synagogue where the rabbi uses the Talmud to talk about homelessness, that davening (praying) is spiritually fulfilling and that perhaps all that stuff about G-d and the chosen people is a bit deeper and more sophisticated than they think. My friends' responses to my kippah reflect Western intellectuals' skepticism toward religious practice. Of course, these same friends respect and honor the religious practices of other cultures or peoples, but that a semi-intelligent person in contemporary American society could be inspired by a Western religion is, to them, a bit puzzling.

So far, I have felt comfortable wearing my kippah everywhere—in front of non-Jewish relatives, all over the United States, in China and Croatia—except in one place: Israel. Why? Do I fear the fiery condemnation of Israeli Orthodox Jews (known, in the past, for throwing rocks at cars driving on the Sabbath and feces on women praying with men at the Western Wall)? Am I troubled by patriarchal stereotypes that preclude women from sharing the same status as men? Not really. In Israel, as in the United States, the most intimidating factor in my wearing a kippah lies not in bias against women, but in the secular population's (understandable) opposition to Jewish religious observance itself.

Before addressing why so many secular Israelis resent—and even detest—religious Jews, and religious practice, it's necessary to acknowledge that Orthodox (and some Conservative) Jews in Israel would definitely disapprove of my kippah-wearing. To them, a woman in a kippah is a horrible desecration of tradition. Among Orthodox Jews, there are clearly delineated roles for women and men (some with halakhic origin, many without) in religion, family and fashion. A violation of these rules is viewed as a threat to the stability of the entire community. I respect the commitment Orthodox Jews have to their religion and way of life, but refuse to alter my own religious practice and dress because it does not conform to their worldview.

For me, the issue in Israel is my strong internal fear of alienating politically and culturally like-minded Jews. No matter how willing I am to explain my relationship to religious Judaism and my reasons for becoming more observant, secular Jewish Israelis who see me donning a kippah will still assume that I somehow support the Orthodox establishment and their conservative political and cultural positions.

Over the last fifty years, a strong association has been established in Israeli discourse between religious observance and political orientation. The less observant Jews are generally more liberal, and the majority of religious Israelis are culturally conservative and politically hawkish. Most secular Jews resent the powerful influence wielded by the Orthodox establishment in the political, cultural and commercial spheres; there is a fierce ongoing battle to preserve the separation of synagogue and state in Israel. The secular population is fighting to eliminate all privileges enjoyed by religious Jews—control over marriage, divorce, burials and yeshiva students' exemption from military service. If I were to walk around the kibbutz in my kippah, lifelong friends and cousins would think, "Emily was always so progressive, but now she's become *datiyah* (religious)." It's easy, in theory, to dismiss such judgments, but much harder to do so when they come from one's family, friends and community.

It is understandable that nonreligious Jews vehemently disagree with religious Jews on many political and cultural issues, and yet it is unfortunate that they have allowed their frustrations with specific people to color their feelings about an entire religious tradition. The politicization of Judaism in Israel has led many secular Jews to view the Jewish religion as a dispensable, outdated relic. Secular Israelis feel anger toward their observant counterparts and are loath to associate with a tradition that they perceive to be factious, extremist and anti-intellectual. They seek their spiritual nourishment elsewhere; they believe that religious Judaism has cultural value, but they have their own country now—so who really needs Jewish religious practice, anyway?

This attitude shaped my perceptions of religious Judaism for a long time. I used to explain to Jewish friends that I was more "Israeli" than "American" in my Jewishness. I turned down their invitations to services, claiming that I didn't need any kind of Jewish religious structure to facilitate my spiritual journey or maintain my identity as a Jew. Cultural Judaism was enough for me. Of course, I had never been to services in my life and, like many secular Israelis, assumed that religious Judaism had little to offer.

It took me a long time to realize that I was reacting to the contemporary political climate in Israel, instead of to the religion itself. I had internalized many of the attitudes held by those around me, both in America and in Israel, and I had closed myself off from a spiritual path because of other people's interpretations of and squabbles over that path. Once I decided to push aside all expectations and stereotypes and connect directly with a religious Jewish community I respected, I found a wellspring of wisdom, compassion and spiritual support—much richer and deeper than I ever imagined.

In many ways, my experiences wearing a kippah reflect the larger struggle of Jewish feminists of my generation. Many of us are working to create and preserve a space in the Jewish community in which women and men from all backgrounds can actively participate in the Jewish tradition without compromising spiritual integrity or denying individuality. The interplay between profound religious ideals and mundane social realities can be frustrating. I put on a kippah to enter more deeply into a religious space, not to be drawn into debates about Arafat and Sharon, or pigeonholed by observers. But alas, it seems impossible to wear a kippah without confronting larger social issues and other people's reactions.

I believe, though, that the greatest potential for tikkun olam, for transforming and healing the world, lies in negotiating the space between our spiritual aspirations and the ongoing struggles of daily life. Religious rituals are not a refuge from the rest of existence, but a source of strength and meaning that help us address difficult issues within ourselves and within the world. Openly expressing my religious observance challenges others to reexamine their view of spirituality; wearing a kippah challenges me to translate my deepest beliefs into compassionate action. These are difficult, ongoing struggles, but they are struggles that bring me closer to my community, and closer to G-d.

United Jewish Feminist Front

Loolwa Khazzoom

I WAS BORN INTO AN ORTHODOX JEWISH FAMILY, with an Iraqi Jewish father and a Jewish mother from an American Christian background. When I was five, my father got a new job in Palo Alto, California, so we settled in the closest area with a Jewish day school for me and my sister. I loved my school and adjusted quickly to the new environment; within days, my teachers adored me and I was one of the most popular kids in the class. This utopia came to an abrupt halt, however, when I entered the second grade. At the age of seven, I learned that I would be accepted as an individual and as a Jew on one condition only: that I keep my "ethnic" identity to myself.

That year, my father and older sister had decided it was time for me to learn about my Iraqi Jewish heritage. That this was necessary is a bit ironic, given that I was enrolled in a Jewish school. Are not Jewish children enrolled in Jewish schools specifically for the purpose of learning about their Jewish heritage?

As I came to understand, however, "Jewish" meant "Ashkenazi." It did not mean my heritage, and it did not mean me. Any people and any traditions that were not from Northern Europe were, according to the messages of my childhood, not really Jewish.

For two years, my parents spoke repeatedly to the principal and teachers, pointing out that what they were teaching as Jewish tradition and Jewish law at times conflicted with Mizrahi and Sephardi practices—specifically, with my family's practices at home. The best response the faculty ever gave my parents was indifference.

When I took on my ethnic identity at the age of seven, my teachers suddenly stopped liking me, though I was the same kid they had adored just days before. Now when they talked about Jewish traditions that in truth were only Ashkenazi, I raised my hand and shared the traditions of my family, noting that not everyone practices Judaism the way they were saying. The teachers responded by either denying the truth of my statements or otherwise invalidating them. They made nasty comments about my culture and embarrassed me in front of the class, clearly annoyed at my "audacity" in pointing out the differences in tradition.

"Why do you pray in that book?" one teacher loudly asked in front of the class, after I began reading silently from my Iraqi Jewish prayer book.

"Because it's my tradition," I answered, lowering my eyes, sensing what was coming and feeling both afraid and ashamed. My teacher looked as disgusted as she might have had I been eating live worms. I wanted to hide.

A few weeks later, my classmates and I were in our Humash (Bible) class. The standard practice during this class was that our rabbi would read to us from the Humash in Hebrew then translate it into English. On this particular day, the rabbi recited the following verses, which I knew did not come from any Bible: "It is against Jewish law to pray from a Sephardic prayer book, and it is against Jewish law to pray by yourself." All but one of the students in the class turned to face me and unanimously said, "Shame, shame, shame on you, Loolwa!" My parents took me out of the school that day; I spent the rest of my life in public school.

From then on, my primary Jewish education came from my father—every Shabbat he taught me Mizrahi prayers, religious songs, holy day traditions and rabbinical teachings. Of course, I continued learning the Ashkenazi traditions by default. Outside of my home, in every Jewish synagogue, camp, community organization and community publication, Ashkenazi religion and culture was the standard; by being an involved Jew, I could not help but learn the Ashkenazi way of life.

By the time I was eight years old, I could sing the Shabbat and weekday evening prayers in the traditional Iraqi tunes; I knew dozens of Iraqi Shabbat and holy day songs by heart; and I could sing a good portion of the Haggadah in the Iraqi melodies, both in Hebrew and Judeo-Arabic (the traditional language of many Mizrahim). I loved singing the prayers, and realized the significance of carrying on the tradition. I was able to lead them for my family, and very much wanted to lead the prayers for the synagogue congregation. At such a young age, however, I not only had to confront the Jewish community's racism but sexism among Mizrahim as well.

My father, sister and I went to the only Mizrahi/Sephardi synagogue in San Francisco. With rare exceptions, my sister and I were the only children and two of the very few females who ever showed up. Our dedication was strong; we walked three miles each way, every Shabbat, on Friday night, Saturday morning and Saturday afternoon. If we had been boys, I believe the entire synagogue would have been ecstatic that we were so committed to Judaism and to passing on our heritage. They probably would have encouraged us in every possible way to continue in our Jewish pursuits. But alas, we were only girls, and therefore not allowed to lead any part of the main prayers. After considerable fuss, I was allowed to lead parts of the supplementary prayers, since those didn't really count.

But there was one catch: Once in a blue moon, a boy would walk in, dressed more for a street fight than for the synagogue, barely able to read Hebrew, stumbling and sputtering through the prayers—a boy who barely knew his tradition from Episcopalianism. Any old boy would do. Whenever one came in, he would be instructed to lead the prayers instead of me, and I would be shoved aside. Once, with ten minutes left in the service, a boy walked in just as I was climbing the steps to the *bimah* (podium) to do my thing. One of the men from the synagogue came and literally pulled me off the bimah—I was just a girl. I tried saying something, but the man only grunted at me as if I didn't exist. There was a communal sigh of relief as several men shoved a prayer book in his hand.

I had no meaningful outlet for this pain, no context for it and no power to fight it. My father kept saying it was not fair the way they treated girls, and he comforted me; yet we kept coming to the synagogue. We had no means to rebel against the system, and we didn't walk out on it. I learned that though this treatment was unfair, it was acceptable. So I accepted it.

With Mizrahi and Sephardi culture fading fast in American society, how could this community have ignored the potential of a child so young and so eager to learn and share the traditions?

I knew the men were just waiting for me to reach *bath mouswa* age and be banished to the back of the synagogue forever. But apparently, out of sight was not enough; I had to be muted, as well. Being cast off to the women's section was a devastating and degrading experience for me. After my bath mouswa I was kept from active participation in the synagogue and thereby stripped of what little Jewish freedom I had enjoyed up to that point. Just as the *brith milah* (circumcision) is the sign of a male Jew's covenant with G-d, just as a boy's *bar mouswa* is a visible ritual rite of passage that ushers a boy into his full place in the Jewish community, so, I feel, the act of being confined to the women's section is a physical, visible sign of a woman's shrinking place in the community. Coming of age as a woman is not an honor, but a punishment. Obviously, it was preferable to this community to lose a potential leader, and thereby further sacrifice ethnic continuity, than to encourage a female Middle Eastern Jew to participate fully in services, even lead.

Singing and chanting the prayers was my last shred of connection to the congregation; I sat in the front row of the women's section, hanging as much over the top of the *mehisa* as I could get away with, heartily singing along. Nevertheless, I felt tremendous sadness, anger and hurt from being shut out. By this point, my sister was off in college, so I was almost always the only woman at services. Accordingly, my voice was the only female voice that could be heard. The rabbi then decided that I was not to sing audibly, for that would violate the law of *kol isha* (a woman may not sing alone if she is within hearing distance of men). As I recall from the arguments that ensued, the kol isha practice was not custom in any of the Sephardi and Mizrahi communities from which synagogue members came. As far as my father knew, it was strictly an Ashkenazi practice. Ashkenazi or not, this ruling conveniently served the purposes of the men in our congregation.

We left the synagogue that Shabbat, and I spent the next two years going to Ashkenazi synagogues. I neither participated in those services nor cared to, as those traditions meant nothing to me. When I was fifteen, I stopped attending services altogether.

In the following years, I had additional experiences where Mizrahi and Sephardi communities bent over backwards to ensure that women could not participate in the prayers, learning and leadership. Where it was permissible by our tradition for women to be involved in these activities, the communities adopted Orthodox and ultra-Orthodox Ashkenazi practices so as to guarantee women's exclusion. I was a Mizrahi in an Ashkenazi world, yearning for any drops of my heritage I could find.

Not one to take discrimination lying down, I launched my own efforts to create a multicultural, egalitarian Jewish community. After trying to work through entrenched patriarchal and racist Jewish establishments ("Can we please include one non-Ashkenazi prayer? Please?"), I jumped ship. At twenty, I founded the Student Organization for Jews from Iran and Arab Countries (SOJIAC) at Columbia University and took it to the greater Los Angeles area upon graduation, where it was co-sponsored by local and regional Hillels. Within two years, it was incorporated into the Jewish Federation and given a complementary office. Doing your own thing and then coming back to the mainstream as a force, I discovered, is much better than trying to be a good girl and working within a system set against you.

At twenty-two, I founded the One People, Many Voices coalition—a group of six interdenominational synagogues in the Los Angeles area. The coalition sponsored monthly programs on Mizrahim and Sephardim. Women artists and dancers were invited to teach programs on Mizrahi and Sephardi culture. Women lecturers were invited to speak about their struggles as Mizrahi and Sephardi feminists. I myself led egalitarian Mizrahi/Sephardi services—to my knowledge the first ever in a public setting—and helped teach women the prayers and songs. In all this work, women participated fully at the forefront.

Though all this work was rewarding, it was also painful and exhausting. I was young, female, Mizrahi and (despite it all) asserting myself out of nowhere as a leader in fractured, assimilated or separatist, patriarchal, old-school Mizrahi and Sephardi communities and an Ashkenazi-dominated mainstream. Talk about banging into walls.

As I found, doing cutting-edge work can come with the price tag of losing one's individual voice. Out of necessity, I became the Jewish Multicultural Machine, the cheerleader for the cause, the voice of optimism. There was no room for my story, my pain, my anger or my needs. The vision I was building was so radical and tenuous that it was like a house of cards, too fragile to take the weight of anything "negative."

As an outlet for my voice (and the voices of other Sephardi/Mizrahi women), I decided to create an anthology of Middle Eastern and North African Jewish feminists, "Behind the Veil of Silence." At the time, I only knew of my sister, myself and four other women who fit the bill. But over the years, the anthology served as a magnet. A virtual community gathered on my computer screen, and I found myself facing the heady task of having to turn submissions away because I had too many!

Compiling the anthology was an incredible healing experience. As I read story after story that reflected my world and my experiences, I felt less alone, often crying and shaking as I read. The anthology received interest from numerous publishing companies—ranging from small feminist houses to prestigious university presses. Ultimately, it was rejected by all but two, where it is still under consideration. Each rejection was a reminder of the need for the project. One company wanted the anthology to be "a cross-sectional anthology, including Ashkenazi viewpoints." As far as I'm concerned, that's comparable to saying an anthology on black women's experiences should include the perspectives of white women.

After taking a post-burnout break, I decided to go independent, billing myself as a Jewish multicultural educator—a term and profession I pulled out of my belly button. "What's that?" people always asked, assuming it meant I taught Jews (that is, white people) about multiculturalism (that is, non-Jewish people of color). Two years ago, I did a series of workshops at a local congregation. I liked them, they liked me, and the religious school director and I were both high-energy women. The match seemed perfect to launch my dream project; and when I ran the idea by the director, she was excited about it. As such, the Jewish Multicultural Curriculum Project—a national pilot project to diversify Jewish education—was born.

Through this project, I taught a fifth-grade class of eighty children, creating curriculum on Jews from Ethiopia, the Middle East and North Africa, Central and East Asia, Southern Europe, Central and South America and Northern Europe. Wherever possible, I brought female figures to the fore, to the extent that the boys in the class called me a sexist, accusing me of liking girls more.

"Yeah," I laughed, "you're right. But don't worry, it will balance out in your lifetime."

While studying Ethiopian Jews, students spent a month learning about Queen Makeda, the queen of Sheba (ancient Ethiopia) and mother of the Ethiopian Jewish community. Our guest speaker on the unit—a scholar on Queen Makeda—was an African-American Jewish woman. When the Iranian family of one of my students came to present on Jewish life in Iran, I continuously asked the women questions, countering the tendency for them to sit quietly while the men did the talking. While studying Mizrahim, students learned about Asenath Barzani, a female rabbi of the late sixteenth and early seventeenth centuries—a Kurdish (today, Iraqi) Jew and head of a yeshiva. Students also learned about how Middle Eastern men preferred fat women—my way of countering the looming body-image problems awaiting the girls.

I did the best I could with the information and resources I had, but so much more needs to be collected. The historical and cultural assumptions in Jewish feminist books and organizations reflect the homogeneity of Ashkenazi heritage—and often don't even acknowledge the existence of Jewish women from Iraq, Yemen, Morocco, Libya or Iran, let alone our rich background or the complex issues we face.

What does this lack of representation mean for our identity as Jewish feminists? Where is our community? Where do we go? Perhaps the existing movement should be called the Ashkenazi feminist movement, just to be honest. And since we cannot turn to it for information about non-Ashkenazi women, maybe we should create a separatist movement for ourselves.

In Israel, Mizrahi women took that step a few years ago, and I was there. Tired of exclusion and condescension from the entrenched Ashkenazi feminist leadership, HILA (an equal-rights organization working in the predominantly Mizrahi and Ethiopian inner cities of Israel) sponsored the first feminist conference for indigenous Middle Eastern and African Jewish women.

"Welcome, *Chah'chahim!*" the leaders crooned at the opening. They were met with an uproar of applause, whistles, laughter and adulation. "Chah'chah" is the ultimate patronizing word describing Mizrahim, embodying the primitive/low-class/tasteless/barbaric image Ashkenazim have ascribed to working-class Mizrahim in Israel. Through this tongue-in-cheek use of the word, it lost its power and became a joke on the Ashkenazim. This charged moment was just the beginning of the first political gathering in my life where my agenda was *the* agenda.

The conference had many rich clashes and volatile arguments throughout the weekend, showing how desperately we had needed the opportunity to "talk amongst ourselves," to move beyond our struggle for basic recognition from Ashkenazim. We delved into topics like the relationship between Ethiopian and Mizrahi women, Mizrahi and Palestinian women, Mizrahi women in Israel and the diaspora, religious and secular Mizrahi women. I found myself crying frequently and gaining strength through each difficult experience, becoming bolder and more outspoken with each round. When I attended Jewish feminist gatherings in the States, I consistently felt alienated, frustrated and somewhat withdrawn as a non-Ashkenazi; at this conference I was fully present and engaged. What a relief to be able to let my hair down and be me, transcending the need to play a role with my standard line, "Um, excuse me, we're not all Ashkenazi."

Of course, every movement has its challenges and blind spots. In this case, I wondered how transformative the conference was for the Ethiopian women, since the Mizrahi agenda seemed to dominate. Though there was a significant Ethiopian presence, there were only a couple of workshops addressing Ethiopian community concerns. I asked one of the Ethiopian women how she felt about this. She was adamant that she felt included and connected; I wondered if she felt that way because the conference was one of the only places in Israel that Ethiopian women were noticed, period. Growing up, I remember flying into fits of glee and gratitude upon simply hearing a leader mention the *existence* of non-Ashkenazi Jews.

Whether the representation was as good as it could have been or not, it was the best there was at the time, and in that sense, revolutionary. The conference participants and organizers nonetheless got a lot of flak from the Ashkenazi feminist leadership, who apparently thought it was racist for us to organize by, for and about ourselves. Then again, men around the world were threatened when women first began organizing the feminist movement. Perhaps this mix of anger and fear is to be expected. But despite the initial friction, the conference helped to shift the radical power imbalance between the Ashkenazi and non-Ashkenazi feminist leaders.

After years of fighting and negotiating, Mizrahi, Ashkenazi and Arab feminist leadership came together four years later, for a united national feminist conference. I had the good fortune of being in Israel the summer before the conference and thus was able to participate in planning meetings. The idea was to split the conference into four equal time slots. Everyone at the conference would spend the first quarter going to Ashkenazi-led workshops, the second quarter going to Mizrahi-led workshops, the third quarter going to lesbian-led workshops and the fourth going to Arab-led workshops.

Initially, I thought the third division was to be Ethiopian, not lesbian. I did not find out until the conference began that an Ethiopian piece did not exist, which I found both illogical and disturbing. By dividing the conference slots along the lines of ethnicity but excluding a significant Israeli ethnic group, I felt that the voices of Ethiopian women were rendered invisible—despite the conference's aim of cultural unity.

A few months later, nestled in my Berkeley habitat, I bought a ticket back to Israel for the conference. But the problems had just begun.

"Loolwa," the Mizrahi women's facilitator wrote in an email just days later, "The Ashkenazi women freaked out about having to present under the banner 'Ashkenazi.' They want to present under a general feminist banner and have us do 'special interest workshops.' After a two-hour fight with them, I walked out of the meeting. I'm not going to the conference, and I have to check with the other women in the group about what they want to do."

Ashkenazi women presenting under the banner of "Ashkenazi" was exactly what I loved about the conference organization. For once, everyone would be crystal clear about whom they represented. Why couldn't the Ashkenazi women deal with speaking only for themselves? What was so threatening to them about Mizrahi women having our own space? Ultimately, with the threat of a Mizrahi boycott looming overhead, the matter was settled, and the conference organization returned to its original plan. But the issue remained unresolved. The Ashkenazi panelists continuously questioned why they should have to speak under an Ashkenazi grouping, given that they did not feel particularly "Ashkenazi."

"I'm just Israeli," they all said. Repeatedly, Mizrahi women in the audience stood up and expressed how the Ashkenazi women did not feel particularly "Ashkenazi" because everything around them reflected an Ashkenazi reality as standard.

"You may not see how Ashkenazi you are," I told the panelists, "but as a Mizrahi woman, I do see how Ashkenazi you are. Even the fact that you resist speaking under an Ashkenazi grouping shows me how Ashkenazi you are. And as an Ashkenazi woman, you cannot speak for me."

Even at a workshop for healing relations between Ashkenazi and Mizrahi women, the argument continued. One very quiet woman, the only Mizrahi employed by a key feminist organization in Israel, surprised people by breaking down in tears while conveying how important it was to have equal slots for representation. "It's always Ashkenazi," she said. "Finally, here, for the first time, I feel represented."

Down the circle, as Ashkenazi women continued to complain, a Mizrahi woman interjected, "Look across the room. A woman is crying over there because this is her first experience being represented! Listen to what the Mizrahi women are saying. Listen to how important and rare this experience is for us!"

Interestingly enough, the Ashkenazi women's workshops all seemed to focus on addressing Ashkenazi racism towards non-Ashkenazim. Whereas I feel it is of the utmost importance to have such workshops, it does not do me any good to see Ashkenazi feminists swing from being blindly racist, patronizing or ignorant to beating their chests, guilt-ridden. I want to see social action and respect for non-Ashkenazi women side by side with self-love among Ashkenazi women. To cancel out one with the other is to continue pitting us against ourselves.

Just a few weeks ago, I was informed that a working-class Mizrahi women's organization has been started in Israel, and a Yemenite friend and I plan to coordinate and co-lead the first ever Mizrahi High Holiday service for women in Israel. So many changes since I was a little girl! We are definitely moving in the right direction, but we're not settled yet.

A few years ago, I helped organize and lead the first-ever egalitarian Mizrahi/Sephardi Rosh Hashanah and Yom Kippur services. They were successful beyond our wildest dreams. By Yom Kippur, there was standing room only, and people were spilling out into the hallway. Because of the obvious excitement about these services, the organizers and leaders went on to follow up on it with a monthly egalitarian Mizrahi Shabbat service.

Currently, I know of just three Mizrahi rabbis who are women and one Mizrahi rabbi-in-training who is a woman. All of these women have faced the choice of either not becoming a rabbi or attending a thoroughly Ashkenazi institution to become ordained. My understanding is that all but one of the Mizrahi and Ethiopian women in rabbinical school in Israel dropped out because they could not stand the Ashkenazicentrism. Others would not even apply for the same reason. Must non-Ashkenazim reinvent the wheel to see ourselves reflected in progressive rabbinic and cantorial schools? Must we take the separatist route and develop our own institutions? Or can the existing progressive Jewish movements open their arms just a little bit more, to embrace all progressive Jews?

An ethnically inclusive rabbinical school would teach the halakha and the traditions of Jewish communities from Argentina to Zimbabwe; texts would include the teachings of the Kes (Jewish priests) of Ethiopia, the Hachamim (sages) of India, and the Kabbalists (mystics) of Spain. Cantorial classes would include Jewish liturgy from Brazil and Afghanistan. History classes would include the story of the lost tribe in Zimbabwe and the recently converted community in Peru. The school would be oriented toward seeking out the special treasure each community offers and delight in its wisdom. Staff would include Jewish scholars from China, cantors from Yemen and priests from Ethiopia, and students would reflect Jewish faces from around the world.

So many Mizrahi, Sephardi, Ethiopian and Central/East Asian Jewish women I know are doing their parts, each on the issues about which they are passionate. We cannot and should not do this work alone. I do not want to see a separatist split between Ashkenazi and non-Ashkenazi women, progressive Ashkenazi and progressive non-Ashkenazi movements. Despite the betrayal and pain of inner strife over the past fifty years, I still believe in *klal Yisrael*—a united Jewish people.

So I call on you to open your eyes and see the many colors of Jewish women. Open your ears and listen to our voices. Open your hearts and take in our stories. There are so many fronts on which our Jewish community needs to heal. Put your hand in ours, and let's heal together.

ON BEING A JEWISH FEMINIST VALLEY GIRL

TOBIN BELZER

I WAS ONE OF SIX JEWISH TEENS in my high school to return from summer vacation with a new nose. On the first day of school, we gathered in the hallway to examine one another's profile, compare costs and enjoy our post-operative popularity. A surgically modified nose was a source of pride amid the white, upper middle-class Jewish students at my high school in the San Fernando Valley. It was my first American Jewish rite of passage.

It was the mid-1980s. Middle-class Americans were prospering in the booming Reagan-era economy, and conspicuous consumption was heralded as the nation's favorite pastime. Financial prosperity was the only economic climate I'd ever known. Until the emergence of the Valley Girl and Jewish American Princess (JAP) stereotypes, I thought everyone shared my aspirations: to be thin and rich. I didn't know that Valley Girl was only the first of many identities I would eventually embrace. I had never heard of women's studies and I'd never met a feminist. I could barely imagine myself in college, much less as a doctoral candidate in sociology. And I never dreamed that I would eventually leave L.A.

At fifteen, I had become almost completely acculturated to Valley Girl life. In the San Fernando Valley—often referred to as simply "the Valley"—having a perfect body was an achievement. I listened to advice from Hollywood and advertising agencies; I believed I would be lovable if I bought the right products. Taking control of my appearance felt empowering, so I shopped and shopped and *shopped*. In my quest for self-improvement, I waxed, painted and polished every inch of my body, changing every part of my self that I could. Cosmetic surgery was my ultimate acquiescence to societal norms about beauty.

Like many of my friends, I contended with Eastern European genes: I was hairy. And since the portrait of ideal womanhood had no discernible body hair, I felt doomed. Remaking myself required a tremendous amount of time, money and effort. I spent countless hours every week removing hair from my body and face, waxing my legs and upper lip, shaving my underarms and trimming my nose hair. My eyebrows were arched and my eyelashes tinted. I had the hairs on my chin permanently removed through electrolysis. And I bought expensive products to cleanse, moisturize and style the kinky Jewish hair on my head.

Grooming was so central to the daily life of a Valley Girl that it evolved into a social event. Once a week, I met my friends at a salon after school to socialize while our nails were manicured. When one of us got our hair cut, the others accompanied her. We did each other's makeup and traded clothes. We attended Weight Watchers meetings and encouraged each other to stick to our diets. We cared for one another by cooperatively improving our appearances.

My friends and I hung out at the mall in packs. We educated each other about the importance of wearing the right clothes and owning the right accessories. As Valley Girls, we luxuriated in our weekly grooming sessions, which we affectionately called "girl bonding time." When I later discovered a feminist community, I was already accustomed to women-centered spheres. Shopping, grooming and dieting are, after all, female-dominated activities.

In my family, Judaism was our ethnicity, but our religion was dieting. We had our own version of keeping kosher: At home, we ate only low-calorie food, but outside the house, we ate anything we wanted. While my peers went to Hebrew school, I went to a nutritionist; I knew that I was learning the more valuable dietary laws. Like everyone I knew, I attempted to transform my body into that of the ideal Anglo woman. I believed that if I were able to fit into the right clothes, I would be popular and happy, I weighed myself twice a day.

Everything around me encouraged and promoted my behavior. In 1982, radio stations played Moon Unit Zappa's parody, "Valley Girl," nonstop; the song title gave a name to the culture I had already internalized. Girls my age made the 1983 movie *Valley Girl* a smash hit. For a brief moment in American history, the Valley Girl became a cultural icon. The Valley was no longer just a place to live; it was a way to be. Bolstered by the media's frenzy, Valley Girl culture saturated mainstream culture. Valley Girl slang became a national fad. The sound bite "Oh, my, gawd!" was heard around the country.

The media hype surrounding Valley Girl culture simultaneously celebrated and mocked us. We were sold products to accentuate our Valley Girl identities while we were ridiculed for our excessive consumerism. Our enthusiastic engagement in mall culture made us famous, but we were disparaged because Valley Girl life was void of the trappings of high culture. Both class- and race-based anxieties were embedded in the criticism of Valley Girls' lack of refinement. The Valley Girl was born in L.A.'s largest suburban Jewish community; Valley Girls were daughters of the Jewish nouveau riche. The stereotype was the most recent permutation of the age-old condemnation of Jews for being crass and money-grubbing.

On the East Coast, the anti-Semitic nature of the insult was less thinly veiled. Girls with our characteristics were called Jewish American Princesses (JAPs); the labels gained popularity simultaneously. Like the Valley Girl, the JAP moniker began as a fairly mild stereotype depicting the over-indulged daughter of newly prosperous parents. A JAP wanted to date the right guy and dress according to magazine styles; she drove an expensive car and used multiple credit cards. Like Valley Girls, JAPs had a dialect that included the exclamation "Oh my gawd!"

JAP jokes were everywhere. (Q: How many JAPs does it take to change a light bulb? A: Two. One to get the Diet Coke and one to call Daddy.) The jokes evolved into JAP-bashing, which erupted on college campuses. Jewish girls were maligned, held up as warnings of what becomes of those who try to acquire social status through consumerism.

On the more tolerant West Coast, we Valley Girls escaped the overt prejudice that accompanied the JAP label; the geography-based nature of the Valley Girl label made the anti-Semitism embedded in the stereotype less obvious. Since the anti-Jewish sentiment remained unnamed, identifying the malice in the stereotype was more difficult.

I was not able to recognize the extent of the psychic damage that I incurred because of this until I left the Valley at age twenty-three. By then I had realized that I would never be thin enough or rich enough, so I decided to leave L.A. altogether. I enrolled in graduate school at Brandeis University in Massachusetts because I was eager to discover another way of life.

Everything I knew about the East Coast I had learned in movies, so I was unprepared for the extent of the cultural differences I would encounter in Boston. I felt like a foreign exchange student. My peers did not wear makeup or openly obsess about their weight. They did not exchange Hollywood gossip, and they detested the mall. I learned that people from the East Coast proudly despised everything about L.A. In order to fit in, I believed I had to disavow the city of my birth, so I enthusiastically colluded with East Coast natives who were eager to delineate the depravity of Los Angeles. I stopped wearing lipstick and I rarely visited the mall.

In some ways, Valley Girl culture had prepared me for the world of East Coast academia. As a Valley Girl, complaining was one of my fundamental methods of communication. As a feminist, I'm empowered to complain. I'm as comfortable now naming a social injustice as I was sending a salad back when the dressing was not "on the side."

The constant criticism of one's self and peers was fundamental to both Jewish and Valley Girl cultures. So even before I became a feminist sociologist, I acquired substantial training in the art of social critique. Acquiring a feminist consciousness and a sociological awareness in graduate school enabled me to turn my critical voice outward, and use that ability to better understand the social world. I began to examine my world through the lenses of race, class and gender. I learned to analyze behavior by looking at social context as well as an individual's actions. In my research as a Jewish feminist sociologist, I aim to dispel stereotypes and correct the misconceptions about young Jewish women.

My stories about L.A. never fail to shock my friends from the East Coast. And my stories about the East Coast are similarly received by my friends from the Valley. When I told my graduate student friends about a new pubic hair waxing fad that was popular in L.A., they were horrified. And when I showed my West Coast friends the alternative menstrual product I bought at a co-op in Cambridge, they thought I was kidding. I feel like an intermediary between two foreign lands. I am simultaneously at home in, and alien to, each world I inhabit.

As a Jewish feminist Valley Girl, I am trying to honor my multiple selves while acknowledging the contradictions inherent in doing so. This can be tricky. My conflicting reactions to the Lewinsky/Clinton scandal are particularly illustrative. My response developed as an internal battle between my differing selves. I was fascinated by the fact that a voluptuous, sassy Jewish girl from L.A. was the focus of international news. I was also excited: the President of the United States was attracted to a girl who was practically my peer. If Bill was attracted to Monica, I reasoned, that meant that the ruler of the free world could be attracted to me!

At the same time, as a young Jewish woman from L.A., I felt embarrassed to be represented by Monica. In the media's eyes, she embodied everything disgusting about being Jewish, wealthy and female. She was depicted as a spoiled-rotten princess whose father (a Jewish doctor) gave her everything. Her appearance, as well as her behavior, was critiqued. She was charged with using her father's influence to forward her career, but she was also accused of sleeping her way to the top. She was described as young, naive and stupid, but was also seen as a manipulative temptress. I regarded the scandal as a reminder that a woman's most potent power is her ability to be sexually objectified (but when she uses that power, she will be vilified).

Even though Monica grew up in Beverly Hills, she was often referred to as a Valley Girl by the press. She was never called a Jewish American Princess. While the two terms are practically synonymous, the use of JAP is no longer socially acceptable. During the late 1980s, Jewish feminists condemned the JAP stereotype as anti-Semitic and sexist. In 1987, *Lilith* magazine devoted its fall issue to analyses of the problem.

After much deliberation, the organized Jewish community made a systematic effort to publicly condemn the image. Jews were called upon to abandon the stereotype, and by the 1990s, JAP T-shirts, buttons, humor books and the like had largely disappeared. The media was cautious when referring to any aspect of Monica's Jewish background. "Valley Girl" was used to evoke the same anti-Semitic sentiment of the JAP epithet without the political or social consequences of using that term directly.

When Monica finally agreed to an exclusive interview with Barbara Walters, I realized, with a moment of pride, that two Jewish women would be the focus of the world's attention. I waited enthusiastically, both to hear Monica's voice and to see what she would be wearing. It was the first time I would learn about her experience from her perspective.

Monica had obviously had a makeover in preparation for the interview. She wore a pink sweater and pink lipstick, and I wondered, from my feminist perspective, if she had been advised to look as feminine and innocent as possible. Yet at the same time, I found myself admiring how meticulously her eyebrows had been manicured, and I wondered which Beverly Hills salon she had visited. I also speculated about where I could purchase that fabulous lipstick. From my friends in L.A., I learned that I was not the only one; after the broadcast, that shade was impossible to find. During the interview, Monica seemed young and insecure. But when she described her sexual experiences with President Clinton, her eyes lit up and her body language became animated. Her nervousness turned to mania. It was clear that she derived a great deal of self-esteem from her sexual prowess. I felt sorry for her, remembering a time in my life when I, too, believed that my self-worth depended on my sexual attractiveness to men. I realized that she was simply adhering to the same lessons I had learned as a girl growing up in L.A.

During my East Coast experience, I acquired a feminist consciousness and met a wonderful therapist. During Monica's East Coast experiences, she acquired a stained blue dress and the negative attention of the nation. Instead of learning to love her body, she made a million-dollar deal with Jenny Craig. I felt grateful for our differing experiences, but saddened by the fact that Monica did not fare as well as I had.

Embracing my Jewish feminist Valley Girl identity has allowed me to honor all sides of my self. As a Valley Girl, I had paid meticulous attention to altering my appearance. When I became a feminist, I decided to learn to love and honor my body, rather than investing all of my energy in trying to improve it. Instead, I set out to change the world. My Valley Girl identity enables me to feel entitled to complain, while my feminist identity compels me to acknowledge the class- and race-based privilege behind that entitlement. As a Jewish feminist, I acknowledge the importance of community and the significance of history while working to critique and correct the myopic attitudes that pervade American Jewish culture.

I have challenged myself to accept the positive aspects from each of my cultures and to leave behind the qualities that are not useful. I now know that critiquing my identities does not necessarily mean rejecting them completely. I listen to National Public Radio as religiously as I read *People* magazine. I critique pop culture through a feminist lens and regard fashion with a Valley Girl sensibility. I am a lipstick enthusiast who detests the beauty industry. And I am a young Jewish leader whose Jewish nose has been altered.

I am one of scores of young Jewish women who use our privilege to make the world a better place. We have defiantly refused to be hindered by stereotypes. In doing so, we are learning to honor the inevitable contradictory realities that come from occupying multiple identities. I wear my contradictions proudly: in my heart, in my mind and on my face.

Sacred Rose

BEFORE THERE WERE WORDS OR MILK or even Mom there was Grandma Rose. She was the first family member ever to see me, retrieving me from the arms of my birth mother's father while Mom and Dad waited nervously in the car. She turned wool into sweaters, powder into cakes, tantrums into paroxysms of laughter. She brought me all the books I could ever want, and let me eat my breakfast cereal with an espresso spoon. She soothed me to peacefulness, the tips of her fingernails gliding softly over my shoulder blades. I worshipped her.

Unlike my parents, whose job it was to make sure I was constantly improving, Grandma Rose's job was to accept me as I was, to revere my gawky little self as a perfect mitzvah (blessing). As much as I detested my untimely hips and those crabapples on my chest, that's how much she loved them. I think she may have been the only one who did.

As the first grandchild I could do no wrong, even when I picked a vase full of dandelions from the front lawn, bringing in hundreds of tiny white aphids to infest her kitchen, or when my aunt's joking caused me to laugh so hard that grape juice came out my nose, all over the white seder tablecloth. Grandma Rose believed that all my traits were special and unique—even the ones that were less socially acceptable. And the one thing she wanted in return, the one thing she wanted most, was to see her eldest granddaughter bat mitzvahed. I couldn't wait to take the *bimah* and show her what kind of strong, solid woman she'd helped to create.

And then one night the phone rang—a darker, more ominous ring than usual—and the heavens broke in half as my mother howled, "Mommy!" with an anguish I wish I could forget. Grandma Rose didn't make it home from the airport, returning from her brother's funeral. It was as though someone had extinguished my guiding star. It was nine months before my thirteenth birthday.

After Grandma Rose, there was Mr. Max Friedman. Every Tuesday afternoon he'd park his Buick next to our manicured hedges and shuffle up to our door in his heavy black shoes. I'd be waiting for him at the piano, Grandma's piano, practicing the haftarah in my tentative soprano. Mr. Friedman's hands were made of hardened wax and his cheeks of translucent paper, and he smelled vaguely of mothballs. His ancient voice wavered but never cracked as he chanted in his Old World accent.

Together, Mr. Max Friedman and Grandma's piano prepared me for my first Torah blessing, singing each phrase of each prayer for me to repeat. When it wasn't a bitter irony it was a small consolation, having Grandma's piano to sing to me so I could learn my prayers. I spent hours and hours praying, chanting those ancient melodies, and hoping as hard as I could that God would hear me and come and speak to me, now that I needed Him more than ever. I had no idea what I hoped He would say; I only knew that the hollow echo of those desiccated prayers was certainly not it.

By the time I ascended the bimah, looking for all the world like a groomless bride with a smile full of shiny silver braces, I knew it all cold, every note. Like every other test I'd ever taken, I'd studied more than enough and was prepared to get an A. And I did. The rabbi nodded approvingly and my parents beamed proudly as their little girl sang open the Holy Book and read from its holy pages.

When it came time to address the congregation, I gave neither an analysis of my Torah portion nor a treatise on world hunger. Instead, I dedicated the day to Grandma Rose. As I invoked my grandmother's memory and my aunts and uncles and cousins sobbed softly into their handkerchiefs, I knew Rose was getting her wish—to attend my bat mitzvah—even though we'd dance the hora without her that afternoon.

I still remember looking up at the ceiling at that moment, as I finished speaking, past the tasteful chandeliers of our suburban New York synagogue, and feeling somehow unsettled. I heard no majestic trumpets that day. I saw no visions of robed seraphim amongst swirling clouds; my hair wasn't blown by doves taking flight. I felt no golden gates swing open to welcome me, no mighty arm outstretched to bless me. I had a bat mitzvah—but God didn't come. When all the dancing and feasting was done, I went to bed feeling betrayed, with a cold knot in my heart that no one could touch.

That cold knot flared into a persistent burning when I told my parents that I wouldn't be returning to Hebrew school after the bat mitzvah. I can't remember what version of the truth I told them, but I'm pretty sure I didn't say that God had deserted me and I was angry about it. I certainly didn't tell them (and I'm not even sure I realized) that I needed to figure out what I believed now that God hadn't come before I could, in good conscience, participate in Judaism.

The problem, of course, was whom I had been waiting for. It didn't make sense to me to worship a vengeful old man who lived in the sky and obviously didn't have time for the likes of me, someone I had to impress regardless or face His wrathful retribution—but I'd been waiting for Him anyway. I'd been as afraid of his showing up, I realized, as of his not showing up.

I spent many hours sitting in my bedroom with the door shut, staring out the window with a forgotten textbook open in my lap, thinking about holy and magical things. I spent almost as many hours laying on my stomach in the basement of the local library, poring over dusty volumes written by dead people about gods that seemed equally dead. That's when I found sacredness—a reflection of my own intellect and spirit staring boldly at me from the pages of a yellowing paperback.

The voice of sacredness was all at once fingers on a harpsichord, honey dissolving in mint tea, the roaring of the tide over the rocks. She told me that God didn't live only in a synagogue or church, but also in mountains and trees and the woman who cleaned our house and the chamomile that sprouted between the cracks in the sidewalk—and that God had a vagina, just like I did. She told me that one does not become a spiritual leader through self-denial, but through experience tempered with responsibility, and solid ties to a community. She told me that I was responsible for my own growth and healing, my own divinity. When she whispered in my ear, the words resounded in my chest—as though I'd spoken them myself.

My relationship with my sacredness developed more intensely than did any of my other first loves. I talked to her, questioned her, played my flute for her, nursed at her breast and brought her offerings of sonnets and sketches and virginity. I learned to create a temple on the beach, in the forest or even in the library, to create sacred space with the force of my own intent. I was awed and humbled at the redwoods in their grove, by a perfect blood orange, a hummingbird's flight, Brahms' *Tragic Overture*. I attended synagogue only under duress, and when I did I went in silence, refusing to speak what I perceived as dead prayers to a dead God. I stopped calling myself Jewish.

Early one spring, many years later, I was sweeping the cobwebs out of the corners of my apartment when I came upon a cardboard box gathering dust on a top shelf. What I found when I opened it brought me to my knees: photos of me at age four, lighting the Shabbat candles with my mother's assistance, designating that time as sacred time; recipes for the potato kugel and matzo ball soup that we had prepared for our loved ones; the menorah I lit in my college dormitory, with new friends who'd never seen a Jew before; the empty glass from the *yahrzeit* candle I'd left burning in my sink all day, every year on the third of November—the day my grandmother didn't come home.

All these were rituals that I had been enacting faithfully for so many years, at my mother's side and on my own, stubbornly insisting all the while that Judaism was my ethnicity and not my spirituality. These were rituals Mom, in turn, had learned from Grandma Rose, who had learned them from her mother, who had brought them over from Russia in steamer trunks full of hope.

What I found, finally, was Judaism. I had kept it safe, kept it nourished, kept it alive for all those years without knowing it, wrapped in my love for my own sacredness—and in my grandmother's blanket. But it isn't a Judaism that sits up on the shelf next to the china plates that are too good to use, or that I need to keep covered in a plastic slipcover to protect it from wear. It is a Judaism as mystical and practical as Great-Grandma's candlesticks—and Grandma's piano. My grandmother's memory—and my mother's persistence—brought spark to a flame that had been all but extinguished, and humility to a proud and privileged woman who thought she knew it all. When next I sit with loved ones around the seder table, I will open the door and set an extra place for my Grandma Rose.

The "Big O" Also Means "Olam"

HANNE BLANK

THE EMAIL CAME FROM EUROPE, from a medical doctor, asking me if I could tell him Judaism's stance on condom use. This wasn't unusual: I'm a sexuality writer and educator who helps run a suite of sex-positive, woman-owned websites. I also write sexuality columns online and off-, so I receive a fair number of questions about more or less esoteric aspects of sex. When it comes to Jewish sexuality, laws and customs, I'm an amateur scholar who tries hard to stay reasonably well-educated. I've written one or two articles about aspects of sexuality as they relate to Judaism, and periodically I get a query about something Jewish and sexual. Confronted with this one, I checked a few sources, then wrote back.

"There is no unified opinion on condom usage within Judaism," I began, since I have often had to clarify that Judaism doesn't have a papacy or other central body that issues decrees on these sorts of things. "Different rabbis and communities have different stances on condom usage as well as other forms of contraception. I urge you to contact, or have the person on whose behalf you are writing contact, a qualified local rabbi, as I cannot predict what a given Jewish community's standards or practices will be like."

Then I continued, noting that Orthodox Jews do not tend to condone the use of condoms, since they feel that anything that results in throwing away semen is tantamount to the Sin of Onan (depositing one's seed on the ground). I also mentioned that this was just one opinion, and that on the whole, since condoms are useful for more than just contraception and have a good track record for preventing disease, many rabbis are happy to permit them.

Imagine my surprise when, the very next morning, I received a reply. The doctor who'd written me was apparently an ardent anti-condom activist, and he ranted on at some length about how condoms actually contribute to the spread of HIV/AIDS and cause uterine cancer and all sorts of other things. This was enough to have me scratching my head. But then he wrote something that just left me speechless. He told me that by not endorsing his (and Orthodoxy's) anti-condom stance and preaching it far and wide from my sex educator's bully pulpit, I was clearly not a good Jew. I was furious, but realized a reply would get me nowhere. I shelved the letter and went on with my day, but the fury lingered. How dare he tell me that promoting condom use was tantamount to betraying Judaism?

"I'm not betraying Judaism," I wanted to yell, "I'm living it!" To me, part of what it means to be a Jew is to promote social change, to educate, to work to better people's lives. Part of the reason I do sexuality work, in fact, is because I am Jewish, and because my *yiddishe neshoma,* my Jewish soul, hates to see the pain and misery that so often and so avoidably stems from human sexuality. As a Jewish sex educator and writer, I sometimes feel pinned between Jewish tradition and halakha on one side, secular tradition and law on the other and, on all sides, the primal human facts of bodies, desire, pleasure, pain and a need for information and education. Negotiating some middle ground where I can help build a basis for a better understanding of sexuality, and perhaps a more nuanced and humane understanding of what is possible for us as sexual beings, is a difficult task and, I think, a Jewish one. Other Jews choose to do their activism in fields such as worker's rights, civil rights for racial and ethnic minorities, Zionism, poverty. I've chosen to do mine in the very nontraditional realm of sexuality, but for the same reasons: Lives are bettered by it.

I've also chosen to do it because it's personal, controversial and, frankly, difficult. I like a challenge. Neither traditional Judaism nor other traditional approaches to sexuality have proven themselves adequate for the amazingly complex task of honoring and teaching it in all its breadth and depth. Judaism's long and rich history of sexual law and custom has its glorious moments, moments of romance and poetry and remarkable logic. It also has instances of stomach-churning sexism, homophobia, and a tendency to make discussions of sexuality outside the context of marriage so taboo that it becomes next to impossible to discuss sex at all. Talking about sex isn't proper, it isn't modest, and it isn't something that nice girls are supposed to do. We're barely even supposed to have it, and we'd better be married when we do. Jewish mamas don't let their babies grow up to be sexual beings who are invested in their own sexuality. They certainly don't let them grow up to be sex educators.

I think that's part of the reason I did, but it wasn't simple rebelliousness that led me here. I, like most other people, reached a point in my life where I needed sexual information, needed to be able to talk about sexuality and not be judged, and after a time I started to work toward providing that for others through sexuality-related outreach. I wanted to believe that when it came to sexuality, simple openness and the ability to speak out in our secular twentieth-century way would eventually cure people of their fear, their small-mindedness, their selfishness and their pain. But over the years, I realized that simply having an arsenal of medical and scientific facts at one's disposal or the ability to discuss sexuality openly didn't necessarily solve the real problems of sexuality any better than shrouding it in layers of misty religious "modesty" and moralistic lockjaw. The truth, however, was simple and confounding: It wasn't enough. Just having the facts is not enough. Speaking honestly about sexuality is not enough. Educating people in a way that makes it possible for them to act more ethically and lovingly toward themselves and others when it comes to sex requires more than that. Much more.

To teach about sexuality is to teach about being human. Object lessons in humility and responsibility, vulnerability and generosity, fear and joy are all part of the package. Anatomy and physiology are the basics. The rest is all human frailties and abilities. Sex is complex. It isn't just "tab A in slot B," and it can't be dumbed down to universally applicable answers. Teaching about sexuality, and doing it well and responsibly, requires a traditionally Jewish viewpoint. One must be learned. One must be prepared to evaluate individual situations carefully. One must know the background. One must be humane. One must be prepared to argue and to entertain divergent opinions. One must bring to it, in short, a perspective not too different from that of a skilled and insightful Talmudist.

In practice, that means that honesty comes first, even when that honesty means complexity: answers that are neither necessarily ideal nor complete. When the doctor who sent me the emails about condoms initially contacted me, I would've loved to have been able to answer him by writing, "Sure, absolutely, Jews use condoms! Jews aren't stupid. Jews think you should use condoms or other applicable barrier methods every time you have sex." But that would've been a self-serving answer, not an honest one—an answer designed to quickly satisfy my own priorities as a proponent of safer sex. Similarly, when I deal with a sixteen-year-old whose hormones are raging and who is self-admittedly desperate to get laid, I can't just say, "Oh, it's your hormones, you'll get over it. Go masturbate." Instead, I try to discuss all the possibilities, from masturbation to mutually desired casual sex to relationships that become exploitive because one partner is only in it for the nookie, letting the potential complexity of the situation make itself obvious and the ethical and personal conundrums come to light. When I get a horny sixteen-year-old kid to pause for a moment and consider what might be best for him or her in the long run, when I get that kid to give some thought to what he or she really wants to do with all that roiling sexual energy, when I can put emphasis on the options that are nonexploitive and least likely to cause pain but still leave room for choice—that, to me, is teaching sexuality Jewishly.

Teaching people to value ethical behavior, ethical impulses and ethical consideration of their fellow human beings over the classification of individual actions as arbitrarily good or bad is as Jewish as the Pirke Avot (Ethics of our Fathers). It is, as I see it, perhaps the best way for us to teach sexuality Jewishly, and it is the only way for us, as Jews, to recognize nontraditional aspects of sexuality. When, as recently happened, a fifteen-year-old boy writes to me asking, "I'm Jewish and I'm wondering, what is kosher sex?" I feel that an adequate answer is not the easy, hasty retreat into the dos and don'ts of halakha. Rather, an adequate answer addresses issues such as respect, the mutual good of the partners involved, care, sharing, vulnerability, risk, contraception, *minhag* (community standards and practices), honesty, communication and physical, emotional and reproductive responsibility. And then, after all that, perhaps it's time for a halakhic discussion about the fact that there are many things that aren't (on the surface, and particularly to a fifteen-year-old in this culture at this time) involved in the letter of the Jewish law that should be part of making Jewish decisions about sex. Even without the halakhic aspect, Jewish sex education regards sexuality as an inseparable aspect of the entirety of our lives, with ethical and personal dynamics that extend far beyond any isolated act.

This kind of teaching is necessary, both in the interest of educational honesty and in the interest of how we live our lives in the world as Jews, as people who love and lust. I'm hardly the first person to notice that traditional Judaic thought and writings simply do not provide adequate responses to issues such as women's sexual independence, homosexuality, bisexuality, transsexuality, nongenital sexual activity (such as fetishes and BDSM—bondage, dominance, sadism and masochism—in its many forms), intergender/intersex issues (that is, regarding people born with indeterminate physical or chromosomal gender), sex toys such as vibrators or dildos or even freely chosen sexuality that takes place outside of (or without the presence of) marriage.

For traditional Judaism, and as encapsulated in the *taharat mishpachah*, or laws of family purity, sexuality begins and ends with married heterosexuality, with a healthy dose of menstrual taboo (the law has strict limits on when during the menstrual cycle married couples are permitted to be sexual). In Ashkenazi Orthodox communities, there is a large body of custom that has built up around this as well, on both the community level and across the board (Mizrahi and Sephardi communities have many similar practices, customs and standards, but I am most familiar with the Ashkenazi). It is not uncommon, for instance, for Ashkenazi Orthodox men and women to practice *shomer negiyah*, which mandates that no unmarried persons of the opposite sex shall touch one another. In general, the idea is that by limiting sexuality to marriage, and even then, within certain times, we discipline our sexual behavior, making it special, holy— forcing us to think carefully before we act on our physical desires, forcing us to consider the role that our relationship with our community and with G-d has in even the most intimate parts of our lives.

Frankly, I have no problem with the idea of wanting to make sexuality more holy, more thoughtful and more responsible. In fact, I advocate it on a regular basis. But I do have a problem with the fact that Judaism only promotes this concept for certain kinds of sexuality, and therefore for certain kinds of people.

It's not as if we've suddenly slipped into a brave new world of sexual possibility that our forefathers and foremothers could never have conceptualized. We haven't, honestly, moved all that far beyond what our sexual capabilities were as human beings 2500 years ago: Even text-based sex, such as cybersex, has its antecedents, only now we often read them (for example, Rostand's *Cyrano de Bergerac*, Richardson's *Clarissa*, good old Abelard and Heloise) as literature, not sordid little on-screen bleeps and blips. Dr. Bernadette Brooten's pioneering work on lesbian relationships in the early Christian world has proven that lesbianism and female bisexuality were nothing new in the Second Temple era, despite the fact that the Torah ignores their existence and Jewish custom regards sex between women as an abomination. Of course, men's carnal love for other men has been extremely well-documented since before the time of the ancient Greeks, and the Torah gives its own evidence—Biblical prohibitions against male/male sexuality prove nothing so much as that man-on-man sex did in fact exist, and existed publicly enough for a public mandate to be made in an attempt to control it. Really, there's precious little that's new under the sun: Even sex toys aren't a modern invention, as proven by Roman vase paintings that bear images of people using dildos.

Richly varied sexual practices have always existed, for you and me and countless millions of our fellow human beings, Jew and non-Jew alike. Frequently, they are a way that we share love and holiness with one another—the poetry of pleasure, the boundless joy that is bigger than any single human being—through the humble vessels of our bodies. Negotiating the holiness and value we know to exist in our sexuality and our lives—as unmarried people, bisexuals, gays, lesbians, transsexuals—through Judaism's traditional blindness to nonheterosexual, nonmarital sexuality is a damned tough job.

One way to do this is to look to traditional Jewish law and custom for models for relationships, loves and sexualities that are not traditional. For instance, in Jewish law, a married man is obligated to give his wife a certain amount of sexual pleasure, or *onah*, per week or month as part of his side of the bargain in taking care of her needs as his spouse.[1] A polyamorous couple—two people who have chosen not to be monogamous, but who openly and responsibly maintain other relationships in addition to their relationship to one another—struggling with ways to honor the primary relationship might well benefit from using this structure; the couple might decide that the primary commitment would benefit from being given onah and commit to a certain number of nights spent together each week. People practicing BDSM might conceptualize negotiations—who takes on what role(s), what acts are and are not acceptable, what parameters of sexual and other activity are to be part of their interactions with one another—as a form of *ketubah,* or marriage contract, specifying what each partner is obligated to bring to the relationship and what each can expect in terms of support and help if things go poorly. Many nonheterosexual couples have already chosen to draw up ketubot for their commitment ceremonies, reappropriating the notion of a private, spiritually-based contract for unions of a type that both secular and sacred authorities largely refuse to recognize.

Another way to reconcile greater individual sexual freedom and Judaism is to recast sexuality as simply one more category of human interaction to be approached with dignity, intelligence, humility, generosity and an awareness of the essential holiness of our fellow human beings. When we do this, we make ethics more important than orientation, marital status, gender or genitals. We set the stage to make teaching sexuality—and experiencing our own sexuality—a force for bridge building, not division, for healing, joy and pleasure rather than shame and pain. In short, it's a matter of *tikkun olam*—of helping to heal the world.

Yes, you heard me right. Given the amount of pain and suffering, sorrow, misunderstanding and loss that sexuality often seems to cause in people's lives, it seems only to make sense that an effort to relieve that pain and suffering, to give people ways to heal sorrow, avoid misunderstanding and both reduce the risk of loss while giving tools to accept it when it happens would be a mitzvah in the colloquial sense, a blessing. And among Western religions, Judaism is uniquely poised to do this, simply because Judaism acknowledges and has always acknowledged the positive value of pleasure. It is not merely the idea of onah that I alluded to earlier, although the recognition that sexual pleasure should be a right for women as well as men is certainly one of the more supportive and generous points of traditional Judaism's take on sexuality. It is the value of pleasure as both incentive and reinforcement when teaching people to do good things: We put sweets into our children's mouths as we teach them their first letters in Hebrew, their first words of Torah. It seems stingy, ungrateful, to toss away other pleasures of which our bodies are capable, to miss the chance to use them as venues for encouraging ethical thought and behavior. We cannot afford to ignore what it means to have bodies that are capable of intense, sometimes overwhelming pleasure. We can't afford to ignore where that pleasure can take us.

After all, sexual pleasure, like food and death, is one of the great levelers. It gives us a uniquely universal venue into the lives and hearts of every person on the planet, Jew and non-Jew alike. The drive toward sex is not merely about reproduction—when we're honest, most of us agree that the drive toward sex is, and always has been, a drive toward pleasure on emotional, physical, spiritual and aesthetic levels. Reproduction may be the biological metasubject of the drama, but pleasure is what fills the seats. I cannot find it in my heart or head to second-guess G-d on this one: There are too many mutually beneficial sex acts that open us to revelatory and valuable intensities of self and spirit for me to think that G-d somehow intends us to choose only the one capable of resulting in pregnancy, or only the ones that take place within the bounds of marriage, or only the ones that take place between opposite-sex partners. And there is too much pleasure involved for me to feel ethical about using shame or other punitive tactics when I talk and teach about it.

What this means in practice, really, is that educating about sexuality Jewishly really does demand that complicated honesty I wrote about earlier, and that it is a way of making life better. It's the domino effect of tikkun: To heal the world, you must heal yourself, and as you heal part of yourself, you can help heal others, until we are all, finally, gluing together the broken bowls of our lives. To heal sexuality, you must be honest about what is beautiful and what is broken, what can be celebrated and what must be healed.

This means, for me, that when an adult comes to me with complaints about not being able to make a partner have orgasms, I don't just talk about clitorises and penises, or limit my questions to what kinds of sexual activities and positions they've tried. I do talk about those things, but I also talk about sexual pleasure as an entity independent from orgasm, about communication, about whether both partners agree as to the nature and scope of the problem, about arousal levels and attention, experimentation and feedback. When people whose illnesses have caused neurological damage to their genitals (as is sometimes the case with diabetes, or treatment for ovarian and uterine cancers) ask me whether they can still have and enjoy sex, I try to walk through their fear with them to the point where they can begin to realize that their entire bodies, not just their genitals, are sexual and capable of feeling sexual pleasure, and work with them to envison different ways to express their sexual selves. I apply perspective, creativity and compassion to a realm of life that is often limited by lack of knowledge and made harsh by cultural prejudice against sexual pleasure.

I also invoke justice, equality, fairness, forgiveness and understanding. Many of the teenage and young adult men I work with want sex, and lots of it. That's pretty normal, and absolutely okay. It's also pretty common for them not to get it, and to be frustrated about that, often taking out their frustration in sexist, abusive, misogynist talk that reinforces sexist cultural stereotypes. That's also common, but not okay. It's hurtful, ignorant and usually inaccurate, and when I talk to teenage boys about it, I find that I am often the first person who has ever challenged their frustrated abusiveness with logic and fairness. I do the same thing with young women, whose own frustration at being ogled, pawed, harrassed and propositioned often evinces itself in similar stereotyping and abusiveness. If you've never watched a couple of teenage boys actually sit down and talk to a couple of teenage girls about how they really feel about gender-stereotyped sexual behavior, I hope you someday have the privilege. Watching people discover that there is a universe beyond the stereotypes, prejudice and misinformation—where men and women are human beings with fears, desires, needs, inadequacies and vulnerabilities—is pretty magical.

Whether I am helping someone evaluate why she feels like adultery would be desirable or ethical, talking with someone about whether he feels his urge to be sexually dominated is healthy for him, or simply explaining (probably for the ninety-ninth time that afternoon) why using a condom is a good thing, I work hard at keeping my Jewish values—respect, honesty and ethics—front and center. It's a Jewish thing, to me, to reach out to someone who has had their sexuality hijacked by an abuser and say, "You can have your sexuality back, it is the way G-d made you, it is your birthright." It is a Jewish thing to help people feel whole in their bodies, and in their relationships. It is a Jewish thing for me when I teach a teenage girl where her clitoris is so that she can figure out how to masturbate, giving herself pleasure without putting herself at unnecessary emotional or physical risk.

The more honest I am about sexuality and sexual pleasure, the less other people can hold up sexual straw men to hide their own inability or unwillingness to act humanely, respectfully and ethically. Sometimes this means debunking the myth of blue balls in part by discussing sexual pleasure and male ejaculatory orgasms and talking about why pleasure might be so important to someone that he would manipulate a sex partner to get it. Or it might mean talking about BDSM openly and honestly enough to say that, yes, it can be done safely, sanely and consensually, and for those who do it that way, it is not assaultive or unkind, sick or wrong, and, furthermore, that it's not okay to label people as "sick" because they find consensual pleasure in practices others may not. It might mean admitting that condoms aren't always fun and that sex with a condom doesn't always feel as good as sex without a condom, but that sex with a condom certainly beats no sex at all, and definitely outweighs the agony of the possible consequences of making an unethical choice—getting or giving an STD, or causing (or having) an unwanted pregnancy.

It's a very Jewish thing to educate people to be healthy and to run their lives and their interactions with others in a way that does not do harm, whether that means educating people about consensuality, tolerance, condoms or any of a hundred other things. The principle I try to teach—the great sage Hillel goes to sex-ed class—is one that should be familiar to all of us: Do not do unto others that which you would not have others do unto you.

To teach ethics and honesty, to facilitate joyful awe in the possibilities of the bodies G-d has given us, is to do the work of helping people live better, healthier lives. This is a Jewish occupation. So, for those who are curious, no, I do not side with the anti-condom faction. I also don't side with the "just say no" or the "wait until you're married" faction; and I don't side with the "open and unregulated sex for everybody" faction, either. I believe that healing ourselves sexually, as individuals, as cultures, and as a world, is part of fulfilling G-d's intent for us as human beings. I believe we must learn to find G-d in pleasure just as we find pleasure in G-d, and to handle both with dignity, awareness, tolerance and caring. Thus, I side with the faction that is willing to treat sexuality Jewishly, as a matter of ethics and thoughtfulness, yesterday's wisdom and today's immediacies, the eternal pull of desire and the ageless variety of human possibility, applied to human interaction in the pursuit of righteous behavior toward one's fellow human beings and toward G-d. And I must say—it feels awfully good.

Notes:

1. The laws of onah are derived from Exodus 21: 7–11 and elaborated in the Talmud, with particularly pertinent passages at Ketubot 47b–48a, 61b–62b, and many elsewhere.

Of These, Solitude

Dalia Sofer

In the summertime she'd spread the small plush carpet under the shade of the cherry tree, place the cool prayer stone on top, wash her hands, feet and face with icy water, and hide the roundness of her body under her black *chador* (veil) in preparation for prayer. She'd tune out the world around her—the mayhem of midday traffic, the repetitive riff of the street peddler, the clamor of children playing soccer. Then she'd kneel before the stone and begin. On afternoons when the heat drowned the city in a sleepy haze I'd stand quietly on the other side of our garden, and watch her, a black shape waxing and waning on the freshly cut grass. Later, she got me a stone of my own, and sometimes I'd unfurl my own carpet beside hers, imitating the movements of her body though I had no idea what they meant.

This was Tehran, 1977, and the lady in black was our housekeeper, Ehteram, a moderate Muslim. The prayer sessions we shared, though devoid of any religious significance for me (as I was five years old and Jewish), still managed to soothe me; I'd curl into a ball, feel the uneven ground under my carpet as I'd kneel on all fours, and engulf myself in the sound of my own breath. So I faced Mecca with her, unsure of exactly why.

It was with the same incertitude that I followed my parents to synagogue, on the rare occasions that my family made the pilgrimage. But where I expected to find reverence I was doused in jabber, at least on the mezzanine, where the collective chatter of twenty or so women would mute the solemn prayer of dozens of men below.

As in all synagogues in Iran, men and women sat in separate sections, the rabbi was male, as was the cantor, and women were forbidden to carry the Torah. I once asked my mother why that was and she said that men and women have different responsibilities, and carrying the Torah was in the male realm. When I pressed her for a reason, she paused, then said that it was too heavy, that was all. "Well why do the women have to sit upstairs where they can't even hear the prayers?" I continued. At which point she rolled her eyes and said, "Because God said so, that's why."

I rarely challenged authority. This included God. Besides, my family's visits to the synagogue were limited enough to allow the question to take a back seat in my mind.

Later that summer we celebrated my brother's bar mitzvah in a swanky hotel on the Natanya seashore in Israel, where my mother's family lived. On a balmy August night we stood in a row to greet the two hundred or so guests. My mother, in a long ivory satin dress, and my father, in a sharp black suit, stood behind me and my sister, dressed like twins in sky blue princess gowns. My brother, in black pants and a frilly shirt designed to be the masculine escort to our dresses, shook hands with each incoming guest, repeating *"Todah rabah"* in his adolescent voice—a refrain that has become the most memorable segment of the surviving videotape. Several rounds of cocktails and a three-course meal later, my brother stood onstage and mesmerized the room with his perfectly rehearsed Hebrew. He was rewarded with a belly dancer named Jamillah.

My own transition to "adulthood" seven years later came and went with as much ceremony as the changing of produce at the local market. Strolling on the Atlantic City boardwalk with my sister, my brother and a dozen of his friends, I sensed pain, until then unfamiliar, in my lower abdomen. An hour or two later, stretched out on picnic blankets on the beach and nibbling on watermelon slices, I noticed the red stain on my shorts, which as luck would have it were also red, sparing me the embarrassment but not the agony. Unlike my brother, whose manhood had been announced by a Torah portion, my womanhood was marked by a maxi pad bought for a nickel at the Caesar's Palace public restroom.

I may question this discrepancy now, but at the time I was grateful to navigate through life without fanfare. Having witnessed Iran's secular regime succumb to Khomeini's Islamic fundamentalist government in 1979, I had learned to attract as little attention to myself as possible. In my new Islamic uniform—long pants, a navy blue overcoat and a scarf veiling every strand of hair—I'd sit in class and listen to sermons about the superiority of Islam to other religions, buying security with silence and a nod. And when my father vanished on a crisp September day only to return from jail a month later, relieved of charges of espionage for Israel but restricted from leaving Iran, I learned that downplaying religious difference isn't an option, it's a requirement. I didn't feel ostracized, however, nor did I feel vengeful. The sorrowful chant of the muezzin announcing prayer time pierced the sky morning, noon and evening, etching in me the feeling that I was somehow different—neither better nor worse. It's true that I no longer accompanied Ehteram during her prayers, and I'd long since lost the perennially cool prayer stone. But as I'd arrive home from school, life seemed unchanged: I'd replace the dark uniform with jeans and a T-shirt, plant myself at the kitchen table and crack open roasted watermelon seeds with my teeth, chatting with my mother and Ehteram as they prepared dinner.

In late 1982, my family and I made our way out of Iran, escaping via the Turkish border. After six hours on horseback and another six on foot through dark, treacherous terrain, we reached a small Turkish village lit by the hesitant hue of dawn. In our muddied garb we boarded a bus to Istanbul, garnering suspicious stares from local villagers. I didn't care. My head resting on my father's shoulder, I watched green pastures whiz by and tried to suspend the heavy slumber that I knew was imminent. It occurred to me then that lives existed outside of Iran—free of the fear and constant vigilance that I had grown so accustomed to.

In Istanbul my parents arranged for a fake entry stamp on our fake passports, which we hoped would allow us to board a plane for Israel. But the ersatz stamp denounced us, causing the airline clerk to raise an eyebrow and ask, "So how much did you pay for this?" Pulled to the side like outlaws, we waited for the "authorities," though not for long. The Israeli embassy, having sent officials to ensure our smooth departure, bailed us out. *"This* is kinship," I told myself as the plane floated over the teal Mediterranean waters. "Jews watching out for Jews."

My first day of school in Israel gave me a different taste, however. I looked at my new classmates—already brash and aggressive at the age of eleven. They yelled when they disagreed, chewed bubble gum in class, and boys in the back row stretched out their sneakered feet on the tables. One of them noticed me looking and winked. When the bell rang, bringing with it a cacophony of screeching chairs, he walked up to me. I felt my face turning shades of pink then red. But my expectations of a romantic encounter were crushed when something hit my head and popped. I looked up and saw him laughing, holding a torn orange balloon. His friends from the back row were a few feet away, snickering. After a while he mumbled something in Hebrew and walked away. The only word I could make out was "Khomeini."

Like all Jewish immigrant children in Israel, I had to attend an *ulpan* to learn Hebrew. This was a League of Nations of sorts. The Argentineans were polite and mostly kept to themselves, the French were fashionable and mischievous, and the Americans were smug and loud but otherwise harmless. There was a solitary Irish boy who'd pace around the school yard and spit in front of us Iranians whenever he passed us. "Do you see what the world's come to?" one of the Iranians would quip. "Even this stringy Irish Jew who's been dumped on by the English and the Catholics all his life thinks he's better than us."

Soon it became clear to me that religious kinship doesn't amount to much. Within Israel itself a German may have disliked a Pole who may have disliked an Egyptian. Everyone, it seemed, disliked Iranians.

In New York City, where we settled after a ten-month stay in Israel, I once again failed to connect with Judaism despite its manifest presence. Enrolled in a French school because French was the only language I spoke other than Farsi, I had few Jewish classmates and only one Jewish friend, who also happened to be Iranian. Still, I complied with the selective observances held in our household: Non-kosher meat at a restaurant was okay, non-kosher meat at home was not; not observing Shabbat was okay, not observing Passover was not; meat and dairy together were acceptable, pork never was. Once, eager to get a taste of the popular BLT everyone ordered at lunch, I asked my mother for some cash instead of the tinfoiled sandwich she'd hand me every morning. It was only after I had the BLT in hand that I realized what it stood for. Quietly I dumped the bacon strips in the corner trash and ended up with a dry lettuce and tomato sandwich. I sensed the void in my stomach for the rest of the afternoon.

In college, I began letting go of the rules. Then I drifted further and faster, settling for the non-kosher chicken from the local grocer, nibbling on a plate of shrimp, and biting into a slice of bread—first ambivalently, then wholeheartedly, during Passover.

Now, living on the Upper West Side of Manhattan, I find clusters of Jews gathered on sidewalks in front of their congregations, and pierce into them, alone, simply to pass through. Momentarily in their nucleus I hear Hebrew words thrown into English sentences, tainted with the twirl of American accents. This is not just a religion congregating, I tell myself. It's also a culture, one that I am not a part of. These groups emit a certain smugness—a clique barricaded from the rest of the world. I've realized that I have no business there. After all, until recently, I had never even had matzo ball soup, didn't know of the bagel-and-lox culture. And I have yet to try gefilte fish.

I lived in Iran for ten years; I will be Jewish for the rest of my life. Yet asked to define myself, my mind drifts to the snow-covered peaks of the Elburz mountains visible from our kitchen window; streets lined with jasmine trees and poplars; bowls of *sholehzard*—a pudding flavored with saffron, rose water and crushed pistachio that neighbors would offer to one another whenever their prayers had been answered. That, to me, was kinship.

In my experience, religion hasn't been a unifying force, but rather a source of rift. As a child I was treated differently as both a girl and a Jew, then had to flee my country; in Israel I witnessed the silent war among people claiming to be united; here I resent the exclusive sphere I see Jews living in. And while I've watched every speck of religious faith leave me—one by one, like Charlotte's children—I still find comfort in a prayer: brief, reassuring, mumbled in a pitch-black room as I lie awake at night, addressed in no particular language to no one in particular.

CONTRIBUTORS

Tobin Belzer is a doctoral candidate in sociology at Brandeis University and the director of the Joining the Sisterhood Project under the auspices of the Hadassah International Research Institute on Jewish Women. She is the coeditor of *Joining the Sisterhood: Autobiographical Writing by Young Jewish Women* (forthcoming from SUNY Press).

Hanne Blank is a writer, editor and sex educator who is also a classically trained musician and cultural historian. The author and editor of several books, including *Big Big Love: A Sourcebook on Sex for People of Size and Those Who Love Them* (Greenery Press, 2000) and *Zaftig: Well Rounded Erotica* (Cleis Press, 2001), she is also the coeditor of Scarleteen.com, a not-for-profit, independently run sexuality education clearinghouse for teens and young adults. Current projects include a sex-positive sex education book for young women ages thirteen to twenty-one and a biography of Jewish red-hot mama Sophie Tucker. Hanne Blank lives in Boston.

Jennifer Bleyer is a writer who lives in Brooklyn. She is editor in chief of *Heeb Magazine: The New Jew Review.* She published the Jewpunk zine *Mazeltov Cocktail* in 1995 and her writing has appeared in *Salon, Adbusters, BUST* and *New Voices.* She covered the protests at both the Republican and Democratic National Conventions in the summer of 2000 for Alternet, and covered Ralph Nader's presidential campaign for Working Assets's *News for Change.*

Sarah Coleman lives and writes in New York City. She has written on Jewish subjects for publications as diverse as the *Jewish Bulletin of Northern California* and *Salon.* She is the literary editor of Feminista.com and a regular contributor to the *San Francisco Chronicle Book Review, Photo Metro* magazine and other journals. A bleeding-heart liberal 'til death, she is currently collaborating with photographer Warren Hukill on a book about women gun owners.

Ophira Edut has been an independent magazine publisher, writer and web developer for nearly a decade. She is the editor of *Adios, Barbie: Young Women Write About Body Image and Identity* (Seal, 1998) and its second edition, *Body Outlaws* (Seal, 2000). Ophira is also a contributing editor to *Ms.*, and has been featured in numerous anthologies and magazines, including *Vibe, Mademoiselle* and *Entertainment Weekly.* She currently lectures nationwide about body image, media, culture and gender. A Detroit native and Israeli-American, Ophira now lives in New York and spends her time speaking publicly, developing her Ophira.com website, writing and consulting on online projects.

Ellen Friedrichs is a Canadian living in New York City where she is pursuing a master's degree in human sexuality education. She runs workshops on sexuality and also hangs up coats at a fancy restaurant.

A. C. Hall's writing has appeared in a wide range of publications, from the *Seattle Times* to the alternative papers the *Stranger* and *Seattle Weekly.* Her essay, "Japan, My Foot," appears in *The Unsavvy Traveler* (Seal, 2001). She recently finished her first novel for adults, a travel adventure of primarily internal terrain, and is currently working on a young adult novel about sexual coercion. She lives in Seattle with the Nicest Jewish Boy, whom she loves very much.

Susannah Heschel is the Eli Black Professor of Jewish Studies at Dartmouth College, the author of numerous studies on Jewish thought and the editor of the classic anthology *On Being a Jewish Feminist* (Schocken, 1983).

Dina Hornreich is currently pursuing a graduate degree in communication sciences at the University of Connecticut. As a result of all her kvetching, she strives to understand how we develop, and endure, in an evolving media culture. In 1997, she graduated with a BA in philosophy, computers and the cognitive sciences (concentration in linguistics) from the State University of New York at Binghamton.

Ursula Katan is a hell-raising, poetry-writing performance artist and activist who has done much art/work around the interlocking issues explored in her essay. She looks forward to a world where it is safe for all people to speak out about who they are and where they've been.

Loolwa Khazzoom continues to be active on as many fronts as humanly possible. She is the program coordinator of the Jewish Multicultural Education Project, the author of *Consequence: Beyond Resisting Rape* (Pearl In a Million Press, 2001) and the singer and bass player for her band, Grrl Monster.

Karen (Chai) Levy is a twenty-nine-year-old rabbinical student at the Jewish Theological Seminary in New York City.

Ryiah Lilith is a feminist lesbian and a Jewish Dianic Witch and Priestess-in-Training, currently living in Takoma Park, Maryland.

Billie Michele Mandel decided when her grandmother died never again to waste another minute. An artist, musician and dancer as well as a poet and essayist, she lives in London where she spends her free time drinking tea, riding motorcycles and marveling at spiderwebs. She spends her weekdays as a senior manager at an Internet company.

Haviva Ner-David lives in Jerusalem with her husband and four children, three daughters and a son. She is the author of the book *Life on the Fringes: A Feminist Journey Towards Traditional Rabbinic Ordination* (JFL Books, 2000). She is working toward her doctorate at Bar-Ilan University in the philosophy of halakhah, and is studying with an Orthodox rabbi in Jerusalem for *s'micha* (rabbinic ordination).

Eve Rosenbaum received her MFA in creative writing from American University, where she edited the literary journal *Folio*. She has published poetry and fiction in journals including *Potomac Review, For Poetry, Caprice, Artemis, Starfish, Affair of the Mind* and *Three Candles*. Her work also appears in the forthcoming anthology *On the Fringes: An Anthology of Young Jewish American Writers* (SUNY Press). She currently lives in Washington, D.C.

Yiskah (Jessica) Rosenfeld teaches workshops combining Jewish mysticism, text and creative writing to youth and adults in the San Francisco Bay Area and Israel. An award-winning poet, she holds an MFA in poetry from Mills College and an MA in jurisprudence and social policy from UC Berkeley.

Dalia Sofer is a writer and editor living in New York City. Her work has appeared in print and online publications including *Woman's Day*, the *American Journal of Nursing*, *Manhattan Spirit* and TheKnot.com. She is currently writing a novel set in post-revolutionary Iran and pursuing an MFA at Sarah Lawrence College.

Sharon Wachsler is a poet, essayist, cartoonist and disability rights activist. Her work has appeared in *Moxie, Sojourner, Ragged Edge* and *Restricted Access: Lesbians on Disability* (Seal, 1999). She lives in the hills of Western Massachusetts with her service dog, Jersey, and her cat, Ferdinand.

Emily Wages believes that many of life's ills can be healed by the Sierra Nevadas, green tea and grandmothers. She is a trilingual law student at UC Berkeley focusing on international human rights and immigrant issues, and is currently participating in a nine-month practice period at the Jewish meditation center Makor Or, in San Francisco.

GLOSSARY

The words in the glossary are primarily of Hebrew, Yiddish or Judeo-Arabic origin. Variations in the spelling indicate differences in spelling and/or pronunciation of different Jewish languages—for instance, Hebrew and Judeo-Arabic spellings of an entry, or Hebrew and Yiddish.

Adonai A "polite" way to refer to the most sacred name of God. Many religious Jews, rather than risk taking God's name in vain, will not even say "Adonai" except in prayer, and instead choose to refer to Divinity as "Hashem."

aleph-bet *also aleph-beth* (lit. the Hebrew letters for "A" and "B") The ABCs; the alphabet.

aliyah (lit. "to go up") To go up to the bimah to recite the prayers over the Torah. Also means to move to Israel, as it is believed that living permanently in Israel is like ascending to a place of spiritual holiness.

Amidah (lit. "standing") A series of prayers said standing up in direct communication with God; a central part of the Jewish prayer service.

apikores *also apikoros* An apostate, a heretic; only a learned person who turns atheist can be deemed an apikores, as only s/he has sufficient knowledge to understand the consequences of unbelief.

Ashkenazi/Ashkenazim (sing/pl) "Ashknaz" means "Germany." Jews of Northern, Central or Eastern European descent.

ba'al teshuvah/ba'ale teshuvah (masc/fem) *also ba'al/e tshuvah* (lit. "master of repentance") A Jew who was not raised observant (generally, Orthodox) but becomes so later in life.

Bais Yaakov The name of a yeshiva for women and girls.

bar mitzvah/bat mitzvah (masc/fem) *also bar mouswa/bath mouswa* (lit. "son/daughter of the commandment") The ritual through which a twelve- or thirteen-year-old attains religious and legal adult status.

Baruch Hashem *also Baruch HaShem* (lit. "Blessed is God") Thank God, i.e. "Blessed is God, responsible for all."

bimah *also teba* (lit. "elevated place") The podium in the synagogue from which the Torah is read, prayers are led and sermons are preached.

blintzes Ashkenazi crepes, often filled with cheese or fruit.

bracha/brachot (sing/pl) *also brachah/brachoth* Blessing.

bris *also brith milah, brit millah* Circumcision ceremony, usually held when a Jewish male baby is eight days old.

cantor *also hazzan* A member of the Jewish clergy who sings or chants the prayer service, often using music to bring worshippers deeper into prayer.

Chabad *also Lubavitch* A branch of Hasidic Jews known particularly for their outreach programs to unaffiliated Jews.

challah A Jewish egg bread, usually served on Shabbat and on holidays. The mitzvah in which one piece of challah dough is separated out and burned in the oven before the rest of the loaf is baked is a nod to practices of the ancient Jerusalem Temple.

chuppah *also huppah, chupah* The canopy under which a wedding ceremony takes place.

chutzpah *also hutzpah* Audacity. Used to describe someone who is strong and tough, or obnoxious and out of line.

Conservative Judaism The branch of Judaism which asserts that, though Jews are still bound to observe ritual law, interpretations and applications of that law can, with attention to the law's tradition and history, evolve to address modern concerns.

crypto-Jews Jews who pretended to convert to Christianity, either voluntarily or under duress, but who secretly practiced Judaism, most commonly during and after the period of the expulsion of Jews from Spain in 1492 and the Spanish Inquisition.

cultural Jews See **secular Jews**.

datiyah *also dati* A Hebrew word for "religious."

daven Yiddish, either from the Latin "divinus," meaning "the Divine", or from the Lithuanian word meaning "gift." To pray with deep intensity.

d'var Torah *also d'bar Torah, devor Torah* (lit. "words of Torah") A sermon or talk based on the week's Torah portion.

dybbuk A demon of Yiddish folklore.

egalitarian Services in which men and women are counted as equal participants in ritual.

fleishig A Yiddish term for "meat." Food which has meat ingredients, or which was prepared with utensils used for meat.

frum Religious; a Yiddish-ization of the German word for "pious."

galut *also galus* Exile; the Jewish diaspora.

G-d Some religious Jews use this "shorthand" for the name of Deity on any object (such as a piece of paper) that could be destroyed, thereby avoiding the possibility of desecrating the Sacred Name.

gevurah Strength; often associated with judgment.

goy/goyim (sing/pl) A non-Jew.

goyishe (adj) Gentile.

hachamim *also Hachamim, chachamim* Sages.

Haftarah/Haftarot (sing/pl) *also Haftorah* The weekly reading from the Biblical prophets, intended to correspond to and comment upon the weekly Torah reading.

Haggadah *also H'gaddah, Haggada* (lit. "telling") The book used during the Passover seder which recounts the Exodus from Egypt.

halakha *also halakhah, chalakah, halachah* (lit. "the way") Jewish law, i.e. the laws set out in the Torah and/or developed through the oral and legal tradition.

Hanukah *also Hanukkah, H'nika, Chanukah, Chanukkah* A holiday in December celebrating a military victory of a group of Jews over a foreign government. On each of the eight days of the "festival of lights," a candle is lit on a Hanukiah, sometimes called a menorah.

haredi/haredim (sing/pl) Religious, often ultra-Orthodox, Jews.

Hashem *also HaShem* (lit. "the Name") The sacred name of God.

Hasid/Hasidic (noun/adj) A strain of Judaism founded by Rabbi Israel Ben Eliezer (also known as the Baal Shem Tov) in the eighteenth century as a way to approach God with both contemplative meditation and fervent joy. There are many sects of Hasidism, most of which are modeled on the teachings of a particular rebbe (spiritual leader).

havurah/havurot (sing/pl) *also haburah* (lit. "society" or "fellowship") A group, with a heavy emphasis on community-building, that forms for prayer, study or social activity. Often emphasizes lay leadership.

hesed *also hessed* Lovingkindness.

hiloni/hilonim (sing/pl) Secular Jews.

hora A dance, often associated with weddings or other happy occasions.

humanistic Jews According to the Society for Humanistic Judaism, humanistic Jews "embrace a human-centered philosophy that combines rational thinking with a celebration of Jewish culture and identity." It is a decidedly nontheistic movement.

Humash *also Chumash* The five books of the Torah (Genesis, Exodus, Leviticus, Numbers, Deuteronomy). A term more commonly used by Ashkenazi Jews.

Kabbalah (lit. "receiving") The Jewish mystical tradition.

Kaddish A prayer that is (among other things) designated for mourners.

kashrut/kosher (noun/adj) *also kushrus* Jewish dietary laws.

ketubah *also k'tubah* The Jewish wedding contract.

kibbutz (lit. "community") A voluntary collective community, usually agriculture-based, with an emphasis on the collective ownership of possessions and a collective responsibility for its members.

kibbutznik A resident of a kibbutz.

kippah/kippot (sing/pl) A yarmulke; a Jewish head covering, traditionally worn by men.

kol ishah *also kol isha* (lit. "The voice of a woman," from the Rabbinic statement, "Kol b'ishah ervah," the voice of a woman is sinful) Certain Orthodox Jews have forbidden women's singing in front of a man, lest he hear the nakedness of her soul and be led to sinful thoughts.

kugel An Eastern-European Jewish casserole.

kvell A Yiddish word perhaps best translated as "To exude pride and joy over the accomplishments of loved ones (usually children)."

kvetch To complain.

Lubavitch See **Chabad.**

matzoh/matzot (sing/pl) *also matzo, massa* An unleavened bread eaten on Passover.

mazel tov *also mazal tob* (lit. "good luck") Congratulations!

mechitza *also mechitzah, mehisa* A partition separating women and men, used primarily in Orthodox synagogues.

Megillah/Megillot (sing/pl) (lit. "scroll") There are five Megillot, but the word Megillah usually refers to the Book of Esther, which is read on the holiday of Purim. Also **megillah,** a slang term for a tediously detailed or embroidered account.

menorah/menorot (sing/pl) A seven-branched oil lamp used in the Tabernacle and the ancient Jerusalem Temple; also used sometimes to describe the eight-branched candelabrum used on Hanukah.

mezuzah/mezuzot (sing/pl) A parchment scroll upon which two paragraphs from the Torah are inscribed; the scroll is rolled tightly, put in a case and affixed to the doorway of one's home or office.

midrash/midrashim (sing/pl) A genre of literature that includes stories, legends, folklore and interpretations on the Bible.

mikveh/mikvot (sing/pl) *also mikvah, miqua* Ritual bath; a pool of water used for purification.

milchig A Yiddish term for "dairy." Food which has dairy ingredients, or which was prepared with utensils used for dairy.

minhag Custom; tradition within a community.

minyan The assembly of ten Jews (traditionally men) required to say certain prayers. Or, a prayer service.

Mishnah An interpretation and explication of the Biblical law handed down through oral tradition, first compiled in written form around 200 C.E. One of the two major divisions of the Talmud.

mitzvah/mitzvot (sing/pl) *also mouswa/mouswoth* (lit. "commandment") One of the 613 directives issued by the Torah; also used more casually as "good deed" or "blessing."

Mizrahi/Mizrahim (sing/pl) Hebrew for "Easterners"; Jews indigenous to the Middle East and North Africa, and their descendants.

mohel/mohalim (sing/pl) The person who performs a Jewish circumcision.

niddah Menstruation; a menstruant.

niggun/niggunim (sing/pl) Melody.

omer The forty-nine days between the holidays of Passover and Shavuot. In ancient Israel, it counted the time from the first barley harvest to the first wheat harvest, and in theological terms counts the time between the Exodus from Egypt and receiving of the Torah. These days are "counted" by saying a particular blessing on each of the forty-nine days.

onah (lit. "span of time") The laws of onah regard a man's obligation to visit his wife sexually: how many times he is required to be with her sexually within a given period of time. Onah is considered to hold irrespective of whether or not the sex is reproductive; "onah" is sometimes used as a trope for "satisfying one's wife sexually."

Orthodox Judaism A stream of Judaism based on the belief that the Divine Law, as reflected in the Torah, is eternal and unchanging—though, within Orthodoxy, there are range of understandings and interpretations of the law. Generally considered the most "traditional" of the contemporary Jewish denominations—though "Orthodox" is less of a movement than a catch-all phrase for those whose beliefs most closely resemble Judaism of times past.

Passover See **Pesach**.

Pesach *also Pesah, Id La F'teer (Holiday of the Massa/Matzoh)* The holiday celebrating the Israelites' Exodus from Egypt.

Purim A spring holiday celebrating the victory of the Jewish people over a plot to destroy them. Esther, a Jew living in a Persian king's court, is the heroine of the tale.

Rashi Eleventh-century Jewish scholar whose commentaries on the Bible and the Talmud are still considered some of the most important in Jewish literature.

Rashi script A particular typeface often used for Rashi's commentaries.

rebbe *also Rebbe* Generally refers to a rabbi or Jewish leader whose teachings are followed by others. Often used in reference to the leader of a Hasidic sect.

rebbetzin *also rebitzin* The wife of a rabbi. In some communities, she has a fairly high status.

Reconstructionist Judaism A movement that defines Judaism as an evolving religious civilization and believes that each generation is charged with the mandate to understand and create the Judaism of its own time. Reconstructionism places a high value not only on the Jewish humanistic and ethical tradition, but on the ability of Jews to reconcile their Judaism with modern-day scientific and philosophic innovations.

Reform Judaism A movement, begun in the nineteenth century, which de-emphasizes adherence to Jewish law and often includes more English in the services than many Conservative or Orthodox synagogues.

Renewal Judaism A recent movement that seeks to renew the relationship between individuals and the Divine, and communities and the Divine; the movement is informed both by Kabbalistic and Hasidic traditions and left-wing contemporary politics.

responsum/responsa (sing/pl) The interpretation and adaptation of Talmudic law; a rabbinical ruling on an issue of contemporary importance which carries the weight of law. Sometimes issued in response to a specific question about the implementation of Jewish law.

Rosh Chodesh *also Rosh Hodesh* (lit. "head of the month") The first day of the new lunar month, the new moon. A holiday traditionally observed just by women.

Rosh Hashanah *also Rosh HaShanah, R'shana* The Jewish New Year and beginning of the Days of Awe; one of the calendar's holiest days.

schmaltz herring A mature, higher-fat herring that is filleted and preserved in brine.

secular Jews Jews who maintain a strong cultural or familial tie to their family's history or heritage, but who don't practice the religion itself.

seder *also Seder* The ritual Passover meal at which the story of the Exodus from Egypt is recounted.

Sephardi/Sephardic (noun/adj) The Jews, and the descendents of the Jews, who settled in Spain and Portugal from roughly the time of the destruction of the Second Temple in 70 C.E. until the expulsion of Jews from Spain in 1492 and from Portugal in 1496.

seraphim Angels.

Shabbat *also Shabbos, Sebbath* The Sabbath, the seventh day of the week, a day of rest. Saturday.

Shabbat Shalom "Have a nice Shabbat."

shanda A shame.

Shavuot (lit. "weeks") An early summer holiday commemorating the giving of the Torah to the Jewish people on Mount Sinai.

shehechianu *also Shehechianu, shehecheyanu, sheheyanu* A blessing thanking God, "who has kept us in life, preserved us, and brought us to this time." Recited in moments of celebration and/or thanksgiving.

Shekinah The Divine Presence; Jewish mystical literature describes the Shekinah as the feminine, immanent aspect of God.

sheva brachot *also Sheva Brachot, Sheva Brachoth* The seven wedding blessings.

shiksa Yiddish for a non-Jewish woman. Not always the politest of terms.

shiva (lit. "seven") The first week of mourning after a burial. Family and friends traditionally visit the home of the mourners and offer support.

Sh'ma (lit. "hear") The prayer, "Hear, O Israel, God our God, God is One" and a number of fixed verses which follow. A central aspect of Jewish liturgy.

shomer negiyah A custom among some traditional Jews which dictates that there be no physical contact between men and women (that means, no hand on shoulder) unless they are married to each other. This rule, however, generally does not apply to family members.

shtetl Central or Eastern European Jewish settlement.

shtup In Yiddish, "to have sex with."

shul *also sla* Synagogue; Jewish house of worship.

simcha *also simha, simchah* (lit. "joy" or "happiness") Often used as a synonym for "joyous occasion."

sniut *also sniuth* See **tsnius**.

spherot *also sefiroth* The Divine attributes or emanations described in Kabbalah. These include the seven "lower," more Earthly attributes and three "higher," transcendent attributes.

sukkah A temporary booth in which Jews eat and sometimes sleep during the week of Sukkot.

Sukkot A holiday celebrating the harvest.

taharat mishpachah *also taharat hamishpacha* (lit. "purity of the family") The laws surrounding menstruation.

tallit/tallitot (sing/pl) *also tallis, tallith* Prayer shawl.

tallit gadol (lit. "big tallit") See **tallit**.

tallit katan (lit. "small tallit") A four-cornered garment with tzitzit, ritual fringes, traditionally worn under the clothes of Jewish boys and men.

Talmud A compilation of the discussions, interpretations, arguments and theological explanations about and including the Mishnah, compiled over the first five centuries of the Common Era (C.E.).

Talmudist A person skilled in the nuances of the Talmud, including its argument and rhetoric.

tchotchkes Yiddish for "knickknacks."

tefillin *also tfeeleen, tefilin* Phylacteries; black leather straps and boxes containing prayers which are affixed to the arm and the forehead during weekday morning prayer.

Temple, The A reference to the Holy Jerusalem Temple, from which Israelites offered animal sacrifices to God. The First Temple was built by King Solomon and completed in roughly 950 B.C.E., and destroyed by the Babylonians in 586 B.C.E. The Second Temple stood from about 515 B.C.E. until 70 C.E., when it was destroyed by the Romans. The rebuilding of a Third Temple is often associated with the coming of a Messianic age.

tichel Scarf, traditionally worn by married Jewish women to cover their hair for reasons of modesty. Mizrahi women tend to cover their hair more loosely than Ashkenazi women.

tikkun olam (lit. "healing the world") Often used today to denote works of positive social activism.

Tisha B'Av *also Tishah B'Av* (lit. "the Ninth of [the month of] Av") A holiday commemorating the destruction of the Temple; a day of fasting and mourning.

todah rabah *also toda rabah* Hebrew for "Thank you very much."

Torah The Five Books of Moses: Genesis, Exodus, Leviticus, Numbers, Deuteronomy.

treyf *also treif* Non-kosher.

tsnius *also sniut, sniuth, tzniut* Modesty (generally in dress).

tsuris Yiddish for aggravation, headache.

Tu B'Shvat The new year of the trees; the late winter/early spring holiday celebrating the time when trees begin to form their first fruit.

tzedakah *also s'daqa, sadaqa* (lit. "righteousness") Often used to describe the act of helping the less fortunate. Or, charity money.

tzitzit *also sisith* Ritual fringes which serve as a reminder of the Torah's commandments.

ulpan An intensive Hebrew-language program.

yahrzeit The anniversary of a death.

yarmulke A kippah, a Jewish head covering.

yedid nefesh Term meaning "beloved of the soul." Also **Yedid Nefesh,** a sixteenth-century Kabbalistic poem about longing for union with God, often sung at the beginning of Friday-night Shabbat services.

yeshiva/yeshivot (sing/pl) *also yeshivah* A center for Jewish learning.

yeshiva bocher A yeshiva student; generally refers to an unmarried young man.

yetzer hara *also yeser hara* The evil inclination; that which draws a person away from his/her highest, most fully-realized self.

yichud *also yihud* (lit. "seclusion") The time spent by bride and groom alone together immediately following the wedding ceremony, traditionally used to consummate the marriage.

Yom Kippur *also 'Kipur* The Day of Atonement, during which Jews fast and attempt to ask forgiveness for their sins and shortcomings. Generally considered the holiest day of the Jewish year.

zav/zavah (masc/fem) A man or woman who has abnormal bodily emissions, usually genital.

Zionism A movement for the return of Jewish people to the patch of land known as Israel, Palestine or Canaan, depending on one's socio-political orientation, and the resumption of the Jewish sovereignty in this land. The movement in support of a Jewish state.

zmirot *also zmiroth, sh'bahoth* Sabbath songs.

About the Editor

Danya Ruttenberg is a San Francisco–based writer, editor and educator. She is a contributing editor to *Lilith: The Independent Jewish Women's Magazine;* her writing has appeared in numerous anthologies and magazines, including the *San Francisco Chronicle, Tikkun* and *Salon.* She also lectures nationwide about religion, spirituality and culture. Danya recently completed her first novel, "The Medieval Body," and is working on a second. She received her BA in religious studies from Brown University and has since studied at the Jewish Theological Seminary, Sarah Lawrence College and the Pardes Institute of Jewish Studies.

SELECTED TITLES

Listen Up: Voices from the Next Feminist Generation edited by Barbara Findlen. $16.95, 1-58005-054-9. In a new expanded edition of the classic collection of young feminist writing, *Listen Up* gathers the women of feminism's "third wave" and allows them to explore and reveal their lives. Contributors address topics such as racism, sexuality, identity, HIV/AIDS, revolution, religion, abortion and much more.

Young Wives' Tales: New Adventures in Love and Partnership edited by Jill Corral and Lisa Miya-Jervis, foreword by bell hooks. $16.95, 1-58005-050-6. *Wife.* The term inspires ambivalence in young women the world over, for a multitude of good reasons. So what's a young, independent girl in love to do? In a bold and provocative anthology, women in their twenties and thirties attempt to answer that question, whether they are trying on the title "wife," deciding who will wear the gown in a lesbian wedding or demanding the space for solitude in a committed relationship.

Sex and Single Girls: Straight and Queer Women on Sexuality edited by Lee Damsky. $16.95, 1-58005-038-7. In this potent and entertaining collection of personal essays, women lay bare pleasure, fear, desire, risk—all that comes with exploring their sexuality. Contributors write their own rules and tell their own stories with empowering and often humorous results.

Cunt: A Declaration of Independence by Inga Muscio. $14.95, 1-58005-015-8. An ancient title of respect, "cunt" long ago veered off the path of honor and now careens toward the heart of every woman as an expletive. Muscio traces this winding road, giving women both the motivation and the tools to claim "cunt" as a positive and powerful force in the lives of all women.

Body Outlaws: Young Women Write About Body Image and Identity edited by Ophira Edut, foreword by Rebecca Walker. $14.95, 1-58005-043-3. Filled with honesty and humor, this groundbreaking anthology offers stories by women who have chosen to ignore, subvert or redefine the dominant beauty standard in order to feel at home in their bodies.

FROM SEAL PRESS

Wild Child: Girlhoods in the Counterculture edited by Chelsea Cain, foreword by Moon Zappa. $16.00, 1-58005-031-X. Daughters of the hippie generation reflect on the experience of a counterculture childhood, presenting a fresh perspective on our current world as seen through the legacy of sixties ideals.

Breeder: Real-Life Stories from the New Generation of Mothers edited by Ariel Gore and Bee Lavender, foreword by Dan Savage. $16.00, 1-58005-051-4. From the editors of *Hip Mama,* this hilarious and heartrending compilation creates a space where Gen-X moms can dish, cry, scream and laugh. With its strength, humor and wisdom, *Breeder* will speak to every young mother, and anyone who wants a peek into the mind and spirit behind those bleary eyes.

The Mother Trip: Hip Mama's Guide to Staying Sane in the Chaos of Motherhood by Ariel Gore. $14.95, 1-58005-029-8. In a book that is part self-help, part critique of the mommy myth and part hip-mama handbook, Ariel Gore offers support to mothers who break the mold.

Valencia by Michelle Tea. $13.00, 1-58005-035-2. The fast-paced account of one girl's search for love and high times in the dyke world of San Francisco. By turns poetic and frantic, *Valencia* is an edgy, visceral ride through the queer girl underground of the Mission District.

Dharma Girl: A Road Trip Across the American Generations by Chelsea Cain. $12.00, 1-878067-84-2. Written to the unmistakable beat of the road, this memoir chronicles the twenty-four-year-old author's homecoming to the commune in Iowa where she grew up with her counterculture parents.

Seal Press publishes many books of fiction and nonfiction by women writers. If you are unable to obtain a Seal Press title from a bookstore, please order from us directly by calling 800-754-0271. Visit our website and online catalog at **www.sealpress.com.**